The Collected Works of
James M. Buchanan

VOLUME 9
The Power to Tax

James M. Buchanan and Geoffrey Brennan,
Blacksburg, Virginia, 1989

The Collected Works of

James M. Buchanan

VOLUME 9

The Power to Tax

Analytical Foundations of a Fiscal Constitution

Geoffrey Brennan
and
James M. Buchanan

LIBERTY FUND

Indianapolis

Foreword and coauthor note © 2000 by Liberty Fund, Inc.
© 1980 Cambridge University Press
All rights reserved
Printed in the United States of America

C   10 9 8 7 6 5 4 3
P   10 9 8 7 6 5 4 3 2 1

Library of Congress Cataloging-in-Publication Data
Brennan, Geoffrey, 1944–
The power to tax : analytical foundations of a fiscal constitution / Geoffrey
Brennan, James M. Buchanan.
p.   cm. — (The collected works of James M. Buchanan ; v. 9)
Includes bibliographical references and index.
ISBN 0-86597-229-x (hc : alk. paper). — ISBN 0-86597-230-3 (pb : alk. paper)
1. Taxation.   I. Buchanan, James M.   II. Title.   III. Series:
Buchanan, James M.   Works.   1999 ; v. 9.
HJ2305.B64   2000
336.2—dc21   99-24061

LIBERTY FUND, INC.
8335 Allison Pointe Trail, Suite 300
Indianapolis, IN 46250-1684

C'est une expérience éternelle que tout homme qui a du pouvoir est porté à en abuser; il va jusqu'à ce qu'il trouve des limites.

—Montesquieu, *De l'Esprit des Lois*

The power to tax involves the power to destroy.

—Chief Justice John Marshall, *McCulloch* v. *Maryland*

Contents

Foreword

The Power to Tax was a book waiting to be written.[1] This is so not just because the tax revolts sweeping across the United States in the late 1970s cried
out for an analytic interpretation that orthodox public finance was apparently incapable of providing. Rather, *The Power to Tax* was waiting to be
written in the more academic-intellectual sense that the Leviathan approach
to taxation filled a logical gap in the array of approaches available at that
time. In this sense, *The Power to Tax* represents a kind of tent peg—or logical
compass point—in the intellectual territory that tax theory marks off.

As of 1980, there were on offer two broad approaches to normative tax
analysis. First, there was the approach provided by the family of orthodox
public finance models. The characteristic feature of these models was the direct application of normative criteria to tax arrangements—sometimes, de-
rivatively, to particular taxes, but, more commonly, to the tax system as a
whole. Within this family, there were distinct strands. The two most important of these were the more traditional Musgravian strand, derived from
R. M. Haig, Henry Simons, and Georg Schanz, in which the central ambition
was the achievement of an equitable tax system based on ability to pay; and
the so-called optimal tax approach, which involved the direct application
of the utilitarian normative scheme to tax design questions. There were
other, less common variants, but all variants shared the implicit benevolent
despot assumption about the operation of political processes. Effectively,
political constraints were ignored in the determination of tax policy (the
despot aspect); and policymakers were assumed to be driven solely by the

---

1. Geoffrey Brennan and James M. Buchanan, *The Power to Tax: Analytical Foundations of a Fiscal Constitution* (New York: Cambridge University Press, 1980), volume 9 in
the series.

desire to "do good" as the public finance policy advisor would discern it (the benevolence aspect).

The second approach of orthodox public finance models on offer was the public choice one. The distinguishing feature of this approach was the rejection of the benevolent despot model of public finance orthodoxy: a formal model of political process was to be an explicit part of any satisfactory approach to taxation, and the actors within any such model had to exhibit the same motivational patterns as were ascribed to taxpayers. Again, there are a variety of strands within this family, many of them derived from Buchanan's own work. One broad division is between those models that treat taxes as essentially *en*dogenous—that is, as themselves emerging from political determination—and those that treat taxes as *ex*ogenous, affecting political outcomes but themselves determined through some other process. For example, in the former camp lie the original Knut Wicksell and Eric Lindahl models. In the latter lies James M. Buchanan's approach in *Public Finance in Democratic Process* and in the papers contained in part 2 of volume 14 in the Collected Works, *Debt and Taxes*.[2]

We can, on the basis of this broad categorization, picture the public choice approach and public finance orthodoxy as lying at opposite ends of a two-dimensional spectrum reflecting the underlying political models in play. The two dimensions of this spectrum reflect, on the one hand, the degree of political constraint and, on the other hand, the motivational assumptions made about political agents—the degree of despotism and the degree of benevolence. In this sense, we could imagine a two-dimensional map of intellectual possibilities, within which various accounts of taxation policy might be located. However, this notional map only had the two possible polar extremes in action: the map lacked, as it were, a cornerpost. And it was that cornerpost that the Leviathan approach to taxation, which *The Power to Tax* laid out and developed, sought to supply. The underlying motivating question was simple: Why not borrow the motivational assumptions standard in public choice theory and put them together with the assumptions about policy-maker discretion taken from public finance orthodoxy? One could then

---

2. James M. Buchanan, *Public Finance in Democratic Process: Fiscal Institutions and Individual Choice* (Chapel Hill: University of North Carolina Press, 1966), volume 4 in the Collected Works.

develop an account of preferred tax policy within that hybrid political model. After all, there is available on the shelf in mainstream economics an extremely familiar model of the exercise of discretionary market power—namely, the standard model of monopoly. Why not adapt that familiar model to the tax context? Responding to that possibility gave rise to the model of the revenue-maximizing Leviathan—and the derivation of a tax constitution specifically in the face of a Leviathan government.

It is difficult now, some twenty years later, to be confident as to what exactly the authors' motivations and expectations for this model were. There is no doubt that at some level the mere exploration of logical possibilities for its own sake initially played some part. But two general considerations also weighed. The first was the force of the public choice insistence that the same basic motivational assumptions should be ascribed to market agents and political agents. The second consideration was that, as a matter of casual empiricism, it seems clear that policymakers have some discretion over policy choice: it is difficult otherwise to explain a market for policy advisors. Putting these two general considerations together leaves the Leviathan model as the logical outcome.

The interesting aspect in the development of the model was its capacity to turn so many of the traditional nostrums of tax orthodoxy on their heads.[3] Moreover, the Leviathan model lent support to some of the more legally derived tax desiderata, such as the absence of retrospectivity, which are difficult to derive from the standard public finance approach. (Specifically, an unexpected retroactive increase in taxes would generate revenue in an efficient way because there would be no behavioral response among taxpayers and, hence, no inefficiency generating substitution effects.) The effect was that the Leviathan approach was construed by critics as a wholesale attack on public finance orthodoxy, both directly by questioning the orthodoxy's central claims and indirectly by exposing its ambiguous stand on issues like retroactivity. Probably for this reason, *The Power to Tax* proved a controversial book.

---

3. The initial summary statement of the central analytics was in article form. See Geoffrey Brennan and James M. Buchanan, "Towards a Tax Constitution for Leviathan," *Journal of Public Economics* 8 (December 1977): 255–73; see also volume 14 in the series, *Debt and Taxes*.

Interestingly, one of the grounds for criticism—or for treating the arguments in the book as irrelevant and therefore ignoring them—was that the model of politics implied was implausible. That such a claim should issue from proponents of public finance orthodoxy is more than a little ironic, since models of politics, plausible or otherwise, play no role in that tradition. But the truth is that *The Power to Tax* is not a model of *politics* so much as it is a model of political agent *motivation:* To the extent that there is a model of politics here, it is borrowed directly from public finance. This is the model of the despot but here an egoistic despot rather than a benevolent one.

Conceivably, as an expositional matter, it may have been better to attempt a reasonably elaborate model of dictatorial government, with a clear specification of the constraints to which such a government is likely to be subject—for example, the need to buy the support of salient groups (including the military), the need to suppress those who might otherwise launch a coup attempt, and so on. Alternatively, the analysis might have been lodged formally within one of the standard public choice models of democracy with imperfectly constrained political agents, such as the strategic-agenda-setter model or the Niskanen bureaucracy model. But each of these courses ran the risk of cluttering the central argument with material that was not absolutely central and of disguising the simplicity of the core logical claims. What *The Power to Tax* provides is a monopoly model of government, with the emphasis on the monopoly connection and with the simple analytics designed to underline the monopoly analogue. The thought was that the central messages would be more arresting if derived from a model of the behavior of a discretionary agency that most readers found familiar—so familiar, indeed, as to be almost unquestionable.

The reception to *The Power to Tax* was so vehement and the authors' purpose so misunderstood that the ink was scarcely dry before it became necessary to begin an exercise of clarification and defense of the whole approach. This exercise initially took article form, but eventually emerged as a more detailed account of the whole constitutional paradigm in *The Reason of Rules.*[4] Of course, there is no sense in which the constitutional approach

---

4. For example, Geoffrey Brennan and James M. Buchanan, "The Normative Purpose of Economic 'Science': Rediscovery of an Eighteenth-Century Method," *International Review of Law and Economics* 1 (December 1981): 155–66, and Geoffrey Brennan and James

presupposes Leviathan government. But, equally, there is no point in constitutional rules if those rules only prevent wholly benevolent persons from doing good. And there is no point in constitutional rules other than simple majority rule if majority rule robustly ensures maximally desirable outcomes.
The whole point of fiscal rules (or fiscal norms), whether of the kind derived
in orthodox public finance or the kind derived from the Leviathan model or
other variants of the public choice approach, is that the rules or norms operate to support better overall outcomes than would prevail in their absence:
they necessarily operate in the face of other, imperfect institutional devices.
In this sense, what is possibly surprising about the Leviathan approach is
how much it shares with orthodox public finance and, for that matter, with
the orthodox theory of the state (in which connection, see Anthony de Jasay's *The State*, which also treats the state as a monolithic actor).[5] Specifically,
both approaches share a similar presumption about the degree of political
agent discretion and a similar presumption about the desirability of politically independent fiscal rules. Where they differ is that in *The Power to Tax*
tax policymakers and taxpayers have identical motivations, whereas in the
orthodox approach, tax policymakers and taxpayers have utterly different
motivations. In this sense, *The Power to Tax* is clearly in the public choice
tradition: the insistence on motivational symmetry is a characteristic feature
of the public choice approach, and it is in this dimension that *The Power to
Tax* and the orthodox public finance approach diverge.

Geoffrey Brennan
Australian National University
1998

M. Buchanan, "Predictive Power and Choice among Regimes," *Economic Journal* 93
(March 1983): 89–105; both articles are in *Economic Inquiry and Its Logic*, volume 12 in the
series. Geoffrey Brennan and James M. Buchanan, *The Reason of Rules: Constitutional Political Economy* (Cambridge: Cambridge University Press, 1985), volume 10 in the series.

5. Anthony de Jasay, *The State* (Oxford: Basil Blackwell, 1985); republished by Liberty
Fund in 1998.

Geoffrey Brennan

The Power to Tax is, I think, demonstrable proof of the value of genuine research collaboration across national-cultural boundaries. Geoffrey Brennan, as a golden-voiced "wild colonial boy" from Down Under, joined our research team in Blacksburg in the 1970s, and his enthusiasm quickly spilled over and generated joint efforts. We discovered that along many, but not all, dimensions of discourse, we were on the same wavelength.

The Power to Tax is informed by a single idea—the implications of a revenue-maximizing government. The origins of the idea emerged first in a paper that we agreed to write jointly for a *festschrift* for Joseph Pechman. Once the idea existed, the book, more than any other of my experience, simply wrote itself. Perhaps, in part, this is how it seemed only to me, since Geoffrey Brennan was the coauthor who provided much of the sometimes difficult technical construction.

James M. Buchanan
Fairfax, Virginia
1998

Preface

The success of Proposition 13 in California was one of the top news stories of 1978, and many commentators interpreted this success as the first major step in a genuine "tax revolt." Politicians seeking either to attain or to maintain elective office were quick to accept such an interpretation, and the political rhetoric of the late 1970s suggested that the era of explosive governmental growth may have been coming to an end.

These events went on about us as we were writing this book. At times we felt as if we were being swept away by political developments that threatened to reduce our efforts to little other than academic exercises, a fate that was not our initial intent. We can, of course, claim some credit for having established our position on the ground floor, so to speak, for having undertaken a specific analysis of constitutional tax limits well before the dramatic events of 1978 took place. And we can, more constructively, argue that this book represents the first serious economic analysis of tax limits, a subject that has been predictably neglected by economists.

Nonetheless, there remains the lingering concern that this is a book that might, ideally, have been completed two years earlier. To offset this concern we are buoyed in the prospect that a book whose time has clearly arrived may be more readily accepted than a book whose message antedates its topicality. Had this book been published in 1960 or in 1970 it probably would have fallen stillborn from the press. It should not suffer such a fate in 1980.

Both of us are public-finance economists, despite our various excursions into the territories of ethics, law, politics, and philosophy. This book marks a return to the fold, but not without our having been very substantially influenced by the detours. The analysis, both in its positive and its normative aspects, lies well outside the limits of orthodox fiscal economics. Our initial efforts were prompted by our growing disenchantment with economists' treatment of taxation and tax reform. This treatment seemed to us to have become increasingly irrelevant, in terms of both its explanatory content and its normative potential. In this respect, the events of 1978 reinforced our initial motivation. The orthodox analysis provides neither an understanding of observed fiscal process nor a basis for improvement on grounds that are acceptable to the taxpaying public.

The normative standards in our analysis are based on the calculus of the potential taxpayer-beneficiary, who is presumed able to control government's "power to tax" by a constitutional selection of tax arrangements that are anticipated to serve his own interest. This approach is contrasted with the more familiar objectives laid down for taxation, such as the promotion of "social welfare," "social utility," or "public interest" without regard for political implementation. As our subtitle suggests, we adopt the *constitutional* perspective, in which the taxpayer is presumed to be unable to identify his own position, either as taxpayer or as public-spending beneficiary, in a sequence of separate budgetary periods. The constitutionally selected structure of taxation may be, and normally will be, quite different from the "in-period" tax-share distribution that might conceptually emerge from some idealized fiscal exchange in the Wicksellian sense.

The methodological-analytical setting is familiar, at least to those who are cognizant with the literature in modern public-choice theory. The constitutional perspective for the choice of institutions has been elaborated by one of the authors in several works, and, more generally, it has been made familiar to many scholars of the 1970s through the work of John Rawls. Where the argument of this book diverges most sharply from almost all previous analysis lies in the predicted workings of the political process in the postconstitutional sequence. We analyze the properties of the political process under the assumption that citizens exercise relatively little control over governmental fiscal outcomes except at the initial constitutional decision stage, where the basic fiscal arrangements are chosen. More dramatically, and more controversially, we model government as a revenue-maximizing Leviathan. We argue that both aspects of our political model gain some plausibility in this era of apparently uncontrollable budgets. Further, and much more important, we argue that our model is the appropriate one upon which to construct reasoned discussion of constitutional alternatives. The current discussion of constitutional tax limits suggests that there is widespread public agreement with at least some central elements of our model of politics. Even for those who categorically reject our formal model of politics, however, the constitutional norms laid down may possibly prove acceptable as embodying a minimax strategy aimed at securing protection against the worst outcomes that might emerge.

We shall discuss the basic constitutional perspective in Chapter 1. In Chapter 2, we develop our model for the working of the political process that will be used for the later analyses. Chapter 3 examines the choice calculus of the potential taxpayer as he confronts alternative rate and base constraints. Chapter 4 extends the analysis to commodity taxes. Chapter 5 extends the analysis intertemporally and specifically introduces capital taxation and public debt. The revenue implications of the money-creation power, including (but not exclusively) the power to use inflation as a means of taxation, are analyzed in Chapter 6. In Chapter 7, the focus is shifted toward possible modification of the incentive structure to ensure that tax revenues are actually spent on providing goods and services valued by taxpayers. Chapter 8 discusses the whole domain of politics, with specific reference to fiscal versus nonfiscal constraints on governmental activity. The structural order of federalism as a means of constitutionally limiting government's fiscal powers is examined in Chapter 9. In Chapter 10, we attempt to relate our analysis to the current proposals for constitutional tax limits, and we suggest necessary avenues for authentic fiscal reform.

Acknowledgments

We expressly thank all of our colleagues at the Center for Study of Public Choice, VPI, particularly Professors Robert Tollison and Gordon Tullock, for providing an atmosphere within which genuinely radical ideas are nourished rather than drowned at birth in either technical detail or methodological straitjackets. We also gratefully acknowledge financial support from the National Science Foundation and the Olin Foundation, which has allowed us time to develop our ideas free from at least some of the standard academic pressures.

We are especially appreciative of the help of Professor Charles Rowley, University of Newcastle, who, during his visiting stint at the Center in 1979, painstakingly read and criticized the manuscript chapter by chapter. The "research team" of Cecil Bohanon, Richard Carter, and David Nellor was essential to our efforts. Members of this group provided not only editorial, stylistic, and bibliographical assistance but also very constructive analytical and substantive criticism. George Uhimchuk was both cooperative and reliable in helping with many stages of the processing of the final manuscript. Donna Trenor was cheerful and efficient in typing several early drafts. And, of course, Buchanan's books could never get written, or be got right, even with a coauthor, without the assistance of Mrs. Betty Tillman Ross.

Geoffrey Brennan
James M. Buchanan
Blacksburg, Virginia

The Power to Tax

1. Taxation in Constitutional Perspective

The interest of the government is to tax heavily: that of the community is, to be as little taxed as the necessary expenses of good government permit.

—J. S. Mill, *Considerations on Representative Government*, in *Essays on Politics and Society*, vol. 19, *Collected Works*, p. 441

This book is about government's power to tax, how this power may be used, and how it may be and should be constrained. The set of issues that we address has been almost totally neglected by public-finance economists. Their concern has been with telling governments how they should tax, how the taxing powers should be utilized. Both the positive analysis of tax incidence and the normative derivation of tax principles have had as their ultimate objective the proffering of advice to governmental decision makers.

We offer no such advice, either directly or indirectly. Our concern is neither with telling governments how they should behave if revenues are to be raised efficiently and/or equitably nor with telling them how public monies should be spent. At this level of discourse, our analysis is necessarily more positive. We introduce models of how governments do behave or how they may be predicted to behave (regardless of the advice that may be advanced by public-finance economics). The subjects of our ultimate normative concern are taxpayers or citizens—all those who suffer the burdens of taxation or who are the potential subjects of government's powers of fiscal exaction.

The stance taken in this book embodies presuppositions about political order that are not necessary in the traditional analysis. For the latter, in order to proffer advice to governments, the minimal requirement is that government exist. By contrast, our effort is premised on the notion that government derives its powers from the ultimate consent of those who are governed; that the structure of government is an artifact that is explicitly constructed or may be treated as if it is so constructed. Further, it is implicit in this model that the authorized agent of coercion, the government, may be limited in its range of action. That is, constitutions may constrain the activities of the political entity.

From such a perspective, questions of constitutional policy emerge that are not present in the traditional approach. What constraints or limits should be imposed on the political agency? That question is not at all akin to asking what an existing political agency should or should not do in this or that setting or circumstance.

Given that he is ignorant about his future position, what sort of tax institutions would we expect the rational citizen-taxpayer to select as elements in the constitution?

This is the central question addressed in this book. The specific aim of this first chapter is to indicate something of what the question involves and why it is an interesting one to ask. As noted, the question is itself a purely positive one. We do not ask the question "What is a 'good' tax system?" We do not specify a set of externally determined, or divinely revealed, criteria by which alternative tax systems may be judged. Nor do we seek to indicate the effects of alternative taxes on the distribution of income or on efficiency in the allocation of resources—although these traditional concerns may be relevant to some parts of our discussion.

The focus of our discussion is logically prior to all this. We are concerned to go back to "first causes"—to think "radically" in the strict sense—of the *nature* of taxation, about what is involved in the *power* to tax and about what is implied by the government's possession of that power.

As it turns out, asking these logically prior questions suggests that much of the traditional economic analysis of taxation is either irrelevant or profoundly misleading. Posing the basic question as we have actually serves to turn much of the familiar folklore of public finance on its head. However, our major object is not to demonstrate that much of the policy advice proffered by current tax advocates to governments may be wrong, even on its own grounds. Rather, we are seeking to offer a different *understanding* of the nature and process of taxation—a different "window" through which fiscal phenomena can be viewed. Once the difference in perspective is established, we can proceed to the analysis and discussion of constructive fiscal reform.

1.1. The Notion of a "Constitution"

One of the characteristic features of the particular perspective on taxation that we wish to develop is its "constitutional" orientation. Throughout our discussion, a "constitution" is conceived as the set of rules, or social institutions, within which individuals operate and interact with one another. The analogy with the rules of a game is perhaps useful here. A game is described by its rules—its constitution. These rules establish the framework within which the playing of the game proceeds; they set boundaries on what activities are legitimate, as well as describing the objects of the game and how to determine who wins. It is clear intuitively that the choice among alternative strategies that a player might make in the course of a game is categorically quite distinct from his prior choice among alternative sets of rules. A tennis player after hitting a particular shot may reasonably wish that the net was lower, yet prior to the game he may have agreed to a set of rules in which the height of the net was specified.

This distinction between choices over alternative strategies in a game, and choices over alternative sets of rules by which the game can be played—the distinction between "in-period" and "constitutional" choice—has several important elements. In constitutional choice, the individual must base his selection upon some prediction about the working properties of alternative sets of rules over a whole sequence of "plays," a sequence that may well be indeterminate. The horizon is necessarily more extensive than in any postconstitutional choice. This extension in the time horizon ensures that, in almost all real-world approximations, the individual chooser is more uncertain about his own private prospects or positions. The utility-maximizing calculus becomes quite different from that which would be required in the simpler selection of one strategy within some predetermined set of rules.

In the limiting or idealized model for constitutional choice, the individual must know the pattern or distribution of positions under differing rounds of play under all sets of rules, while remaining ignorant about his own position under any one of these patterns. This is, of course, the choice setting made familiar by John Rawls in his derivation of the principles that satisfy criteria of *fairness*.[1] The constitutional choice is made behind a "veil of ignorance" in the sense that particularized identification is absent. For our purposes, description of the idealized setting is useful primarily as an analytical benchmark rather than as a model that is expected to prevail. As the constitutional-postconstitutional distinction is recognized at all, some elements of the idealized choice setting enter into the calculus of behavior. Once we acknowledge that the choice of a strategy within rules differs from the choice of rules, some partial veil-of-ignorance construction must inform any evaluation of alternative sets of rules.

We are here, of course, interested in the idea of a constitution in its "political" or social sense, as a set of rules that establish the setting within which the whole range of individual interaction takes place. Why do we need such a constitution? Wherein is the logic of the constitution to be found?

1.2. The Logic of a Constitution

We do not intend to retrace here ground that has been extensively covered by one of us elsewhere.[2] Since a certain amount of that approach is being taken as given, however, it may be useful to indicate the central notions that establish the logic of a constitution.

The point of departure is the Hobbesian insight that in the absence of collective enforcement of basic property rights (including the right to one's own life) and of rules by which those property rights might be exchanged, the state of nature would ensure that man's life is ". . . nasty, brutish and short." To Thomas Hobbes, the only logical alternative to anarchistic chaos is the assignment of power to government—or some other institution of authority. In this sense, the essential feature of the establishment of order, of the leap out of anarchy, is the monopolization of the use of coercive power. Anarchy can be viewed as a situation in which there is complete freedom of en-

1. John Rawls, *A Theory of Justice* (Cambridge: Harvard University Press, 1971). This setting was also used in a context perhaps more closely related to our analysis in James M. Buchanan and Gordon Tullock, *The Calculus of Consent* (Ann Arbor: University of Michigan Press, 1962).

2. James M. Buchanan, *The Limits of Liberty* (Chicago: University of Chicago Press, 1975).

try in the exercise of coercive power; "order" as a situation in which coercive power is monopolized.

The perspective that has become characteristic of the so-called "Virginia school," however, involves a blend of this Hobbesian view with the notion of social contract. If the leap out of anarchy into order is indeed to be preferred by the citizenry, it must be possible to examine the establishment of government *as if* it emerges from the voluntary consent of those who are to be subject to it. Yet once the "voluntary exchange" view of government is taken, it is also reasonable to ask what is the nature of that government to which the citizenry would *agree* to be subject. In particular, would citizens voluntarily agree to allow government to exercise power quite *unreservedly*? Or would they rather seek to impose constraints on the behavior of government—constraints that restrict the ability of government to take actions that it would otherwise take?

Of course, to the extent that government could be predicted to act "perfectly"—whatever that may mean[3]—in all periods, there would be no conceptual or logical basis for imposing constitutional limits; such limits could only prevent government from taking actions that are, by definition, "desirable." In this sense, the constitutional perspective is irreconcilably at odds with the benevolent despot model, which in its various guises underlies the orthodox analysis of public policy generally and of conventional tax theory in particular. The logic of constitutional restrictions is embodied in the implicit prediction that any power assigned to government may be, over some ranges and on some occasions, exercised in ways that are at variance with the

---

3. Social-choice theorists have attempted to define reasonable properties that might be expected for a "social" or "governmental choice function." However, all such efforts have foundered on the central contradiction involved in any shift from the preference or value rankings of a single person to an ordering designed to reflect the potential choice bases for a group or community of persons. The focal point for much of the analysis in social-choice theory has been Arrow's famous impossibility theorem. The theorem demonstrates that no social-choice function based on individual evaluation can exist that does not violate one or more of the reasonable conditions or properties imposed on such a function at the outset. See Kenneth Arrow, *Social Choice and Individual Values* (New York: John Wiley & Sons, 1951). In our terminology, government cannot, even conceptually, work "perfectly" because there is more than one person or citizen affected by its operation. That pattern of governmental activity deemed to be "perfect" by Mr. *A* might be deemed just the opposite by Ms. *B* or Mr. *C.*

desired usage of such power, as defined by citizens behind the veil of ignorance. As emphasized throughout modern public-choice theory, persons who act in agency roles, as "governors," are not basically different from their fellow citizens, and methodological consistency suggests that the same motivations for behavior be imputed to persons in public and private choices. We need not, of course, rule out the possibility of "moral" (or, more accurately, "altruistic") behavior on the part of those persons who make governmental decisions. Our approach does rule out the presumption of such behavior as the basis for normative analysis. Those who might argue that governments should be analyzed on such a presumption of agent benevolence are denying the legitimacy of *any* constraints on government, including electoral ones. In this setting, there is no logical basis for a constitution.

1.3. The Means of Constitutional Constraint

Once the need to constrain the power of government is accepted, the question automatically arises as to the sorts of constraints—or constitutional rules—that are available. By what means might the citizen hope to limit the exercise of public power so as to ensure that outcomes fall within tolerable bounds?

To a very substantial extent, modern economists have implicitly accepted the prevailing twentieth-century presumption (or faith?) that nominally democratic electoral processes are sufficient in themselves to guarantee that government activity remains within acceptable limits.[4] Constitutional analysis in economics has consequently focused on the choice between alternative electoral procedures as the major element in the citizen's constitutional calculus. For this reason, it is worth emphasizing at the outset that nonelectoral rules are conceivable, that they do in fact play a significant part in most recognizably democratic constitutions currently operative, and that it is not obvious on prima facie grounds that they are less significant in controlling govern-

---

4. Both Lord Hailsham and Professor Hayek have recently argued strongly to the effect that the presumption is invalid. See Lord Hailsham, *The Dilemma of Democracy* (London: William Collins Sons & Company, 1978); and F. A. Hayek, *Law, Legislation and Liberty,* vol. 3, *The Political Order of a Free People* (Chicago: University of Chicago Press, 1979).

ment than are purely electoral constraints. For example, most constitutions involve constraints on the *domain* of public activity: rules are set that specify those things which governments may and may not do. One aspect of such rules is the application of restrictions on the possible misappropriation of public funds by legitimate public officials. Apparently, the possibility that politicians (even elected ones) might simply pocket tax revenues is sufficiently significant to merit the extensive accounting procedures and explicit rules of conduct that are provided for in most allegedly democratic constitutions. Further, restrictions are typically placed on the legitimate activities of government, in terms both of the nature of the services that government provides and of the type of laws that governments may enact. In some cases, constraints are also placed on the *structure* of government by assigning specific functions to specific units, as is the case with the decentralization of political power evidenced in a federal political structure. In general, we see such nonelectoral constitutional rules existing side by side with electoral ones, and there seems no particular reason for elevating the latter to a position of primacy.

In the ensuing chapters, we shall be concerned with one particular subset of nonelectoral rules—those which deal specifically with the taxing power. We should note, however, that there is *one* case in which electoral processes would, if enforced, be sufficient to restrain government within bounds totally acceptable to the citizenry. This is the case in which all public decisions were taken by unanimous consent. By contrasting this conceptual ideal with actual electoral processes, the crucial role for nonelectoral, and specifically fiscal, constraints can be exposed.

1.4. The Wicksellian Ideal and Majoritarian Reality

One condition necessary to ensure a citizen that the government would never impose injury or damage on him, while ensuring all citizens in the same fashion, is the requirement that all governmental decisions be made by a rule of unanimity. Knut Wicksell was the first to recognize the importance of the unanimity rule as an idealized benchmark—since it would be necessary to ensure that all governmental actions represented genuine "improvements" (or at least no damage) for all persons, as measured by the preferences of the

individuals themselves.[5] Only through general agreement could the preferences of citizens be revealed; there is no other way of "adding up" the individual evaluations; there is no other means of ensuring that collective action
will always be "efficient" in the welfare economists' usage of this term.

For our purposes, it is important to note that, in this idealization of political order, "government" possesses no genuinely coercive power. In this
setting, each and every public activity is considered separately, together with
a specific cost-sharing arrangement. And the activity proceeds only when
unanimous consent is reached. No individual can be coerced in such a setting, either by some entity called the "government" or by some coalition of
other individuals in the electorate. Each activity publicly approved necessarily
represents the outcome of a complete multilateral trade from which net benefits are received by all parties. The Wicksellian approach is rightly termed the
voluntary-exchange theory of the public economy.

But the Wicksellian world is far removed from the worlds we inhabit and
observe, where transactions costs and free-rider problems are ubiquitous. As
emphasized in earlier work,[6] the costs of achieving unanimous approval for
public activity are so enormous that the rational citizen can be expected,
when making his constitutional choice over the set of voting rules, to trade
off some of the narrow in-period "efficiency" of the unanimity rule in return
for workability in political processes. Whether a simple majoritarian process
would be the natural outcome of this trade-off seems highly doubtful. But
this *is* the decision rule widely observed in practice, and much modern public choice takes majority rule as given. What has not perhaps been sufficiently
emphasized in the public-choice literature is that the move from unanimity
to majority rule involves a drastic weakening of the power of purely electoral
constraints. Indeed, it may be suggested that commonly observed majoritarian rule can best be modeled as if it embodies *no effective constraint on the
exercise of government powers at all.* (We shall defend the use of such a model
in Chapter 2, particularly as applied to constitutional tax issues.) In the familiar majoritarian world, the exercise of political power does indeed involve
the capacity to coerce. Some citizens may coerce others, as when the decisive
majority operates to overrule the desires of the minority. Quite apart from

---

5. Knut Wicksell, *Finanztheoretische Untersuchungen* (Jena: Gustav Fischer Verlag, 1896).
6. See Buchanan and Tullock, *The Calculus of Consent.*

this, those individuals who make up the institution of "government" possess the power to coerce the citizenry at large.

The sum of this introductory discussion is the simple and probably unexceptionable proposition that, in all practically relevant cases, governments—or more accurately the individuals involved in governmental process—do possess the power to coerce. They do exercise genuinely discretionary power, and it is both empirically reasonable and analytically necessary to assume that over some range they will exploit that power for their own purposes, whatever these may be.

Given this constitutional setting, how are we to understand tax matters? What is involved in the power to tax? And by what means can that power be constrained? More generally, to pose our central question again, what sort of tax institutions would we expect the rational taxpayer-citizen to select in determining the constitution to which he is to be subject?

1.5. The Power to Tax

For the ordinary citizen, the power to tax is the most familiar manifestation of the government's power to coerce. This power to tax involves the power to impose, on individuals and private institutions more generally, charges that can be met only by a transfer to government of economic resources, or financial claims to such resources—charges that carry with them effective powers of enforcement under the very definition of the taxing power. To be sure, governments may use tax revenues for financing public goods or transfers that citizens-taxpayers desire. But we must distinguish sharply here between a *rationalization* for the government's possession of the power to tax and an *understanding* of that power in and of itself. The power to tax, per se, does not carry with it any obligation to use the tax revenue raised in any particular way. The power to tax does not logically imply the nature of spending.

Seen in this way, the power to "tax" is simply the power to "take." If the government wishes to obtain a particular piece of property, it is of no account whether it does so simply by direct appropriation or by purchase together with a tax imposed on the original owner amounting to the full purchase price. Both government and the owner are in an identical position after government action, irrespective of the precise details of the means of appropriation. If any distinction between taking and taxing is to be sustained, therefore, the tax alternative must involve certain additional requirements not present with direct appropriation. For example, if the power to tax is constrained by some generality-uniformity requirements that all individuals in similar circumstances (e.g., with the same aggregate net wealth) should pay an identical tax, then it may be that, whereas the direct appropriation alternative might survive electoral scrutiny, the tax alternative would not do so. In this case, the generality requirement ensures (or, more accurately, increases the likelihood) that electoral processes will operate within tolerable limits: fiscal constraints complement electoral constraints.

In other examples, the precise analytic details of which are spelled out within the body of this book, fiscal constraints may actually *substitute* for electoral constraints, in the sense that they are effective even when electoral constraints are not. In all cases, however, the role of fiscal rules is to limit and appropriately direct the coercive power of government, as embodied most conspicuously in its power to tax.

Historically, of course, governments have possessed genuine powers to tax, although representatives of the citizenry seem to have recognized the sweeping import of such powers. Controls over the sovereign have been exercised through constraints on the taxing authority. The ascendancy of the British Parliament through its ability to restrict the revenues of the monarchy is a part of our political heritage. Even in the collectively dominated era of the late twentieth century, in most countries there remain nominal legal constraints on government's taxing activities.

All constitutional rules may be interpreted as limiting the potential power. That focus rules out explicit consideration on nonfiscal constitutional constraints in this book. We must drastically restrict the domain of our discussion to get within manageable bounds. Similarly, the power to tax is not the only dimension to the government's coercive power, although it is a major one. As we have emphasized, our focus here is on the power to tax and on constraints on that power. That focus rules out explicit consideration on nonfiscal constitutional rules, such as those that might be imposed through definition of franchise, voting rules, legislative and judicial powers, and so on. We cannot, however, rule out the possibility of significant interdependencies between fiscal constraints and other constraints. The assumptions made about other constraints assumed to be operative will vary somewhat from chapter to chapter. We shall, at the relevant points, attempt to specify clearly what these assumptions are—but by and large, we will not seek to justify them, since in the main they serve only an analytic function. There is, however, one crucial assumption which clearly underlies the whole constitutional construction—that of enforceability.

1.6. The Enforceability of Constitutional Contract

Our whole discussion depends critically on the assumption that constitutional choice is relevant, that the behavior of governments as well as the behavior of individuals and nongovernmental entities can be constrained by rules laid down at a constitutional level of deliberation. Without some such assumption, normative argument must necessarily be directed at those who hold political power currently and who are, personally, wholly unconstrained as to the uses to which such power might be put. In such a nonconstitutional model of the political process, there are no formal or legal protections against fiscal exploitation or other arbitrary action on the part of the state. Reformers must "preach" to the powerful, and the hope for moderation rests only with the moral-ethical precepts that the powerful might have come to acknowledge, and to live by, as taught to them by the "preachers" of all ages. In such a model, "limited government" is a contradiction in terms; by its monopoly on coercion, government is by nature unlimited.

To Thomas Hobbes, unlimited government is the only alternative to anarchistic chaos. He argued that all persons would willingly submit to the unchecked will of the single sovereign in exchange for the personal security that the latter promises to ensure, and which, indeed, is consonant with the sovereign's own interest. The Hobbesian despot is preferred by everyone to the Hobbesian jungle, where life, for everyone, tends to be poor, nasty, brutish, and short.

We reject the Hobbesian presumption that the sovereign cannot be controlled by constitutional constraints. Historically, governments do seem to have been held in check by constitutional rules. The precise reasons why this has been so need not concern us here. But our whole construction is based on the belief, or faith, that constitutions can work, and that tax rules imposed within a constitution will prevail.

We do not deny that major problems of constitutional enforceability may emerge, particularly under situations where the whole idea of constitutional choice is not well understood in the prevailing public philosophy. To discuss problems of enforceability would, however, distract attention away from the main purposes of this book.

1.7. Normative Implications

So far in this preliminary discussion, we have indicated something of what is involved in an analysis of taxation from a constitutional perspective. We have not, however, indicated why we believe this perspective to be either empirically relevant or normatively desirable.

We could in part justify our particular approach in the negative sense by appeal to the intellectual poverty of the standard alternative—the failure of orthodox tax analysis to incorporate a plausible political-institutional framework; its naive application of the "equi-revenue comparison"; its appeal to external and apparently arbitrary ethical norms; its obstinate neglect of the expenditure side of the budget; and so on. All of these justifications would have some validity. The benevolent dictator–ethical observer–philosopher king model of political process that underlies the standard tax theory *is* pretty much bereft of empirical relevance in observable governments— Western or otherwise. The assumption that the aggregate level of revenues remains invariant with respect to alternative means of raising it, however convenient analytically, *is* an extremely dubious and potentially very misleading one. The neglect of the public-spending benefits and costs, and the distribution of them, does emerge as a significant gap in the standard analysis.

We think that we can offer positive justification for adopting the constitutional perspective on tax questions, however. We think that there is substantive analytical content in the taxpayer's constitutional choice problem, both conceptually and empirically. We think that our analysis sheds considerable light on the attitude of taxpayers that is reflected in the tax revolt of the late 1970s. Perhaps more important, however, we think that the taxpayer's constitutional choice calculus offers the only legitimate basis for the derivation of possible norms for tax reform. The use of this calculus allows us to indicate directions for what may be called authentic tax reform, changes in tax structure that may prove beneficial to all citizens-taxpayers when evaluated at the constitutional stage of decision.

The preoccupation of the standard analysis with the distribution of tax burdens "in-period" effectively denies the possibility of agreement among taxpayers. Each identifies his own economic position fully; and the tax reform "game" is strictly zero-sum. In this setting, the only possibility is to call down external norms that specify what a "fair" tax system would be—what tax burden each taxpayer "should" face. And such norms *must* be external, because the (internal) judgments about the desired distribution of tax burdens (even if tempered by moral or altruistic concerns) held by different individuals are necessarily mutually exclusive.

As we move to the constitutional setting, however, the scope for agreement seems naturally to expand. The presence of extensive ignorance about his future position separates each individual from the identifiable special interest he holds for himself in any in-period setting. In this constitutional setting it becomes possible to apply the generalized contractarian criterion for ultimate "tax reform." Particular fiscal institutions can be designated as "good" or desirable because individuals *agree* that they are desirable. The normative judgments to be applied emerge out of the constitutional consensus itself, rather than from the moral perceptions of one who deems himself close to God.

To be sure, the veil of ignorance may not be complete, and interpretations and predictions about the workings of alternative rules may differ. Agreement may emerge only after much discussion, compromise, and complex trading in alternative constitutional provisions. It could not be expected that everyone or indeed anyone would find any agreed-on constitution "perfect"— but for desirability in our sense, it is enough that the constitution be agreed.

The ultimate test of desirability can of course only be agreement itself. Purely presumptive reasoning alone cannot be expected to define a set of tax rules that *would* be mutually advantageous—only a set of tax rules that might be *predicted* to be so. In this sense, the normative conclusions that issue from our discussion are strictly provisional. All that we can be seen as doing is offering a set of tax rules that might form an agenda for the fiscal constitutional convention. This may seem to be a rather modest object! But it is, we believe, both ethically superior to and practically more relevant than the orthodox tax advocacy alternative.

2. Natural Government
A Model of Leviathan

The very principle of constitutional government requires it to be assumed that political power will be abused to promote the particular purposes of the holder; not because it always is so, but because such is the natural tendency of things, to guard against which is the especial use of free institutions.

—J. S. Mill, *Considerations on Representative Government*, in *Essays on Politics and Society*, vol. 19, *Collected Works*, p. 505

The aim of this chapter is to introduce, and to justify in some measure, the model of government or political process within which our discussion is to be conducted and which provides the basis for the derivation of the analytical foundations of a tax constitution. The model embodies the predicted behavior of government in its postconstitutional operation. Some such model clearly must inform any consideration of constitutional choice. The selection among alternative tax rules or arrangements to be made by the prospective taxpayer-voter-beneficiary at some constitutional stage must depend critically on the predictions made about how the political process may operate during periods when the rules to be chosen are to remain in force. This statement remains true whether the prospective taxpayer-beneficiary considers a change in the constitutional rules from the perspective of a well-identified and historically determined position or some *de novo* selection of a whole set of constitutional arrangements from an "original position" and behind at least a partial veil of ignorance.

We should first emphasize that our whole analysis falls within what may be called the "economic" approach to governmental process. This term is used to distinguish the basic conception of government and politics from that which might be called the "truth-judgment" or "scientific" approach. Politics or governmental process is viewed as an institutional setting within which persons and groups interact to pursue their own ends, whatever these might be, and whatever might be the roles or positions persons may take, either as decision makers or as those forced to adjust behavior to the decisions of others. In such a conception, there are no "solutions" to political-governmental problems in any sense akin to those encountered in problems of "science," as ordinarily understood. And governmental-political institutions are inappropriately modeled if they are interpreted as devices or mechanisms for finding the independently "best" or "optimum" answers or solutions to problems that arise.

Even with the inclusive economic approach to politics, however, the model we describe and use is highly unconventional in its basic assumptions. In the first place, we reject the benevolent, potentially efficient despotism that is the implicit political model dominant in the conventional normative policy framework, in fiscal theory and elsewhere. Such a model is variously articulated in terms of the "social welfare function" of the Samuelson-Bergson type; in the "theory of the public household," familiar to public-finance–taxation specialists in either the Pigovian or the Musgravian tradition; in the form of policy setting devised by Tinbergen and Hansen with its focus on assignment problems and ends-means distinctions; or in the work of the modern-day utilitarians, writing under the rubric of "optimal taxation."

One may, of course, argue that these variants of the orthodox normative approach do not need to incorporate a model of how political processes operate since they are all designed for the purpose of proffering advice to governments, in any shape or form, advice grounded on ethical norms. Nonetheless, there is contained in all of these variants the implicit belief, or faith, that the politicians-bureaucrats, the audience for whom the normative advice is designed, not only have the power to determine governmental-political outcomes, but also are likely to find the ethically based arguments compelling.

It is perhaps not surprising that our model of political process departs from the above-mentioned variants of fiscal orthodoxy. But our model also requires that we jettison the image of the fully constrained politician-bureaucrat that emerges in the major alternative to these variants, the model represented in the work of early public-choice specialists, notably those in the Wicksellian tradition. In such a public-choice model, the median voter in majoritarian democracy is presumed to drive the whole political machine so as to generate results that are broadly reflective of the wishes of the electorate, or at least the relevant subset of it. Relatively little of the emphasis in this literature has been devoted to arguing for the efficacy of the political mechanism as modeled, and, indeed, considerable effort has been aimed at demonstrating the major inadequacies of majoritarian democracy as a means of making efficient collective decisions. These early public-choice models are severely limited, however, in that they have been almost entirely demand-driven. Political competition among politicians and parties along with periodic elections are presumed to constrain outcomes within a narrow range of possibilities. In these models, government is neither despotic nor benevolent; in a very real sense, "government," as such, does not exist.

Our approach returns us somewhat more closely to the traditional model of the benevolent despot, discussed above, than to the public-choice alternative. In our conception, "government" in the sense of "governing" does indeed exist; and it is viewed as monolithic, at least in the model used for derivation of the tax constitution. We depart from the traditional approach simply by dropping the presumption of benevolence. And who would want to proffer advice to a nonbenevolent entity? Our shift of emphasis toward problems of constraining government follows almost directly from the shift of image from benevolence to indifference or even possible malevolence.

Specifically, we assume that the political process, as it operates postconstitutionally, is not effectively constrained by electoral competition as such, and that the electoral process can appropriately constrain the natural proclivities of governments only when it is accompanied by additional constraints and rules imposed at the constitutional level. The major objective of this book is to delineate the subset of these other, nonelectoral constraints relating to the taxing powers that might be selected by the citizen-taxpayer.

2.1. Leviathan as Actuality and as Contingency

Because the model of political process is unconventional, especially in the English-language tradition,[1] it may be useful to try to justify our underlying

---

1. The monopoly-state models developed by several Italian public-finance theorists have some common features with our construction. These models were presented alter-

perceptions before presenting the basic analytics. In so doing, we emphasize the distinction to be made between a justification of theory as a description of reality on the one hand and as an analytic device to be employed in providing foundations for constitutional construction on the other. From theory in the first sense, refutable implications may be derived that will, when tested, add to our positive understanding. And we do not, by any means, wish to reject the explanatory potential of the state-as-monopoly model. In the second sense, however, theory only allows implications to be drawn concerning what might occur rather than what will be predicted to occur. For example, it may be difficult empirically to test the hypothesis that a flood will occur in a particular locality with a 0.01 probability each year. Nonetheless, the theory from which such a predictive hypothesis is derived may be used as the normative basis for taking action toward avoiding disastrous flood damage.

Another example much more familiar to economists may be suggested here, even if its many complexities must be acknowledged. Consider *Homo economicus*—the selfish brute who devotes himself single-mindedly to maximizing the present value of his measurable wealth. As a psychologically descriptive hypothesis of the way that individuals do in fact behave, this model of man may be unacceptable. Any theory that depends for its predictions on the hypothesis that all persons behave in such fashion at all times and in all circumstances must, of course, be rejected out of hand from ordinary introspection. It is difficult to deny, however, that this simplistic model of pure economic man has been shown to have powerful explanatory potential.

More important for our purposes, even if the model of pure economic man should be severely limited in its positive explanatory usage, it may prove to be, and has proven to be, very helpful in the comparative analyses of alternative social orders and arrangements. As Sir Dennis Robertson observed, we need not deny the existence of "love" to believe that love is indeed something precious and worthy of preserving and hence something to be economized upon. As he suggested, the task of the economist is to point out insti-

---

natives to the democratic-state models by both de Viti de Marco and Fasiani. For a general discussion of the Italian contributions, with appropriate citations of the relevant Italian works, see James M. Buchanan, "La scienza delle finanze: The Italian Tradition in Fiscal Theory," in *Fiscal Theory and Political Economy* (Chapel Hill: University of North Carolina Press, 1960), pp. 24–74.

tutional ways and means of economizing on love.[2] Or if we prefer to return to Adam Smith's illustration, we may acknowledge that our butcher and our baker are occasionally, and perhaps frequently, benevolent, but surely we should all feel more secure if the institutional structure is so organized as to make their self-interest coincident with our own rather than the opposite.

In this way, what may appear to be a highly cynical or skeptical model of politics may be justified in much the same way that classical and neoclassical economic theory justifies its economic-man hypothesis, particularly in the context of comparative institutional evaluation. The monopoly-state model of government may be acknowledged to be useful, not necessarily because it predicts how governments always, or even frequently, work, but because there are inherent tendencies in the structure of government to push it toward that sort of behavior implied in the monopolistic model, tendencies that may emerge in settings where constraints are wholly absent. That is, natural government is monopoly government, with all the implications that the word "monopoly" suggests.

2.2. Monopoly Government and Popular Sovereignty

The essence of the problem at the constitutional level is how to constrain the natural proclivities of government so as to achieve results that are consonant with those which are desired by the potential taxpayer-voter-beneficiary, as he views his own role in postconstitutional periods from the initial constitutional perspective. As we have noted earlier, current public-choice theory, as well as the prevailing political ethos or public philosophy, has concentrated its attention largely on voting rules and arrangements as the primary means of constraining governmental behavior. Our analysis shifts emphasis to nonelectoral means of achieving these ends. Our object is, of course, not to deny that electoral processes *may* constrain in some cases over some range, any more than we would seek to deny that dictatorial governments may exercise their discretionary power benevolently in some cases over some range. Rather, we are seeking to show that the assumption that electoral processes

2. Dennis H. Robertson, *Economic Commentaries* (London: Staples Press, 1956), pp. 148–49, 154.

are *sufficient* to constrain self-seeking government is extremely vulnerable. We do so by appeal to a sequence of observations which, taken together, seem to us to support this position fairly thoroughly.

These observations are of three basic types. First, there is the observation that for certain types of decisions in relation to the use of resources, electoral processes are inappropriate even where those processes do generate outcomes congruent with electoral demands. Second, there is a set of purely analytic questions about majoritarian political processes which raise doubts as to whether such processes can be predicted to constrain governments effectively, in all or most cases. Third, there is a set of observations about historical experience—about the growth of government in Western democracies, and attempts by the electorate at large to limit that growth—which suggest that, in fact, democratic electoral processes may not have been constrained. We examine each of these basic types of argument in turn.

Analytical justifications for nonelectoral decision processes. Our point of departure here is the observation that electoral processes *could* conceivably be used to constrain governments much more severely than is typically the case in Western democracies. Decisions could be taken by popular referenda much more commonly. Nor, as James C. Miller[3] has recently argued, are the reasons for avoiding the referendum option entirely technical: computer and telephone voting techniques seem to provide inexpensive means of popular voting (or large sample voting) on an extensive range of issues over which politicians and bureaucrats currently exercise discretion. One might argue— and indeed the whole theory of "representative" democracy must now be dependent on such an argument—that the reason for *not* relying more extensively on popular government is that it is simply undesirable to do so. Accordingly, one set of arguments that merit investigation here relates to the question as to why one might avoid reliance on majoritarian political process, even where this is taken to provide effective constraint. We offer three arguments along such lines.

1. *The constitutional domain.* There are aspects of in-period activity that should not be and cannot be, within the terms of constitutional construc-

---

3. See James C. Miller III, "A Program for Direct and Proxy Voting in the Legislative Process," *Public Choice*, 7 (Fall 1969), 107–13.

tion, subject to determination by in-period political process. For example, to the extent that the constitution lays down private property rights and laws against interference with those rights, these laws must be interpreted and enforced essentially independently of in-period politics. (Otherwise, a decisive majority might conceivably simply suspend the property rights of minority members—murder of a Republican may become legitimate under Democratic rule.) Once this point is admitted, however, and once it is recognized that the enforcement of such laws requires resources, possibly of some magnitude, it becomes clear that questions of the extent of resources so allocated, and how they are to be used, must over some range be *independent* of simple majoritarian consent. They must therefore be made independent of in-period political process.

This is an important point and has far-reaching implications. The machinery by which laws are enforced, including not only the judiciary but also the police force, cannot be made obedient to simple majority will. Yet they must clearly be constrained in some way. Their powers must be set forth, and means of enforcement must be found. The "separation of powers," the presence of courts of appeal, and no doubt purely internal moral constraints all have to be relied on here—in addition to the fiscal constraints we set out in the ensuing chapters. Our point at this stage is simply that electoral constraints, as such, cannot be relied on.

2. *Differences between "constitutional" and "in-period" preferences.* The rational individual may have preferences at the constitutional level which at the in-period level will have changed in a systematic way. For this reason, he may wish to set aside some in-period electoral outcomes that would emerge, in favor of his constitutional judgments. One of us has explored two examples of this possibility[4] in detail elsewhere, but a simple case here may be useful. Suppose that the citizenry feel benign toward the "poor" and, at either the constitutional or postconstitutional level, would desire that substantial welfare payments be financed from tax revenues. Quite apart from the tax costs, these welfare payments would have a net cost in terms of disincentive effects,

---

4. See the discussion of the "punishment dilemma," in Buchanan's *The Limits of Liberty* (Chicago: University of Chicago Press, 1975), chap. 8, and the discussion in Buchanan's paper, "The Samaritan's Dilemma," in *Altruism, Morality and Economic Theory,* ed. E. S. Phelps (New York: Russell Sage Foundation, 1975), pp. 71–85.

and at the margin the total of these costs would be equated to the net utility gains attributable to the altruistic inclinations of the citizenry at large. At the constitutional stage of choice, the costs and benefits over the whole sequence of future periods could be taken into account in arriving at some optimal level of welfare. Suppose, however, that no constitutional determination of welfare spending is made and decisions are left to period-by-period politics. In this case, there will be a higher level of welfare or transfer payments than in the case where the determination is made constitutionally. The reason for this difference is that the benefits of the welfare transfers to the current and directly observed generation of recipients (those out of work last period, for example) will be reckoned without adjustments for the disincentive effects on welfare recipients themselves. Potential recipients are observably "poor"; transfers will not make them "poor." At the constitutional level, however, the possible effects of a transfer program in creating potential recipients can be fully taken into account. The program can be examined *ab initio* and abstractly.[5]

The interesting feature of such cases is that individuals may be led to make period-by-period choices that produce a situation that no one of them wants. Further, this result arises *not* from free-riding prisoners' dilemma elements in social interactions, but rather from genuine differences between the constitutional and in-period perspectives. These cases are collective analogues of the purely private inclination to create binding "moral" rules by which the individual may constrain his own future actions. The characteristic feature of all such examples is the conflict between the individual's current and fu-

---

5. In a constitutional choice, the desired level of welfare payments will be that level which maximizes the expression:

$$\int_0^\infty (B_t - C_t)e^{-rt}\, dt,$$

whereas period-by-period decision making will produce the result

$$B_0 + \int_1^\infty (B_t - C_t)e^{-rt}\, dt,$$

where B_i is aggregate dollar benefit in period i and C_i is aggregate dollar cost in period i.

ture preferences, as revealed by his actions taken at *different* times in relation to choices at a specific point in time.[6]

One additional example of such differences relates to redistribution as "justified" by Rawlsian-type preferences exhibited behind the veil of ignorance. Armed with information about his position in society, the individual may (and generally will) adopt profoundly different attitudes to redistribution from those he might have adopted behind such a veil. In such a setting, *constitutional* preferences over the income distribution may be embodied in specific fiscal rules that will generate results quite different from those that would be produced under unconstrained majority voting. In general, transfer policies may need to be set constitutionally: in-period electoral process will simply not generate the constitutionally desired results, and this failure will be predicted at the constitutional level of cognition.[7]

3. *Rational ignorance.* As emphasized by Downs,[8] and elaborated by many other scholars, information about politically provided goods and services is a "public good" in the technical sense. Because the acquisition of such information is costly at the margin, and because the benefits are not fully appropriable to the informed voter, all individuals will rationally remain underinformed[9] about the issues involved in elections and about public policies more generally. This fact has two possible implications. First, recognizing the likelihood of such ignorance on the part of the electorate, the constitutional decision maker may prefer a set of institutions in which effective political

6. For an attempt to model this problem for the individual formally, see A. M. Shefrin and Richard Thaler, "An Economic Theory of Self-control," Working Paper No. 208, Center for Economic Analysis of Human Behavior and Social Institutions (Stanford, Calif.: National Bureau of Economic Research, October 1977).

7. In a setting where individual sovereignty is accepted, the precise normative authority of constitutional as opposed to in-period preferences is by no means clear. One cannot say whether the one should take precedence over the other without appeal to additional value judgments. One can, however, at a purely positive level, observe that decisions about in-period outcomes may be taken at the constitutional level that would never emerge out of ordinary political process, whatever the electoral rules, because in-period preferences would not endorse them. By their nature, such constitutionally preferred policies (including potentially much of redistributional policy) must emerge independently of current *electoral* processes.

8. Anthony Downs, *An Economic Theory of Democracy* (New York: Harper & Brothers, 1957), chaps. 11, 13.

9. That is, they will possess less than Pareto-optimal levels of information.

power is more narrowly held than under genuine majority rule. Rather than choose to constrain politicians to behave in accordance with grossly underinformed electoral preferences, he may prefer to assign discretionary power to a smaller number of (representative) politicians-bureaucrats over some range and to depend on nonelectoral constraints to ensure that this power is used in the interests of the electorate.[10] Second, the necessary asymmetry between information held by the electorate as distinct from the politician-bureaucrat offers scope for misleading the electorate, and a differential power which can within limits be exercised by politicians-bureaucrats in whatever way they choose.

Theoretical analysis of majority rule and its inadequacy to constrain. Each of the foregoing arguments was designed to illustrate the possibility that individuals might, at the constitutional level, explicitly choose nonelectoral means of constraining government in preference to relying on electoral processes, given that those electoral processes generate outcomes in line with electoral preferences. There is, however, no guarantee that majoritarian democracy will operate in this way. Even where electoral processes are *intended* to constrain the exercise of government power, will they necessarily do so? How do majoritarian political processes actually work? Do they in fact constrain the behavior of those who hold the power of government, and if so, to what extent? There are at least two matters here that merit discussion: one relates to the way in which it has become customary to model majority rule, the other to the role of bureaucracy in determining political outcomes.

1. *The operation of majority rule.* As is well known, unless preferences are single-peaked[11] or parties have to announce policies simultaneously,[12] majority rule generates cyclical "social preferences." In other words, there are at least three positions, A, B, and C, such that a majority exists that prefers position A to position B, a majority exists that prefers B to C, and a majority

10. This is, in essence, the argument typically put in favor of *governmental* decision making, rather than decision making by means of continual referenda. The absence of continual referenda does, however, undoubtedly lead to greater discretionary power held by bureaucrats and politicians.

11. To secure single peakedness in preferences, substantial restrictions on both the domain of public spending and the permanence of tax institutions would be required, restrictions that need not characterize the "fiscal constitution."

12. See Downs, *An Economic Theory of Democracy,* chap. 10.

exists that prefers *C* to *A*. Much of public-choice theory has indeed been pre-occupied with this simple majority cycle. For example, in the simplest of the Downsian two-party models, one party, party I, has to announce its policy before the other, party II, and the announced platforms are binding.[13] Downs shows that party II will always defeat party I. Suppose that we consider a simple three-voter world, with no utility interdependence, and party I announces a payoff to the three voters, *a*, *b*, and *c*, of $100 each. This platform can then be depicted as the payoff vector (100, 100, 100), where the first term indicates the payoff to *a*, the second term the payoff to *b*, and the third term the payoff to *c*. Party II can then announce a policy involving the payoff vector (101, 101, *m*), where *m* is less than 98 (or any permutation of these payoffs) and win the election. This possibility leads Downs to the conclusion that interparty competition does not in general lead to Pareto optimality, except perhaps by accident: a party can always ensure victory by announcing its policies last and by organizing appropriate transfers from some minority to the corresponding majority.

One important feature of this model, however, is an implicit inconsistency in the behavior of politicians. Politicians are postulated to maximize their expected returns, which depend on their election—and hence are modeled as maximizing the probability of being elected. It is therefore somewhat bizarre that they are not postulated to maximize the advantages of election when they are successful. Since party II *knows* that it can win the election if it has the right to announce its policy platform after party I, then II will respond to party I's platform involving payoff vector (100, 100, 100) with a platform that *both* assures II of being elected *and* maximizes the "surplus" that it has at its disposal. In this case, party II's "best" policy is one involving the payoff vector (101, 101, 0) (or any permutation of these payoffs), with the party itself appropriating the excess of total product over that product which is required to be left in the hands of voters in order to secure election. The implications of this simple model are then twofold: first, the rational party will exploit the maximal minority to the maximal extent feasible; and second, it will expend in payments to the majority the minimal sum necessary to secure election. As a result, a significant proportion of total resources is available for discretionary use by the successful party. In the non-single-peaked case, therefore,

13. Ibid.

with sequential announcement of policy platforms, important dimensions of "monopoly government" emerge out of simple majority rule.

A number of questions might be posed about the foregoing model. One that arises out of the original Downsian discussion is whether the problems of majority rule in this setting might be avoided by requiring parties to announce their policies simultaneously. In the setting in which parties seek to maximize the probability of election, it does seem as if simultaneous announcement would serve to constrain parties fully. If, for example, we retain the three-voter case in which aggregate income is $300 and in which income can be costlessly transferred among voters, it seems clear that each party will aim for a platform in which two of the three voters share the $300 between themselves and the third receives nothing (the precise identity of the majority being determined at random). A party choosing this strategy would certainly expect to defeat one that chooses to distribute the $300 randomly among the three voters. What is significant in this particular case, however, is that if the party chooses to retain some of the $300 for its own use, the probability of being elected *does not fall to zero.* If we postulate that parties aim to maximize the expected returns from election, *R,* then

$$R = P_E \cdot S,$$

where P_E is the probability of being elected and S is surplus obtained from election, and it can be shown that neither party would ever select a strategy that involved a zero value for S.[14] Each party would rationally appropriate some of the $300, even where the other party did not—and as each party rationally increases its surplus, so the other party will increase its own. A sort of independent adjustment equilibrium may emerge in this setting, in which both parties (being essentially identical, by hypothesis) have identical surplus

14. Suppose, to take a simple case, that party I distributes $280 randomly between two voters (let them be *A, B*), the identity of whom is unknown to party II, and retains the remaining $20 for itself. To establish the proposition that choice of this strategy does not reduce to zero party I's chances of winning, all we need to ask is whether party II can be *certain* of victory if it distributes the full $300 to the electorate. The answer is clearly no. If II distributes $150 to *either B* or *C* and nothing to *A,* I will win if he pays more than $150 to *either B* or *C* and the remainder to *A.* Party I's offer could be (120, 160, 0), and II's (0, 150, 150); and I would win the election. There is clearly a whole range of possible arrangements in which I defeats II, even though the *sum* of the payoffs to electors is smaller for party I.

and identical probability of victory. At this equilibrium, it will be true for both parties that the elasticity of probability of victory with respect to surplus changes is -1; that is,

$$\frac{dR}{dS} = 0 \text{ implies that } \frac{dP_E}{dS} \cdot \frac{S}{P_E} = -1.$$

Thus, simultaneous announcement of policies in this setting is not fully constraining, as Downs claims.[15] Rather, scope is left for genuinely monopolistic behavior on the part of noncooperating parties.

Beyond this, of course, one can hardly rule out the possibility of explicitly cooperative behavior. Politicians of all persuasions do have interests in common, and the potential for them to exploit these interests at the expense of the electorate is very considerable. As standard duopoly theory suggests, increasing the number of "firms" from one to two is not usually sufficient to ensure results analogous to pure competition: the costs of cooperation in the two-party case are surely too low to rule out collusive behavior.

It seems, therefore, that the prevailing views of majoritarian processes and electoral competition under majoritarian rule may be unduly sanguine about the capacity of electoral rules to constrain the exercise of political power. The reasons for this may be largely analytical—theorists have perhaps been overly preoccupied with the equilibrium properties of various electoral arrangements, while ignoring the role of the politicians as players in the political game. As a result, politicians have been mere cardboard cutouts, and the notion of constraining their behavior has been of less real interest than the puzzling conundrums of voting theory. To be sure, public choice has not been particularly optimistic about the possibility of the political mechanism generating outcomes with desirable welfare properties: majority rule has been recognized to generate outcomes that may be nonoptimal or inefficient by ordinary Paretian standards. This notwithstanding, it is clear that we may not have been pessimistic enough.

2. *The role of the bureaucracy.* Just as politicians have the power, through selection of policy platforms, to secure results distinct from those desired by the electorate (or even, as we have seen, those desired by the decisive major-

---

15. Downs, *An Economic Theory of Democracy,* chap. 10.

ity), so do bureaucrats exercise genuinely discretionary power in the selection and implementation of policy proposals. Moreover, whereas the actions of politicians may be somewhat constrained by the threat of electoral defeat, the actions of bureaucrats are not.[16] Indeed, by their very nature, bureaucrats act as monopolistic suppliers. Whether their role is to supply politicians with information about alternative policies, or to design the specifics of policies to be implemented—by appeal to their special skills and information—or to implement the policies (i.e., directly produce public goods) themselves, they do so in a setting in which competitive provision of such expert advice, or alternative sources of supply of the relevant public goods, are unavailable.

One could, of course, imagine a setting in which politicians contracted out the provision of public goods to the lowest-cost provider under a system of competitive tenders. Such a setting does, in fact, apply in some cases—for example, in highway construction or public works. Tasks might be contracted out to firms which do not work solely or even predominantly for the government, and which certainly have no right of tenure in public employment. But such a setting is the exception rather than the rule. Most of the human resources that are used up by governments are in permanent employ by government and do have right of tenure. They are in an inherently monopolistic position in the provision of public goods and services.

The precise way in which this monopoly power is exercised may, of course, vary. In one version of the theory of bureaucracy,[17] bureaucrats are modeled as seeking to maximize the size of their budgets—a model that has some analytic features in common with those used in the book and developed subsequently in this chapter. In others, direct income maximization is taken to be the motivating force behind bureaucratic behavior. For our purposes, it hardly matters. What does matter is that the power that bureaucrats possess by virtue

16. Political appointees may populate the upper echelons of the bureaucracy (as they do in American institutions), in which case they may be constrained in much the same way as politicians are (or are not) by electoral proceedings, depending on their tenure. But in some parts of the bureaucracy (the military establishment, for example) and in all parts of the bureaucracy where the executive is officially apolitical (as in British institutions), bureaucrats are not at all subject to electoral constraints—whether those constraints are effective or not.

17. William Niskanen, *Bureaucracy and Representative Government* (Chicago: Aldine-Atherton, 1971).

of their position as monopoly suppliers of public goods and services and of their role as "agenda setters" in the political arena[18] is to be viewed as lying predominantly outside the coverage of electoral constraints: the potential for nonelectoral constraints to "improve" outcomes in line with the expected desires of the typical citizen-taxpayer at the constitutional level is considerable.

The broad brush of history. All of the foregoing analytics would be hardly to the point if there were clear empirical evidence to the effect that electoral processes have in practice worked pretty well in reflecting citizen preferences. But the facts, to the extent that they can be determined, hardly seem to support such a conclusion. On the contrary, the basic story seems to be an unambiguously sorry one for majoritarian political institutions. Over the last century or so, government has grown enormously in almost every country for which information is available, and probably to a magnitude completely unimagined by the Founding Fathers of the United States or any others of that period in history. In order to give a feeling for rough orders of magnitude, in 1902 the United States expended 7 percent of GNP on government activities at all levels—by 1970, the proportion was well over 30 percent. Of course, the precise interpretation of these figures is fraught with hazards. To the extent that the relative cost of publicly supplied goods has been rising, the increases in expenditure shares may reflect this cost increase alone. On

---

18. The importance of this role is emphasized and an interpretation of Niskanen's theory along such lines offered in ongoing work by our colleagues Robert Mackay and Carolyn Weaver. See, for example, their "Monopoly Bureaus and Fiscal Outcomes: Deductive Models and Implications for Reform," in Gordon Tullock and Richard E. Wagner, eds., *Deductive Reasoning in the Analysis of Public Policy* (Lexington, Mass.: Lexington Books, 1978); "Agenda Control by Budget Maximizers in a Multi-bureau Setting," *Public Choice* (Summer 1981), forthcoming; "Commodity Bundling and Agenda Control in the Public Sector: A Mathematical Analysis," Virginia Polytechnic Institute and State University Working Paper CE 79-6-1; and "On the Mutuality of Interests between Bureaus and High Demand Review Committees," *Public Choice*, 34 (1979), 481–91. See also Arthur Denzau and Robert Mackay, "Benefit and Tax Share Discrimination by a Monopoly Bureau," *Journal of Public Economics* (1980). For an analysis of constitutional limits as a control on the monopoly power of agenda setters, see Arthur Denzau, Robert Mackay, and Carolyn Weaver, "Spending Limitations, Agenda Control and Voters' Expectations," *National Tax Journal*, 32 (June 1979), 189–200; and "On the Initiative-Referendum Option and the Control of Monopoly Government," *Papers of the Committee on Urban Public Economics*, 5, 1980.

the other hand, to the extent that much public-sector output is of the nature of Samuelsonian public goods, where total output is consumed equally by all consumers (or, less restrictively, where there are economies of scale in consumption), the expenditure share figures might disguise a larger share of public output in total output, due to the growth in GNP alone. Nor does the growth of government per se imply that government is too large: there is no presumption that government was the "right size" in 1902, or that increases in size do not accurately reflect electoral wishes. Moreover, it needs to be emphasized that the dimensions of our argument are essentially static. Even if it could be shown that electoral constraints had failed, our argument could not in itself explain the high growth of government, because to do so it would need to explain why electoral constraints have become less constraining over time.

However, as the size of government increases (for whatever reason) the question of whether standard electoral constraints are adequate to keep government power within acceptable bounds does naturally arise. Could the trend be reversed even if the citizenry wanted to reverse it? And if so, what means would be required?

It is in the light of these questions that another important facet of recent history suggests itself for consideration. This is the so-called "taxpayers' revolt" which attracted widespread attention in 1978 in the wake of California's Proposition 13. Regardless of the long-term significance or insignificance of this movement, several aspects of it are noteworthy for our purposes. First, the revolt emerged *not* from within normal "parliamentary" process and interparty competition but from *outside* this sytem. The enormous success of Proposition 13 in California in the face of indifference and even opposition from most of the political establishment must surely raise some doubts about the extent to which normal political processes reflect the popular will. And these are doubts that are not entirely allayed by the spectacular policy reversals of a considerable number of the movement's original antagonists. Second, the revolt took the form not of once-and-for-all tax and expenditure cuts but of explicit *constitutional* constraints designed to be operative over an indefinite future. The avowed intention was to constrain the size of government *below the level that would prevail under normal electoral processes*. The obvious implication is that a significant body of citizens—and the overwhelming majority in some places—do not trust the in-period political process to produce results in accord with the electoral will, for whatever reason.

On balance, the appeal to the experience of history, and not least to recent events in the United States, does suggest that government, in its current institutional setting, is close to being out of the control of the electorate. Governments today seem to be substantially closer to the revenue-maximizing margins of behavior than they were in preceding decades and centuries. From this we might infer that a specifically designated and more explicitly restrictive tax constitution may now be appropriate, whereas it was not in prior periods. Whereas little or no attention might have been given to such matters in the nineteenth and early years of the twentieth century, a relative neglect that may well have been more or less rational, the forces of history may now have moved such problems into places of importance and relevance. With reference to the United States in particular, the absence of a more complete set of tax rules in the initial constitutional document may be at least partially rationalized in this fashion. The writers of that document simply could not bring themselves to imagine governments with the authority and appetites that the modern Leviathan is observed to possess.

The various arguments that we have put together in the foregoing discussion represent, we believe, sufficient grounds for taking seriously the role of non-electoral constraints in the analysis of constitutional choice. The line of reasoning makes a persuasive case, we think, for a general model of the political mechanism in which majoritarian electoral processes are not effective in constraining the power of government.

We should emphasize, however, that the model of government which we set out in the next section and on which our analysis is based is not offered primarily as a description of political reality. Our basic aim is not to effect a revolution in the study of public choice—to overturn the newly emerged orthodoxy about how majoritarian democracies actually work. Even if such a revolution were feasible and desirable, it could only represent a digression from our main argument here. We do believe that there *is* explanatory potential in our model, and in other settings we should not be averse to exploiting that. Our point here is simply that we do not need this stronger positive or empirical case to establish that the model is both interesting and directly relevant to the issues of constitutional choice.

2.3. The Model of "Leviathan": Revenue Maximization

Given that government, as it is observed to operate in-period, is taken to be effectively unconstrained by electoral considerations, the question arises as to how such government is to be modeled. What model of government behavior is to be used as the basis for deriving rules that make up a "good" tax constitution? This question is not as easy to answer as it may seem. In a very general sense, the model incorporates the presumption that governmental decision makers maximize their own utilities subject to the constraints that they face, including those that may or may not be imposed by means of the constitution. To make this presumption operationally meaningful, however, we need to define the relevant arguments in the utility functions, or at least to define the surrogates for such arguments.

The simplest version of the model presumes that governments maximize revenues from whatever sources of taxation are made available to them constitutionally. If there are no constraints on the uses to which revenues may be put, revenue becomes equivalent to private income to the governmental decision makers. If such constraints are operative but are independent of the tax rules which form the object of our study, we might also model government as attempting to maximize revenue, because revenue becomes a proxy for "surplus."

If, for example, constraints on the use of revenue require effectively that some proportion, α, of total revenues be spent on specified public goods and services, then government "surplus," S, the income that accrues to government for discretionary use, is the excess of revenue collections over spending on specified uses, G:

$$S = R - G, \tag{1}$$

and since $G = \alpha R$,

$$S = (1 - \alpha)R. \tag{2}$$

Presumably, the taxpayer would prefer to have α set at unity, so that the entire revenue collected is expended on goods and services from which he and/or other taxpayers benefit. But even if α were nominally set at unity, it seems unlikely that no slippage would occur. And even if it did not, in the absence of specific restrictions on the tax side, revenue maximization remains a good approximation for Leviathan's maximand. Suppose, for example, that a constitutional rule stipulates that tax revenues shall be spent only for the financing of genuinely public goods and services, defined in the polar Samuelsonian sense. Suppose further that such goods and services exist and can be readily identified in some objectively agreed-on way. In this case, governmental decision makers maximize their utilities by financing public goods and services in such quantities as to attain their own satiation levels if they can manipulate the tax system so that they themselves pay no tax. In most plausible settings, those satiation levels will be sufficiently high to make revenue maximization a satisfactory proxy for governmental behavior. Clearly, the decision makers would never find it advantageous to attempt to increase tax rates beyond the maximum revenue limits because, in so doing, they would reduce the quantity of public goods and services financed.

The expenditures of government are not, of course, restricted to the financing of genuinely public goods and services; and there are also serious questions that may be raised concerning the very existence of such goods and services, at least in the form implied by the polar Samuelson definition. Yet once we move outside the pure polar case, the possibility of governments using revenue to redistribute in their own direction because of purely private dimensions to goods publicly supplied implies that incentives to expand budget size are more striking still; and the satiety limits are further expanded because of the possibility of retrading private benefits. Revenue maximization remains a suitable simplification of government behavior.

We may now consider a setting that may seem more descriptive of real-world budgetary experience, one where government finances public and quasi-public goods and services, which presumably yield some benefits to large numbers of the members of the political community, but also finances direct monetary transfers. Suppose, however, that there are constitutional constraints on the direction of transfer flows. Direct monetary payments from tax revenues are constrained to flow toward those members of the community who somehow qualify on criteria of poverty. This constraint implies that governmental decision makers are not allowed to transfer tax revenues directly to themselves. Such revenues are not, therefore, equivalent to private incomes as they are in the nonconstrained transfer setting. Utility maximization on the part of the governmental decision makers here will tend toward the minimization rather than the maximization of the direct payments to the poor. However, in the guise of assistance to the poor, governmental decision makers may secure indirect transfers via the "welfare bureaucracy." Indeed, such a bureaucracy is the predicted result of utility-maximizing government here; direct payments to the poor are not. In this setting, as in the other ones discussed, utility maximization on the part of those who make governmental decisions will predictably embody revenue maximization.

There is, however, one situation in which revenue maximization and surplus maximization diverge. This is where the α of Equation (2) is dependent on the level of revenue, or spending. We examine one particularly interesting variant of this case in Chapter 7. And in the federalism setting discussed in Chapter 9, no constraints on the use of public funds are required. But in the analysis of Chapters 3 through 6, the revenue-maximization model is employed as the most logical and least complex expression of the objectives of Leviathan government.

2.4. The Model of Leviathan as Monolith

In incorporating revenue maximization as the central feature or characteristic of government behavior, we are, as previously noted, making a heroic leap from individual utility maximization to the presumption of a single maximand for "government" which is in almost all circumstances best modeled as a collectivity. Even in nondemocratic states, it is rare that "government" can descriptively be modeled as a single unit, analogous to a single person. If we allow for the interaction of many, several, or even a few separate utility-maximizing individuals within the set of those who effectively make governmental decisions, we are thrown directly into the complexities of public-choice–social-choice theory. "Government," as such, cannot exist, and "governmental outcomes" may exhibit relatively little internal consistency or stability.

We do not, of course, deny the relevance and the importance of the various attempts to look at the political process from within the public-choice–social-choice framework or paradigm. (This statement should be obvious to those familiar with some of our own previous efforts.) But we have chosen, quite deliberately here, to cut through some of these complexities of interpersonal interactions that take place within the set of governmental decision makers and to impose the "as if" model of "government as an entity." In so doing, we are not implying that "government" is something that does, in fact, exist separate and apart from and somehow independent of those persons who act on its behalf, who are individually responsible for the particular results to be observed. These persons are presumed to be maximizing their own utilities, and we are not claiming that each politician-bureaucrat or even any politician-bureaucrat accepts revenue maximization as an explicit objective. Quite the contrary. It seems unlikely that any governmental decision maker will embody such an explicit revenue objective in his utility function, at least directly. Our logical construction is not inconsistent with the utility-maximizing models of the politicians and bureaucrats that are to be found in the modern public-choice literature. The decision makers, individually, in our model do not try to further "Leviathan's interest" directly, any more than they try to further the more familiar "public interest."

The analogy with the interaction of separate buyers and sellers in the competitive market may be helpful. Since Adam Smith, we have known that something that might be called the general "public interest" is promoted by the operation of competitive markets, even though no single participant need explicitly try to promote such an objective. Our model of governmental operation is based on the presumption that something close to "Leviathan's interest," revenue maximization, emerges from the interaction of the whole set of governmental decision makers even if no person explicitly sets maximum revenue as the goal of his own action.

We construct our model of the revenue-maximizing Leviathan in an attempt to bring the observed results of modern governmental decision structures into an analytical pattern that will allow us to initiate reasonable discussion of constitutional alternatives. As we have previously noted, analyses of the complexity of the interactions among individuals in producing collective outcomes may lead to the normative evaluation of constitutional alternatives described in terms of voting rules, procedures, and processes. And it is surely within the realm of the possible that some subset of such alternatives may produce predicted fiscal results such as to make any model of the revenue-maximizing Leviathan wholly inappropriate. But we do not propose to discuss these aspects of the more inclusive constitutional challenges confronted in modern societies. We present our model of the revenue-maximizing Leviathan as a reasonable setting within which the alternative elements of a tax constitution might be discussed: nothing more, nothing less.

There are two steps involved in a shift from the benevolent despotism model of politics to that of revenue-maximizing Leviathan, and many critics may be prepared to go halfway but no further. These critics recognize that persons who act in public-choice roles can best be analyzed as utility maximizers, but they may object to the methodological "leap to Leviathan." These critics may propose that "government" behavior can best be modeled as some sort of "unconstrained random walk" over the potential policy space, without a meaningful maximand, even for "as if" analysis. We should acknowledge the inherent plausibility of such a model of political process, and we can appreciate the challenge of trying to derive the foundations of an appropriate fiscal constitution in such a setting. In many respects, such a constitution would probably be quite similar to that which might emerge under Leviathan assumptions; in other respects, differences might appear. The point of emphasis, however, is that the desirability of constitutional limits is in no way reduced by a switch to such a model of politics. In at least partial defense of the Leviathan model by comparison with a "random walk" model, we might point to the empirical record of governmental growth, in both a relative and an absolute sense.

2.5. The Constitutional Criteria

Before we proceed to the analysis of constitutional choice among alternative tax institutions in the setting provided by our somewhat unconventional model of political processes, we need to offer some remarks on the "welfare characteristics" of this model. More specifically, we need to ask whether we can be sure that constraints designed to limit the behavior of naturally monopolistic government, as modeled here, would in fact emerge from constitutional contract. Is it inconceivable that the future citizen-taxpayer might prefer to leave the taxing power unconstrained even if government is modeled as a revenue-maximizing Leviathan?

At one level, such a question might seem absurd. Surely, the potential citizen-taxpayer would desire fiscal outcomes closer to those he expects to want over the sequence of budgetary periods. But once it is recognized that the citizen-taxpayer may *himself* be a member of the ruling class—a politician-bureaucrat in future periods—then the answer ceases to be self-evident.

Consider two simple examples. If Leviathan is conceived as a monopoly supplier of public goods which, by "perfect" discriminatory tax pricing, can appropriate the full benefits from public-goods provision (which in the limit are the entire benefits accruing from the leap out of anarchy), then the benefits from public-goods provision are internal to the community provided that the monopoly supplier is expected to be a member of the community. Although postconstitutionally each citizen-taxpayer is virtually no better off than he would be in anarchy, the public-goods suppliers are very much better off. If, in fact, the one's loss is the other's gain, and the citizen-taxpayer, who is not a member of the ruling group, is indifferent as to the distribution of the net benefits from public-goods provision, then unconstrained Leviathan government could indeed emerge from a constitutional calculus. From behind a genuine veil of ignorance, the gain to potential politicians-bureaucrats exactly offsets the loss to potential citizens-taxpayers in each individual's calculations. Constraints designed to secure a greater share of benefits for the latter group would not offer any expected benefits at all.

A similar conclusion might be reached from our discussion of the operation of majority rule in Section 2.2. In the standard Downsian model of democracy, where preferences are non-single-peaked and policy announcement by parties is sequential, "political failure" results because the party that has the right to announce its policies last can win whether it chooses an optimal point or not. This phenomenon Downs refers to as "positive blocking." If political parties are conceived as *within* the relevant total group, and if those parties are surplus maximizers as in our alternative to the Downs model, then a Pareto optimum will *always* be aimed at, because the winning party will not allow unnecessary waste which it can convert into personal surplus. To the extent that the citizen at the constitutional level is interested solely in expected returns, therefore, it seems that exploitation of citizens by the government would be quite acceptable to him; aggregate expected returns, including the payoff to parties, are actually higher if parties maximize surplus than if they are simply motivated in the Downsian fashion to secure election.

The implications of posing this problem are of course very broad indeed. To the extent that *electoral processes* are seen as imposing constraints on government, what is at stake is nothing less than the issue of why genuine democracy—where it works perfectly, and setting aside problems of rational ignorance and the like—is to be preferred to dictatorship. And one might well assert that, if the two are equally acceptable within the constitutional setting, then so much the worse for the constitutional approach.

Our response might be that consideration of these issues would divert us from our main purpose—that we can simply take it as given that the role of electoral processes is to constrain naturally monopolistic government and examine nonelectoral rules from the same perspective and according to the same criteria. Our whole argument would, however, remain vulnerable to the charge that the analytic setting we have chosen indicates no underlying rationale for the existence of constraints on government of any form, and that consequently there can be no normative justification for our version of the fiscal constitution at all.

As a result, although we do not seek here to explore "the case for democracy" even in the most general terms, we do need arguments to suggest that Leviathan unconstrained is *not* an "efficient institution" in our sense (i.e., that it would *not* emerge from the constitutional contract unless constraints are inordinately costly). We may offer three basic arguments in this connection.

First, individuals in the constitutional setting may not be indifferent as to the distribution of benefits. To the extent that they are risk averse, they could be presumed strongly to favor constrained government and to oppose the narrow distribution of enormous gains that pure monopoly government would imply. This argument is, we feel, quite persuasive enough on its own. However, we do not seek to rely solely on Rawls-like distributional arguments either to justify fiscal constraints or to specify the form those constraints should take. The fiscal constitution we explore here is *not* essentially Rawlsian in its normative embodiments.[19]

Second, to the extent that taxes impose an excess burden over and above the revenue released to government, transfers from citizens-taxpayers to politician-bureaucrats will not be costless. Setting distributional issues aside therefore and anticipating that each individual will make his consti-

---

19. A Rawlsian fiscal constitution could be devised in which the rules that we develop would play a role. But this is not what we have attempted here. Such an effort would, however, represent a promising line of inquiry.

tutional choice solely in terms of expected returns, the constitutional calculus would generate an institutional setting in which pure transfers from citizens to government were minimized (i.e., transfers of resources over and above those required for public-goods provision). In other words, citizens *would* aim to constrain Leviathan to the maximum possible extent. Since, in fact, virtually all feasible tax arrangements *do* involve "excess burdens," this seems to be a decisive argument for the imposition of constraints generally and of fiscal constraints in particular.[20]

Third, an element of efficiency cost that has recently emerged under the rubric "rent seeking" seems to be of particular relevance.[21] The existence of profits to be obtained from occupying positions of power in government generates competitive processes to obtain those profits—processes which themselves involve the use of economic resources. The establishment of a completely unconstrained Leviathan under a voluntary constitution would involve the creation of a monopoly franchise of enormous proportions: it would be an example of the creation of potential rents par excellence. Just as the competition for a monopoly franchise in the conventional setting involves the creation of incentives to expend resources to obtain that franchise (conceivably many times larger in value than the value of the monopoly rent involved), so the establishment of powerful monopoly government would create incentives to fight over who will occupy the seat of power. History— military history in particular—is replete with examples. History is also

20. Such reasoning does not, of course, rule out the possibility of redistribution entirely. Where altruistic attitudes prevail, or where for other reasons "donors" derive benefits from transfers that are not fully excludable, redistribution through the public sector may be thoroughly justified on efficiency grounds over some range. What the reasoning *does* rule out is the neutrality of transfers that are purely random in terms of the directions that citizens desire. In other words, transfers that are zero-sum when the redistributive process is costless are negative-sum in practice. The constitutional contract would naturally seek to minimize these negative-sum elements.

21. See Gordon Tullock's pathbreaking paper "The Welfare Costs of Tariffs, Monopolies, and Theft," *Western Economic Journal,* 5 (June 1967), 224–32; also see Richard A. Posner, "The Social Cost of Monopoly and Regulation," *Journal of Political Economy,* 83 (August 1975), 807–27, and Anne O. Krueger, "The Political Economy of the Rent-seeking Society," *American Economic Review,* 64 (June 1974), 291–303. These basic papers, along with other contributions to the general theory of rent seeking, are collected in *Toward a Theory of the Rent-Seeking Society,* ed. James Buchanan, Robert D. Tollison, and Gordon Tullock (College Station: Texas A&M University Press, 1980).

eloquent on the magnitude of the costs. From his disembodied vantage point behind the veil of ignorance, the typical citizen would surely prefer to minimize the expenditure of resources in this utterly wasteful manner. The only way of doing so is, however, to minimize the rents that accrue from "governing"—that is, by constraining Leviathan so that its surplus is minimal.

These arguments seem to us to constitute a persuasive case for predicting that all rational individuals, behind a veil of ignorance, would seek to constrain exploitation by revenue-maximizing government to the maximum possible extent. Our construction is based on this hypothesis. To the extent that individuals model government in other than revenue-maximizing terms, our analysis is broadly suggestive rather than definitive. As long, however, as there is predicted to be some feedback effect between the availability of revenue sources and the amount of revenue raised, the substantive implications of our analysis remain valid.

3. Constraints on Base and Rate Structure

> In constraining any system of government, and fixing the several checks and controls of the constitution, every man ought to be supposed a knave, and to have no other end, in all his actions, than private interest.
>
> —David Hume, "Of the Independency of Parliament," *Essays, Moral, Political and Literary,* pp. 117–18

As we have noted, traditional normative tax theory applies external criteria for economic efficiency and equity to evaluate alternative taxing arrangements. In the standard comparisons among alternatives, the problem is posed in equirevenue terms. Government is presumed to require some exogenously determined amount of revenue per period, with the analysis having as its purpose the identification of that taxing arrangement that will generate such revenue most effectively as measured against the criteria chosen. In all essential respects, the standard analysis is institutionally vacuous. No attention is paid to possible feedback effects that specific tax instruments may exert on government itself in determining how much revenue it seeks to raise. By contrast, such possible interdependencies between the form of tax instruments and the behavior of governments in demanding revenues become central to

Some of the central ideas developed in this chapter were initially presented in a more general format in our paper "Towards a Tax Constitution for Leviathan," *Journal of Public Economics,* 8 (December 1977), 255–74.

any constitutional approach, including specifically one in which a Leviathan model of governmental process is adopted.[1]

To emphasize the dramatic difference that the change in assumptions about political process makes, it will be useful to summarize the "principles" for tax structure that emerge from the orthodox analysis. As noted, government is implicitly assumed to require a fixed amount of revenue per budgetary period, an amount that presumably will finance some efficient or optimal quantity of public goods and services, considered independent of the spending side of the account. In this framework, the ideally efficient tax is taken to be the lump-sum levy which, by definition, exerts no behavioral influence.[2] Since persons do not adjust their behavior in any way in response to the tax, there can be no excess burden, no inefficiency that is tax-induced. Furthermore, within groups of taxpayers that are biologically homogeneous (with respect to features that cannot be modified by behavioral adjustment, features such as age, sex, race, and measured natural capacities and skills), the lump-sum tax must be uniform over separate persons. Hence, the central criterion of horizontal equity, equal treatment for equals, is satisfied along with that of economic efficiency.

The lump-sum tax serves as an analytical benchmark in the orthodox normative theory despite the widespread acknowledgment that it does not exist in practical reality. When it is recognized that all taxes must exert some behavioral influence, efficiency and equity criteria may come into conflict in

1. Modern public-choice theory has incorporated the effects of tax instruments on public-goods supply in a constitutional choice approach. Almost exclusively, however, the public-choice model for constitutional fiscal choice has embodied the assumption, explicitly or implicitly, that postconstitutional budgetary decisions conform to the public-goods demands of the median voter or his representative in a legislative assembly. For this approach, see James M. Buchanan, *Public Finance in Democratic Process* (Chapel Hill: University of North Carolina Press, 1967). The analysis in this book differs critically from the public-choice theory analysis, in that we substitute a revenue-seeking Leviathan for the demand-driven and essentially passive government which that analysis assumes.

2. If the spending side of the account is taken into account, the ideally efficient tax becomes the Lindahl tax price. In one sense, the element of coercive taxation is removed in this "fiscal-exchange" approach. The latter approach is, however, not properly classified as falling within the orthodox tax analysis summarized here. For a discussion of the fiscal-exchange approach, as it is contrasted with the orthodox, see James M. Buchanan, "Taxation in Fiscal Exchange," *Journal of Public Economics*, 6 (July–August 1976), 17–29.

the evaluation of alternative arrangements. On strict efficiency grounds, separate persons should be taxed in accordance with their separately predicted behavioral responses. Overall, excess burden is minimized only when the least responsive persons are taxed more heavily than are those who are more responsive. In such a case, however, equals, as measured by pretax situations, may not be treated equally, and equity considerations dictate uniformity of treatment regardless of behavioral response. Similarly, equity considerations may suggest relative differences in the tax treatment of "unequals" that run counter to the requirements for strict economic efficiency. If, for example, persons at lower ranges of the income or wealth scales should prove to be less responsive to tax than persons at the upper ranges, efficiency norms would suggest regressive rate schedules. Only such schedules would minimize excess burdens in this setting. However, equity norms might indicate that regressive rate schedules should be rejected out of hand and that persons should be confronted with rates that are at least proportional or possibly progressive in relation to pretax measures of tax base.

This orthodox normative evaluation of the characteristics of tax structures depends critically on the equi-revenue postulate, one that is untenable when we substitute a revenue-maximizing government for the passively benevolent politics implicitly assumed in the standard treatment. At the constitutional stage of decision in the Leviathan model, potential taxpayers will recognize that government may be held back in its fiscal appetites only by limits on tax bases and on allowable rate structures. Even the analytical benchmark, the idealized and abstract lump-sum tax, loses its "efficiency" features in constitutional perspective.[3] If indeed a tax could be located that exerts no behavioral influence, and if a revenue-maximizing government should be granted access to such a source of funds, all persons would be totally vulner-

---

3. In its most general meaning, "efficiency" must be related to conceptual agreements among all members of the community. At the level of standard policy discussion, it is relatively easy to translate the familiar Paretian criterion into such consensual terms, especially when the possibility of actually organizing a set of compensations is allowed. In constitutional choice, however, the consensual definition of efficiency (i.e., an efficient position or rule is one upon which no agreement for change can possibly be reached) does not readily map into familiar concepts in modern welfare economics. An "efficient" tax arrangement, one that would emerge from agreement at a constitutional state of deliberation, need not, and normally would not be expected to, satisfy orthodox criteria for efficiency defined at the in-period or postconstitutional level.

able to the fiscal authority, with all potential economic value subject to overt confiscation in the taxing process.

As actual tax institutions rather than the idealized models are evaluated, the constitutionally derived efficiency ranking becomes quite different from that which emerges from the orthodox equi-revenue comparison. By contrast, the constitutional perspective tends to be consistent with and hence to reinforce the equity norms that emerge from the more limited, and more naive, orthodox discussion. The principle of horizontal equity, equal treatment for equals, or, put simply, uniformity of treatment for similarly situated persons, becomes a feature of any tax structure that can begin to constrain Leviathan's exactions. If government is constitutionally required to follow precepts of generality in its fiscal dealings with citizens, the revenue potential that could possibly be derived from sophisticated discrimination among separate persons and groups of taxpayers is foreclosed.

Much the same conclusion arises with respect to rate schedules that confront the potential generators of tax base. If we make the plausible assumption that the potential taxpayer secures diminishing relative marginal utility from generating taxable base, whether this base be money income, money outlays, or specified items of spending or earnings, it follows that government can maximize revenue collections only by imposing an ideally regressive tax-rate schedule. Hence, a constitutional constraint against regressive schedules can serve to limit government's taxing power, defined in gross revenue terms. Note that the requirement for uniformity or generality in tax treatment among persons as well as the possible requirement that rate schedules be nonregressive become possible characteristics of an efficient "tax constitution," quite apart from any explicit introduction of external norms for tax equity or tax justice.

Over and beyond constitutional constraints on rate schedules, some limitations on the allowable bases for tax may be desired. In the orthodox normative theory, comprehensiveness in the actual bases of a tax is a highly ranked attribute of a fiscal structure. The logical support for such comprehensiveness is straightforward. To the extent that individuals, as potential taxpayers, are allowed to shift from taxable to nontaxable options, excess burden arises which represents deadweight loss to the community. Furthermore, to the extent that some potential taxpayers shift into nontaxable options while others do not, inequities seem to be created. Within an equi-revenue frame of reference, the argument for comprehensiveness in tax base is valid. But in the constitutional perspective taken in our analysis, the traditional support for tax-base comprehensiveness disappears.

Our purpose in this chapter is to examine in somewhat more formal terms the revenue-maximizing model of government and to analyze possible tax-base and tax-rate constraints that will serve to keep fiscal excesses within tolerable limits.

3.1. Government as Revenue Maximizer Subject to Constitutional Tax Constraints

As Knut Wicksell noted, no persons would approve the imposition of taxes, either at a constitutional or a postconstitutional stage of decision, unless they anticipate securing some benefits from the goods and services that they expect government to finance with the tax revenues collected. Taxes are coercive instruments that allow governments to levy charges on persons without any corresponding expression of current willingness to pay. Furthermore, even in the most effective models of political democracy, the consent of only a majority of the members of a representative assembly is needed for tax legislation.

Perhaps at one period in history it may have seemed reasonable to rely on the operation of majority rule in legislatures to hold governmental fiscal activities in bounds. And, of course, majority-rule models remain in formal theories of collective decision making and in popular discussions of democracy. However, confronted with public sectors of modern scope and bureaucracies that demonstrably possess power quite apart from specifically legislated authority, the democratic-limits model of governmental fiscal restraint becomes increasingly naive. Some of the reasons for questioning the efficacy of electoral constraints were discussed in Chapter 2. A more acceptable model for rational constitutional choice would seem to be one in which the political-bureaucratic process, as it is predicted to operate postconstitutionally, involves the maximization of revenues within tax constraints that are imposed through the fiscal constitution.

Such a model of political process, one that may be termed a model of Leviathan, has been introduced in Chapter 2. The citizenry has no effective control over government, once established, beyond the constraints that are imposed constitutionally. It is assumed that such constraints are binding, but that postconstitutional or in-period fiscal decisions within these constraints are made entirely by the budget-maximizing or revenue-maximizing politicians-bureaucrats.[4]

Our stylized constitutional choice setting is characterized by the further and familiar assumption that each person has well-defined predictions about the aggregate level and the distribution of incomes and consumption patterns in all postconstitutional periods, but that he possesses no knowledge about his own future position within the distribution or about the characteristics of his own taste pattern.[5] The general, nonindividualized knowledge is sufficient to allow the person to make some estimate, within broad limits, both of the "efficient" levels of budgetary outlay on public goods, and of the aggregate revenues that might be obtained under alternative tax arrangements. Since the individual remains ignorant concerning his own predicted income or tastes, he cannot identify a cost share for himself under any particular tax system. He cannot, therefore, predict whether, postconstitutionally, he might prefer a larger or a smaller public-goods quantity than that which he predicts would be "efficient" for the whole community. Hence, each individual, rationally, will prefer institutions that generate roughly the "efficient" quantity, $\overline{G}$, given an independent estimate of the costs of provision. The actual outlay on desired public goods and services is defined by

$$G = \alpha R, \tag{1}$$

where α is the predicted proportion of tax revenue spent on actually providing goods and services desired and R is aggregate tax collections or revenues. Throughout the analysis of the model to be discussed in this chapter, the value for α will be taken to be exogenous, by which we mean that it is fixed

4. There are evident similarities between our model and that developed by William Niskanen in his theory of bureaucracy. See his *Bureaucracy and Representative Government* (Chicago: Aldine-Atherton, 1971).

5. In the most extreme setting for constitutional choice, we may assume that the individual is in some Rawlsian "original position" and behind the "veil of ignorance." See John Rawls, *A Theory of Justice* (Cambridge: Harvard University Press, 1971). We do not need to impose such rigid requirements, however, for the constitutional setting to be relevant. Somewhat more plausibly, we may assume only that the individual is highly uncertain about his own future position. See James M. Buchanan and Gordon Tullock, *The Calculus of Consent* (Ann Arbor: University of Michigan Press, 1962).

by the operation of constraints other than those here analyzed.[6] As we have indicated, α is such that

$$1 > \alpha > 0. \tag{2}$$

Hence, the outlay on desired public goods and services is some direct function of total revenue raised, and the problem that the individual faces at the constitutional stage is to organize tax arrangements so that the revenue raised, when adjusted by α, will yield the quantity of public goods and services estimated to be "efficient" at the given estimated new costs—costs that will, of course, be dependent on the value of α.[7] Thus, R will be chosen so that

$$\alpha R = \overline{G}. \tag{3}$$

The characteristic assumption of the Leviathan model is that, in each post-constitutional budgetary period, government will attempt to maximize total revenue collections (and hence total spending) within the constitutionally appointed tax regime. That is, government will make

$$R = R^*(b, r), \tag{4}$$

where R^* is the maximum revenue that can be raised from the tax regime and is a function of b, the tax base, and r, the allowable rate structure to be imposed on this base. Formally, the problem facing the individual at the stage of constitutional choice is to select b and r so that

$$R^*(b, r) = \frac{\overline{G}}{\alpha}. \tag{5}$$

3.2. Tax-Base and Tax-Rate Constraints in a Simple Model

Initially, we restrict the analysis to a single individual who is assumed to be exercising his constitutional choice between only two potential definitions of

6. The use of tax constraints to ensure that the value of α will be high will be specifically analyzed in Chapter 7.

7. The interrelationships among $\overline{G}$, α, and various aspects of tax institutions will be discussed in some detail in Chapter 4.

the tax base—one that is fully "comprehensive" and another which falls short of this limit. We shall relax these assumptions later, but at this point the simplification is convenient. It is immaterial for our argument precisely what the noncomprehensive base is and whether the tax is levied on the "uses" or the "sources" side (i.e., whether it might be an income tax or an expenditure tax). Let us consider a simple model in which labor is the only factor of production. Suppose, further, that the noncomprehensive tax base is money income derived from labor effort in the market, and that the comprehensive base includes such money income and also the imputed money equivalent of the individual's nonmarket production of valued end products, including leisure; in other words, the comprehensive base is full income or potential income. The question to be examined is whether the person would prefer a tax constitution that embodies the comprehensive base over the one that restricts the base of tax to money income.[8]

The situation may be depicted as shown in Figure 3.1. The indifference curves, labeled with i's, indicate the individual's preferences as between money-income-earning activity, Y, and, say, leisure activity, L. These preferences exhibit the standard properties.[9] As is customary in orthodox tax analysis, in this introductory discussion we ignore income-effects feedbacks generated by the provision of public goods. The pretax situation is characterized by a relative trade-off between L and Y that reflects the productivity of income-earning activity. The initial pretax equilibrium is at E (Y_0, L_0) on i_0.

Consider next the prospect that the individual would face if the government acquires access to the fully comprehensive tax base. In such an event, the individual would be exploitable up to the full limits of his potential income-earning ability over and beyond some minimal subsistence. Apart from this minimum, all of the "income equivalent," $0Y_a$, is potentially available for

8. The analysis holds equally for the case where the comparison is between a more comprehensive and a less comprehensive base, even when the former is itself less comprehensive than the "ideal," when defined in the orthodox terms.

9. By the assumptions of the model, the individual cannot predict his precise preference pattern as between money-income-earning and alternative activity in postconstitutional periods. All that is required for our analysis here is that these preferences are predicted to be standard.

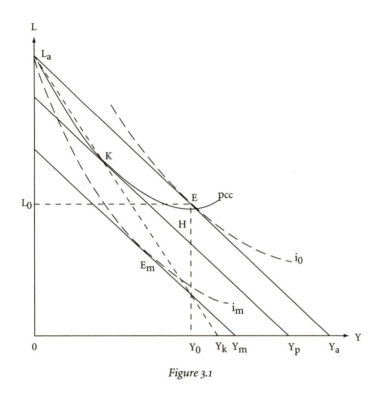

Figure 3.1

governmental use. The government bent on maximizing revenue could levy a tax that expropriated the individual's maximum potential earnings beyond the allowed subsistence level.[10]

Since it is inconceivable that anyone could ever anticipate an "efficient" public-sector–private-sector mix that would require all potential income above subsistence for governmental purposes, it seems clear that a potential taxpayer-beneficiary would *not* select the comprehensive tax base if he predicts postconstitutional governmental behavior of the type that we have pos-

10. It should perhaps be noted at this point that we are assuming that the revenues collected, as these accrue to the agents of government, are not included in the comprehensive base of the tax itself. In the simple conception of Leviathan as the ruling class or monarch, the assumption here is tantamount to allowing the king to be exempt from taxation. In a dominant majority conception of political process, the comprehensive tax may be presumed to fall on all income, but not on the special benefits, transfers, and so on, that accrue to members of the majority coalition as a result of disbursements from total revenues collected.

tulated. He will seek instead to impose constitutional constraints on the fisc, on the ability of government to tax. He can do so, in our simple case, by allowing the government to levy an income tax only on the ordinary sources of earnings—only on money incomes. The maximum revenue that can be secured from this narrowed tax base is depicted by Y_mY_a in Figure 3.1. Clearly, if the government imposes a tax on money income with revenue in excess of Y_mY_a, the individual would be better off by ceasing to earn income at all; he would improve his position by switching to position L_a. If limited to the money-income base, therefore, the government can secure revenues only up to this new maximum limit, Y_mY_a, and it can secure this amount only if it levies an "ideally" structured *regressive* tax, in which the rate for each level of Y is equal to the slope of i_m. This would involve creeping down i_m to the maximum revenue equilibrium shown in the limit at E_m, allowing the taxpayer a minute slice of surplus to ensure that his final equilibrium in the neighborhood of E_m is preferred to L_a.

Recognizing this prospect, the potential taxpayer may wish to impose the further constitutional constraint that the rate schedule should not exhibit regressivity. This choice would clearly emerge if the money-income base, together with the predicted value for α and the revenue-maximizing regressive rate schedule, should be predicted to generate outlays on desired public goods and services in excess of predicted efficient levels of provision. If, for example, the government should be required to stay within the confines of a rate structure that exhibits *proportionality*, at the least, it would effectively be confronted with a locus of potential equilibria along the individual's "price-consumption" curve for varying "prices" of Y, depicted by L_aKE in Figure 3.1. The revenue-maximizing arrangement in this case is shown where a line drawn parallel to L_aY_a is tangent to the price-consumption curve, indicated at K, with the associated revenue-maximizing proportional rate of tax on Y being $Y_kY_a/0Y_a$, and the revenue collected being Y_pY_a. The precise characteristics of this case and the analytic resemblance to familiar results in price theory can be isolated by appeal to the corresponding partial equilibrium diagram shown in Figure 3.2.[11]

---

11. The construction in Figure 3.1 can be used to demonstrate how the constitutional choice setting under our political assumptions transforms the familiar excess-burden argument made in support of a comprehensive tax base. A solution at point K, in the

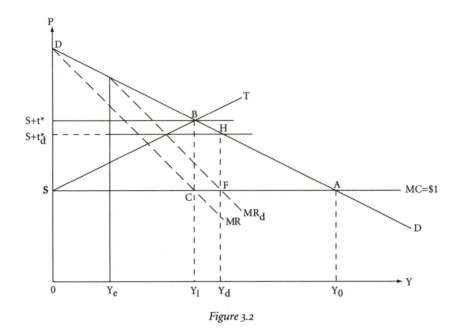

Figure 3.2

Curve *DD* in Figure 3.2 indicates the individual's demand for the income-yielding activity; this curve might be derived from a preference mapping exhibiting the properties depicted in Figure 3.1. Confronted with the requirement that it must levy a proportional tax, what tax rate will the revenue-maximizing government select? The question is clearly analogous

---

traditional argument, is shown to be inferior to that which might be attained with a comprehensive base or general tax that will yield the *same* revenue, producing an ideal solution at a point such as *H* in Figure 3.1, which may lie on a higher indifference curve than *K*. This argument must presume, however, that the government, once empowered to levy the comprehensive base tax, will, in fact, restrict its attempt to raise revenue to the collections dictated by the equi-yield comparisons.

The partial equilibrium version, based on the Marshallian demand-curve construction, can be used to illustrate the revenue-maximizing regressive rate structure, but because of income-effect feedbacks on demand, more restrictive assumptions must be made. For similar reasons, the area under the demand curve cannot accurately reflect consumer or taxpayer surplus; nor can the standard welfare triangle measure welfare loss accurately, except in the case where the income-consumption curve in Figure 3.1 is a horizontal line. We set such problems as these aside in the analysis here since they have no particular relevance to our discussion.

to that asked about the behavior of the monopoly firm that seeks to maximize profits, with the same answer. We derive a "marginal revenue" curve, *MR*, in Figure 3.2, and the quantity of *Y* at which revenue is maximized is determined by the intersection of this curve with the horizontal dollar-price line (which is marginal cost), indicating a posttax equilibrium level of money income at Y_1 and a revenue-maximizing tax rate of t^*. (Note that, when evaluated in the money-income *numéraire*, the cost of earning a dollar of income is simply a dollar. The "consumer's surplus" area between the demand curve and the cost curve in Figure 3.2 measures the utility value of money income relative to that of leisure, again evaluated in the *numéraire*, over and above that of leisure.)

The construction reveals the precise analogy between our model of postconstitutional governmental process and monopoly theory—in an analytic as well as a conceptual sense our model is appropriately designated a "monopoly theory of government." The revenue-maximizing tax rate, t^*, can be derived algebraically as follows. We know that $R = tY_1$, where t is the proportional tax rate and R is tax revenue. Further,

$$Y_0 - Y_1 = Y_0 \cdot \eta t,$$

since

$$\eta = \frac{\Delta Y / Y_0}{\Delta P / P}, \tag{6}$$

and $\Delta P / P = t$. Therefore,

$$R = tY_0(1 - \eta t), \tag{7}$$

and differentiating,

$$\frac{dR}{dt} = Y_0(1 - 2\eta t). \tag{8}$$

Setting (8) at zero, we have

$$t^* = \frac{1}{2\eta}, \tag{9}$$

and substituting t^* in (7), we have

$$R^* = \frac{Y_0}{4\eta}. \tag{10}$$

Hence, as we might expect, maximum revenue is directly related to the initial size of the taxable base and inversely related to the value of the elasticity coefficient.

As we have indicated, the revenue raised from the given base under a proportional tax is less than that which might be raised under an ideally regressive rate structure. We are then led to ask what might be the influence of a progressive rate structure on revenue. In its dealings with a single taxpayer, the revenue-maximizing government will have no incentive to shift from the equilibrium proportional rate to any rate structure that embodies progression, since this latter would imply increasing rather than declining marginal rates of tax with income. The revenue effect can be demonstrated most easily by thinking of the simplest of all progressive rate structures, one that involves only two marginal rates, with the first being zero. Consider such a structure, sometimes called a degressive one, where income over some initial range, Y_e, is wholly exempted from tax. With this additional constraint, the revenue-maximizing proportional rate on remaining units of income falls and total revenue collections fall correspondingly.

Diagrammatically, this result can be indicated by drawing the new marginal revenue curve, MR_d, over the range where the nonzero proportional rate is to be applied—as in Figure 3.2, with the maximum rate being t_d^*, with equilibrium total income at Y_d. Observation of Figure 3.2 reveals that the revenue-maximizing degressive structure generates less total revenue than under the strict proportional tax and, also, that the excess burden is smaller. Under proportionality, the excess burden is measured in Figure 3.2 by the area ABC. Under the postulated degressive structure, excess burden falls to AHF.

Not all forms of progression yield this result for the change in excess burden. For example, a linear progressive rate schedule (of the form shown by line ST in Figure 3.2) will yield a revenue-maximizing marginal rate, t^*, that is equal to the revenue-maximizing proportional rate, with the same posttax equilibrium income at Y_1. Note that, in this case, the total revenue obtained under progression is a constant share of that which would be obtained under proportionality where the marginal rate levied at income Y_1 would be applied over the entire income range. Hence, under the rate structure, ST, total revenue raised under progression is one-half that raised under proportionality. Note that the excess burden in the two cases is identical.

It may be useful to summarize the basic arguments of this section. We have observed that the constitutional decision-making calculus of the taxpayer-beneficiary, operating under the expectation of a Leviathan-like postconstitutional fiscal process, involves his opting for institutional devices that will limit the revenue-raising potential of the tax system. We have explored in some detail two ways that might accomplish this purpose. One is by limiting the size of the tax base—increasing the size of the tax base will be, beyond a point, clearly undesirable. The other is by imposing constitutional constraints on allowable rate structures on any given base. These constraints may rule out the imposition of regressive rate schedules. The argument stems, of course, both from the constitutional perspective within which our whole analysis is developed, and from the unconventional, but uncomfortably plausible assumptions that we have made about the predicted working properties of the political process.

3.3. One among Many

In the simple model analyzed in the preceding section, attention was focused on the single individual's choice calculus. This model need not be nearly so restrictive as it might appear, since we have examined choice in a constitutional setting, where the chooser is not expected to know just what his own position will be in subsequent postconstitutional periods. Nonetheless, we have neglected the problems that arise when the individual recognizes that, regardless of what his own position might be, he will be one among many taxpayers, with differences in public-goods preferences and in tax-base characteristics.

We may first consider whether or not our earlier results concerning tax-base limitations will hold in this setting. We may look at a highly simplified two-person illustration. In Figure 3.3, we assume that two persons, A and B, will earn identical amounts of money income in some pretax or no-tax equilibrium, in the amount Y_0. (Recall that, under our constitutional-stage assumptions, the individual will know only that the two persons will have the

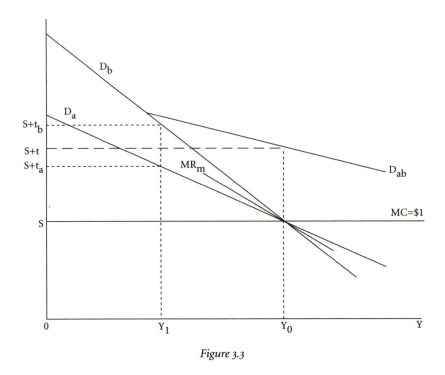

Figure 3.3

characteristics depicted; he will not know which of the two positions he will personally occupy.) The two persons are predicted to differ substantially in their response to the imposition of a tax on the limited or money-income base, with leisure (and/or other valued end products) exempted from tax. This differential responsiveness is indicated by the slopes of the "demand curves" for money income, as shown by D_a and D_b.

The first point to be noted here is that so long as any responsiveness at all is predicted, the argument for the noncomprehensive base developed earlier holds without qualification. Each of the two persons whose preferences are depicted in Figure 3.3 will be protected against the exploitation potential of government that would be present under the full income as opposed to the money-income tax scheme.

Let us now examine the revenue-maximizing government's predicted tax-ing behavior in this two-person situation. If the government could treat A and B differently, and separately, and if it could levy a proportional tax on the money income of each person (we assume that a regressive schedule is not allowed), it would impose a tax rate of t_a on A and a rate of t_b on B. This sort of differential treatment would, under almost all circumstances, allow scope for the extraction of more revenue from the community than would be possible if the government were constitutionally required to levy the same proportional rate on each person, or, stated more generally, to confront each person with the same rate structure or schedule.

On the assumption that positive revenue is extracted from both persons in the uniform-rate case, that uniform rate will lie strictly between t_a and t_b $(t_b > t > t_a)$. The revenue-maximizing uniform proportional rate, t, is determined in Figure 3.3, where the "market" marginal revenue curve, MR_m, cuts the dollar-price line, with "price" set at the intercept of the vertical drawn from this intersection and the aggregate "demand curve," D_{ab}.

As suggested in the introduction to this chapter, the requirement that all persons in the community be confronted with the same tax-rate schedule, or, in other words, that persons be treated uniformly, becomes an institutional means of reining the revenue-seeking proclivities of Leviathan. Such an argument for uniformity, which is related to but different from the more familiar "horizontal equity" norm, has not, to our knowledge, been developed in normative tax theory. With respect to horizontal equity, it is perhaps interesting to note that no constitutional rationalization for this principle, per se, emerges from our analysis.

The construction in Figure 3.3 can also be used to illustrate a proposition that seems at variance with that reached in models that assume institutional fixity. In the latter conventional framework, the behavior of individuals within the structure of given tax institutions is analyzed, and any attempt on the part of one person or group of persons to avoid or to reduce tax payments, through recourse to nontaxable sources or uses of income, is interpreted as imposing an external cost or diseconomy on less responsive taxpayers and/or on public-goods beneficiaries.[12] Behavior in reducing tax liability generates costs for others in the community by making higher rates of tax and/or lower rates of public spending necessary than would otherwise be required.

But now consider the same issue in our constitutional framework. An individual seeks to limit the revenue potential of Leviathan, while remaining

12. For an explicit discussion in such an externality setting, see James M. Buchanan, "Externality in Tax Response," *Southern Economic Journal*, 33 (July 1966), 35–42.

uncertain as to his own position. In such a case, he is benefited by the fact that at least some taxpayers in the community will be able to reduce tax liabilities by shifting into nontaxable options because this will lead to a lower revenue-maximizing uniform tax rate. This result may be shown easily, as in Figure 3.3. Compare the revenue-maximizing uniform rate, t, with that rate which would be revenue-maximizing if the two taxpayers were predicted to be equally responsive in the manner indicated by D_b. The uniform rate would rise to t_b, with higher revenue collections by government. Therefore, B benefits by virtue of the fact that A responds along D_a rather than D_b, thereby ensuring that the tax rate is t, not t_b. To the extent, therefore, that a person in constitutional choice predicts that some members of the whole set of taxpayers will be able to shift to nontaxable sources or uses of income in postconstitutional periods, his own concern about the fiscal exploitation of Leviathan is correspondingly reduced.

As a final point in this section, we want to consider whether or not our earlier result concerning the relationship among progression, proportionality, and maximum revenue holds in the many-person setting. Recall that, in the one-person setting, the introduction of any progressive features into the tax-rate schedule would tend to reduce the potential maximum revenue that government might extract from the single taxpayer. The problem in the many-person setting becomes much more complex because both the differing behavioral responses and the differing pretax levels of income must be taken into account, within the requirement that uniformity in tax treatment be preserved. Recall that, in the simple two-person setting depicted in Figure 3.3, $t_b > t > t_a$, where t_a and t_b were revenue-maximizing proportional rates upon the two persons treated in isolation from each other, and where t was the revenue-maximizing proportional rate uniformly imposed on both persons. Can total revenues be increased above those raised by rate t if government is allowed to or required to introduce progression? By lowering the rate over some initial ranges of income, revenue collections from A, the most responsive person, will increase. But offsetting this increase in collections from A, there must be, over this range of incomes, a reduction in collections from B, who must be treated uniformly. Beyond this limit, however, collections from B may be increased by setting some rate above t. Whether or not the increase in revenue collections exceeds or falls short of the decrease clearly depends on the relative elasticities of the two persons' "demand curves" where they cut the horizontal at $s + t$, the revenue-maximizing proportional rate of tax. If the person designated as *A* in Figure 3.3 is much more responsive to the reduction in tax below *t* than *B* is to the increase in tax above *t* over the higher income ranges, progression may increase revenues above those raised by uniform proportionality. In other cases, this increase may not be possible.[13] The limitations imposed by dealing with a two-person model should be stressed here. What is of importance is the tax-adjustment elasticities of different groups of taxpayers. In terms of the representation in Figure 3.3, the addition of a third person equivalent to *A* would increase the likelihood that progression would be revenue-enhancing. On the other hand, adding a third person equivalent to *B* would reduce such a prospect. This result suggests that the relative revenue-generating properties of revenue-maximizing proportional and progressive rate structures depend critically on the distribution of taxpayers among the separate response groups, with separate levels of taxable income.

3.4. Tax Limits and Tax Reform

We have argued that the bases for taxation, as well as the rate structure, will be constrained constitutionally by the person empowered to choose among tax arrangements who does not know his own position and who adopts a revenue-maximizing model for the behavior of government in postconstitutional periods. Our analysis provides support for the *noncomprehensiveness* of the allowable tax base. To the extent that activities which yield value to taxpayers remain outside the allowable reaches of the fiscal authority, the appetites of Leviathan are checked. Persons may resort to nontaxable options, and in the knowledge that they will do so, government necessarily curbs its revenue extraction.

The danger of allowing government access to revenue-raising instruments that generate budgets in excess of those necessary for financing some roughly efficient levels of public goods and services has been central to our model. We should, however, recognize that constitutional tax constraints might, through time, prove to be overly restrictive. In this case, postconstitutional pressures

---

13. Algebraic derivation of the conditions under which different results apply is presented in the appendix to this chapter.

will surely arise for escape through constitutional-style adjustments designed to widen the bases and to allow for more flexible rate structures, to move generally from specificity to comprehensiveness. Empirically, it will always be difficult to distinguish between genuine constituency demands for a relaxation of such constraints and the ever-present demands of the revenue-seeking politicians-bureaucrats. For the latter group, and for their spokesmen, efforts will tend to be directed toward widening bases, toward increasing the number of sources upon which taxes may be imposed. "Tax-reform" advocacy on the part of the "bureaucratic establishment" will tend to be centered on "tax-base erosion." Indeed, one indirect test of the empirical validity of our model of the political process lies in the observed lack of reformist concern about relative rates of tax within tax-law limits that currently exist.

In the discussion of proposed tax-base changes, the attitudes of the traditional normative tax theorist and the members of the taxpaying public differ more sharply than anywhere else. Our analysis is helpful in "explaining" the attitudes of the taxpayers. For example, they are likely to react negatively and emphatically to proposals to move toward taxation on the basis of full income, as, for example, by including the imputed rental values of owned residences in the base for personal income tax. The normative tax theorist, who advocates such inclusion from reasoning based on equi-yield comparisons, responds to taxpayers by arguing that overall rates of tax may be lowered simultaneously with the widening of the base. But the taxpayers may be implicitly, but correctly, rejecting the equal yield postulate, in their predictions that *any* widening of the tax base must open up further taxing possibilities for a revenue-seeking government.

Illustrations might easily be drawn from American fiscal experience. For example, in late 1979, a proposal was widely discussed aimed at the introduction of a broad-based value-added tax with offsetting reductions in payroll taxes and individual and corporate income taxes. If such a proposal is adopted, it may be predicted that, ultimately, the value-added tax would be used to generate revenues greatly in excess of the revenue reductions under other taxes. In fact, of course, almost any widely advocated tax change tends to be justified in terms of its greater "efficiency," or its greater "fairness," springing from the extension of the tax base. As our analysis indicated, if our perception of postconstitutional political process bears any relation to reality at all, it is precisely on such grounds that the change should be rejected.

Appendix: Progression in the Multiperson Setting

The question of interest here is this: Can a progressive tax system raise more revenue than the revenue-maximizing proportional system, when there are many taxpayers? We have already shown that the revenue-maximizing proportional system always gives more revenue in the single-taxpayer case, or equivalently in the many-taxpayer case when all taxpayers are identical. Is this true more generally?

To investigate this question, we examine a simple two-person example, denoting the two individuals by A and B. We shall assume that B is "richer" than A—that Y_b exceeds Y_a at all tax rates. We further assume, for analytic convenience, that the individuals' demand curves for nonleisure activity have constant elasticities. We can therefore write

$$Y_1^a = Y_0^a(1 - \eta_a t_a)$$
$$Y_1^b = Y_0^b(1 - \eta_b t_b), \tag{1}$$

where

Y_0^i is i's pretax income

Y_1^i is i's posttax income (expressed in dollars net of tax)

t_i is i's tax rate expressed as a rate on net income

η_i is i's elasticity of demand for "income,"

so that

$$\eta = \frac{\Delta Y}{Y_0} \cdot \frac{p_0}{\Delta p},$$

and $\Delta p = t$, $p_0 = 1$, by assumption. The individually revenue-maximizing proportional rates, t_i^*, can be derived by maximizing $t_i Y_1^i$ in each case by simple calculus. On this basis, we obtain

$$t_a^* = \frac{1}{2\eta_a} \tag{2}$$

$$t_b^* = \frac{1}{2\eta_b}.$$

The uniform proportional tax rate that maximizes revenue, t^*, is obtained by maximizing the expression

$$R = Y_0^a(t - \eta_a t^2) + Y_0^b(t - \eta_b t^2), \tag{3}$$

which yields

$$t^* = \frac{Y_0^a + Y_0^b}{2\eta_a Y_0^a + 2\eta_b Y_0^b}. \tag{4}$$

From (4), it is clear that t^* is a weighted average of sorts of t_a^* and t_b^* and must lie between t_a^* and t_b^*.

In fact, recalling that Y^b exceeds Y^a by assumption, a necessary condition for progression to yield more revenue than the revenue-maximizing proportional rate is that

$$t_b^* > t_a^*. \tag{5}$$

If this is not so, a departure from t^* by lowering the rate for earlier units of income or raising the rate on later units of income (to B) must reduce revenue. From this it follows directly, using (2), that

$$\eta_a > \eta_b. \tag{6}$$

To derive *sufficient* conditions, consider the revenue-maximizing "progressive" rate structure, which consists of two rates: t_1 over the range in which both pay tax and t_2 in the range where B only pays tax. Any additional progression must lose revenue. We can examine aggregate revenue in this case and determine the conditions that must hold for t_2 to exceed t_1. Accordingly, we examine

$$R = 2t_1[Y_0^a(1 - \eta_a t_1)] + t_2[Y_0^b - Y_0^a(1 - \eta_a t_1) - Y_0^b \eta_b t_2] \tag{7}$$

$$\frac{dR}{dt_1} = 2Y_0^a - 4\eta_a t_1 Y_0^a + Y_0^a \eta_a t_2 \tag{8}$$

$$\frac{dR}{dt_2} = Y_0^b - Y_0^a + Y_0^a \eta_a t_1 - 2t_2 \eta_b Y_0^b. \tag{9}$$

Setting (8) and (9) at zero, we have the equation system

$$\begin{bmatrix} 4\eta_a & -\eta_a \\ -\eta_a & 2\eta_b \cdot Y \end{bmatrix} \begin{bmatrix} t_1 \\ t_2 \end{bmatrix} = \begin{bmatrix} 2 \\ y - 1 \end{bmatrix}, \tag{10}$$

where $y = Y_0^b/Y_0^a \ (> 1)$. Thus, we have

$$\frac{t_1^*}{t_2^*} = \frac{4\eta_b y + \eta_a(y - 1)}{4\eta_a(y - 1) + 2\eta_a}. \tag{11}$$

For $t_2^* > t_1^*$, therefore, we require that

$$4\eta_b y + \eta_a y - \eta_a < 4\eta_a y - 4\eta_a + 2\eta_a$$

or

$$\frac{\eta_b}{\eta_a} < \frac{3y - 1}{4y}. \tag{12}$$

Since $1 < y < \infty$ (by construction), (12) requires that η_b/η_a be less than three-fourths, or that η_a be at least one-third larger than η_b.

We should note that if η_a is too large relative to η_b, then the revenue-maximizing arrangement in the proportional tax case may ignore A entirely and simply levy t_b^*, and the progressive tax system becomes "proportional" anyway. That is, we require that $t^* < 1/\eta_a$ (since at $t = 1/\eta_a$, individual A ceases to pay tax entirely). In other words, we require that

$$\frac{Y_0^b + Y_0^a}{2\eta_a Y_0^a + 2\eta_b Y_0^b} < \frac{1}{\eta_a}$$

or

$$\frac{y + 1}{2\eta_a + 2\eta_b y} < \frac{1}{\eta_a}. \tag{13}$$

That is,

$$\frac{\eta_b}{\eta_a} > \frac{y - 1}{2y}.$$

Combining (12) and (13), we can specify the general requirement on η_b and η_a as

$$\frac{3y - 1}{4y} > \frac{\eta_b}{\eta_a} > \frac{y - 1}{2y}. \tag{14}$$

For y in the neighborhood of unity, we require η_a to be more than twice as large as η_b. As y becomes very large, we require only that η_a be more than one-third larger than η_b—but not more than twice as large, since then the tax system will force A to earn no taxable income at all.

It is however clear that, for any value of y, there is a value of η_b/η_a that satisfies (14). Progression *can* therefore yield more revenue than proportionality, under the appropriate relative values of η_b and η_a.

It is interesting at this point to contrast the results under the simple two-tier rate structure with those that emerge under a progressive tax system in which the marginal tax rate is a linear function of Y_1. Such a "linear" progressive tax is depicted in Figure 3.4 by the line SM. Now, under such a rate structure, the largest amount of revenue in the two-person case that could conceivably be obtained is exactly one-half of the maximum revenue obtainable under a regime in which the revenue-maximizing proportional rates, t_a^* and t_b^*, are imposed on A and B, respectively. This situation is depicted in Figure 3.4—the revenue obtained from B is at most $\frac{1}{2}R_b^*$, from A at most $\frac{1}{2}R_a^*$.

Let the revenue under this "linear progressive" rate structure be R_L. Then

$$R_L \leq \tfrac{1}{2}(R_a^* + R_b^*). \tag{15}$$

Let the revenue derived from the revenue-maximizing uniform proportional rate structure be R_p. Then we know that B can be treated as if he were identical with A, so that R_p must be greater than or equal to $2R_a^*$; and A could be ignored entirely, so that R_p must be at least as great as R_b^*. In other words,

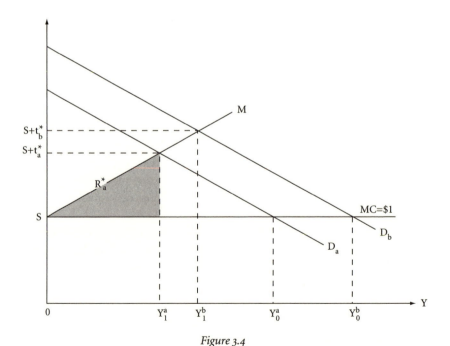

Figure 3.4

$$R_p \geq \max \, [2R_a^*, \, R_b^*].$$ (16)

Suppose that $2R_a^* \geq R_b^*$. Then

$$R_p \geq 2R_a^* \text{ and } R_L \leq \tfrac{1}{2}(R_a^* + 2R_a^*),$$

so that

$$R_p \geq 2R_a^* \geq \tfrac{3}{2}R_a^* \geq R_L.$$ (17)

If, on the other hand, $R_b^* \geq 2R_a^*$, then

$$R_p \geq R_b^* \text{ and } R_L \leq \tfrac{1}{2}(\tfrac{1}{2}R_b^* + R_b^*) = \tfrac{3}{4}R_b^* \leq R_p.$$

In the two-person case, then, the linear progressive tax derives unambiguously smaller revenue than the revenue-maximizing uniform proportional system.

We can add a third party, C, where $R_c^* > R_b^* > R_a^*$ by construction. Then, by analogous reasoning,

$$R_L \leq \tfrac{1}{2}(R_a^* + R_b^* + R_c^*),$$

and

$$R_p \geq \max \, [3R_a^*, \, 2R_b^*, \, R_c^*].$$

Let $3R_a^* \geq 2R_b^* \geq R_c^*$. Then

$$R_L \leq \tfrac{1}{2}(R_a^* + \tfrac{3}{2}R_a^* + 3R_a^*) = \tfrac{11}{4}R_a^* < 3R_a^* \leq R_p.$$

And similarly, if $R_c^* \geq 3R_a^*$, $2R_b^*$, or $2R_b^* \geq 3R_a^*$, R_c^*. More generally, it can be shown by induction that

$$R_L^n \leq R_p^n$$

(where R_L^n is the linear progressive rate for n taxpayers). Assume that $R_L^n < R_p^n$. Then

$$R_L^{n+1} \leq \tfrac{1}{2} \sum_{i=1}^{n+1} R_i^* < \tfrac{1}{2}R_p^n + \tfrac{1}{2}R_{n+1}^* \leq \max \, [R_p^n, \, R_{n+1}^*].$$

Now, R_p^{n+1} must exceed R_p^n, since R_p^n is feasible (one could simply ignore individual $n + 1$). Moreover, R_p^{n+1} must exceed R_{n+1}^*, since R_{n+1}^* is feasible. Therefore,

$$R_L^{n+1} \leq R_p^{n+1}.$$

So $R_L^n \leq R_p^n \Rightarrow R_L^{n+1} \leq R_p^{n+1}$; and since the result is true for $n = 2$, and $n = 3$ it is true for all n, by induction. Thus, the "linear progressive" schedule always derives less revenue than the revenue-maximizing proportional rate structure.

A third variety of progression is worth mentioning here. This is the degressive system mentioned in Chapter 3. Any such system, combining a flat exemption with a uniform proportional rate, must raise less revenue than the revenue-maximizing uniform proportional rate structure, since less revenue is obtained from each and every taxpayer.

4. The Taxation of Commodities

But what is government itself, but the greatest of all reflections on human nature? If men were angels, no government would be necessary. If angels were to govern men, neither external nor internal controls on government would be necessary. In forming a government which is to be administered by men over men, the great difficulty lies in this: you must first enable the government to control the governed; and in the next place oblige it to control itself.

—James Madison, *The Federalist No. 51, The Federalist Papers,*
p. 160

In Chapter 3, we examined the question of how we might expect the individual citizen-taxpayer to choose among alternative bases and rate structures at the constitutional level under ignorance concerning his future position. The analysis in that chapter can be most directly applied to an income tax. In this chapter, we use essentially the same analytic framework to examine commodity taxation. As in Chapter 3, the analysis will be conducted in a setting that abstracts entirely from the time dimension. All taxes are current, and all tax rates are known with certainty in advance, permitting the appropriate behavioral response. We shall relax these time-dimension restrictions in Chapters 5 and 6.

Our purposes in this chapter are twofold. First, we wish to examine questions concerning the commodity-tax arrangements that would be selected by the potential taxpayer, given our constitutional setting and our assumptions about the motivations and actions of government. Because of the directional similarity in behavioral responses on the sources (income) and the uses (expenditure) side of the taxpayer's account, many of the implications here tend to mirror those derived in Chapter 3. This varied reiteration of the earlier analysis may be useful in itself but it also offers a springboard for discussion of a different issue—which brings us to our second purpose. Here and elsewhere, the focus of our discussion is primarily on the selection of tax instruments that are suitably constraining. But clearly there may be a variety of tax instruments that are equally constraining—instruments that will, when exploited to the fullest by government, yield *identical maximum* revenue. Are some of these arrangements to be preferred to others by the potential taxpayer? Are the standard techniques for "equi-revenue" comparison applicable to the subset of tax instruments that yield identical maximum revenue? Specifically, can excess burden considerations be used to rank these instruments? If so, how do these considerations intervene in evaluating alternative tax institutions more generally? Is it possible to determine some "optimal" trade-off between smaller excess burden and larger welfare loss due to excessive spending? To answer such questions and to predict what tax institutions might emerge from the constitutional contract, we need to evaluate alternative means of achieving desired constraints. This part of our discussion has the added heuristic advantage of allowing us to indicate how our basic analysis incorporates, or may incorporate, the standard equi-revenue construction.

4.1. The Conventional Wisdom

It will be useful to begin our discussion of commodity taxation with a brief review of the central elements of orthodox doctrine. This procedure will allow us to point up the contrasts between the standard normative results and those which emerge under the alternative constitutional perspective on taxation applied within a Leviathan or Leviathan-like model of political process. In commodity-tax analysis, as elsewhere in orthodox tax literature, the point of departure is some presumed requirement that government raise a fixed and exogenously determined amount of revenue. Given this fixed-revenue requirement, the question is: How should taxes be levied so as to minimize welfare loss? As noted earlier, the orthodox procedure is to attempt to answer this question independent of any consideration concerning the uses to which tax revenues may be put. This analytical weakness aside, the traditional argument has concentrated on the efficiency aspects of differing commodity-tax arrangements. Equity and/or distributional implications have been less emphasized in commodity-tax analysis than in income-tax analysis. The issue of the normatively desired form of commodity taxation has been treated largely as a problem of minimizing excess burden, with some consideration of horizontal equity (i.e., of avoiding discrimination among individuals on the basis of tastes or other "irrelevancies"). Vertical equity issues have tended to be effectively ignored. The literature has noted the equivalence between a uniform tax on all commodities and a personal tax on consumption expenditure with a proportional rate structure;[1] nonetheless, within the indirect tax analysis, as such, the concentration has remained on the efficiency properties of alternative tax arrangements.

Basically, the application of the same normative framework to both commodity and income taxes tends to generate policy recommendations of the same type and direction. Personal taxes should allegedly be broadly based so that there is no (or minimal) discrimination among individuals on the basis of how income is earned; similarly, commodity taxes should allegedly also be broadly based—and ideally should tax all "goods," including leisure, equally—so as to minimize discrimination among individuals on the basis of how income is spent. Likewise, just as failure to tax all income sources equally under direct taxation is adjudged to lead to efficiency losses as individuals attempt to substitute less productive but relatively lightly taxed activities for those more highly taxed, so failure to tax all *goods* equally under commodity taxation is taken to lead to efficiency losses on the consumption side.

In both cases, or so says the prevailing tax-analysis orthodoxy, lump-sum taxation represents the idealized benchmark. Given the infeasibility or even the impossibility of lump-sum taxation, the practical question necessarily becomes one of selection among second-best options. Whereas with personal taxes the "second-best" arrangement is normally assumed to be the broadest-based income tax (or consumption-expenditure tax) that is feasible, with in-

---

1. Or an intertemporally neutral "income tax" of the type recommended by J. S. Mill, *Principles of Political Economy* (London: Longmans, Green, 1926); Irving Fisher and Herbert W. Fisher, *Constructive Income Taxation* (New York: Harper & Brothers, 1942); W. D. Andrews, "A Consumption Type or Cash Flow Personal Income Tax," *Harvard Law Review,* 87 (April 1974), 1113–88; and most recently by James E. Meade, *The Structure and Reform of Direct Taxation,* report of a committee chaired by J. E. Meade (London: George Allen & Unwin, 1978).

direct taxes the possibility of using differential rates on goods according to their degree of complementarity with leisure (relatively high rates on leisure complements, and lower rates on goods relatively highly substitutable with leisure) naturally presents itself. As emphasized by Corlett and Hague, Harberger, Lerner, Baumol, and Bradford and in much of the "optimal-taxation" literature in general,[2] a set of differential excises can be devised that involves a smaller welfare loss or "excess burden" than does an equi-revenue tax falling equally on all the directly taxable commodities (i.e., excluding leisure).[3] It is always more efficient to raise a given amount of revenue by means of a set of taxes in which the tax rate applied to each good is appropriately related to the degree of substitutability between that good and the untaxed good, leisure, than by an equal rate on all taxed goods.[4]

4.2. Constitutional Tax Choice

As in our discussion of income taxation, our quarrel is not with the *logic* of the orthodox conclusions. It is, instead, with the *setting* within which the questions are posed. Once the implicit "benevolent dictator" conception of political process is rejected, the appropriate role for normative tax analysis

2. See W. Corlett and D. Hague, "Complementarity and the Excess Burden of Taxation," *Review of Economic Studies,* 21 (1953–54), 21–30; Arnold Harberger, "Taxation, Resource Allocation and Welfare," in National Bureau of Economic Research/Brookings Institution, *The Role of Direct and Indirect Taxes in the Federal Revenue System* (Princeton: Princeton University Press, 1963), pp. 25–70; Abba Lerner, "On Optimal Taxes with an Untaxable Sector," *American Economic Review,* 60 (June 1970), 284–96; and W. J. Baumol and D. F. Bradford, "Optimal Departures from Marginal Cost Pricing," *American Economic Review,* 60 (June 1970), 265–83.

3. There is, of course, an exactly analogous horizontal equity argument applicable in all cases except where tastes are identical. See Geoffrey Brennan, "Second-Best Aspects of Horizontal Equity Questions," *Public Finance/Finances Publiques,* 27, no. 3 (1972), 282–91. Of course, the precise policy implications for horizontal equity will in general differ from those for efficiency (unless all individuals have homothetic preferences) because goods that may be complementary with leisure at the margin will not be complementary with leisure over the entire range.

4. On the other hand, an arbitrary set of excises is worse in an expected sense than a uniform tax on all goods (excluding leisure). Thus, if the complement-substitute relations are not known, uniformity of rates is to be preferred. See Y. K. Ng, "Towards a Theory of Third Best," *Public Finance/Finances Publiques,* 32, no. 1 (1977), 1–15; and G. Brennan and T. G. McGuire, "Optimal Tax Policy under Uncertainty," *Journal of Public Economics,* 4 (February 1975), 205–9.

becomes that of offering assistance to the individual, the potential taxpayer, who, at a constitutional level of deliberation, is presumed able to select among the alternative fiscal powers and instruments to be made available to government. Such assistance is not, however, in the form of ethical-moral principles telling the individual how he "should" behave in a constitutional choice situation. For the most part, constitutional tax analysis becomes technical and is designed to provide a basis for an understanding of how alternative fiscal arrangements may be predicted to operate, a basis from which some choice must ultimately be made.

Given a model of revenue-maximizing government, the implied normative conclusions about commodity taxation follow the spirit of those outlined in Chapter 3. And they are diametrically opposed to those that emerge from the standard treatment. For example, the lump-sum tax does not constitute the "efficiency" ideal. Under lump-sum taxation, the individual can expect only maximum exploitation by the fisc. Under almost any projection of demands, revenue collections would be predicted to be grossly in excess of those that might be required to finance expenditures on public goods and services. In much the same sense, the minimally distorting set of excises (i.e., with rates related inversely to the degree of substitutability with leisure) serves to raise maximum revenue limits above those implied by a uniform commodity tax and almost certainly to increase total revenue beyond desired levels. Indeed, a restriction that all rates on taxable commodities be identical might well be instituted precisely as a means of restricting Leviathan's fiscal appetites.

In the more formal analysis that follows, we offer analytic support for these conclusions. More specifically, we deal with two sorts of questions. First, what are the effects on maximum revenue yield of alternative forms of restriction on commodity-tax institutions? Second, given a choice among various forms of commodity tax all of which yield the same maximum revenue, which, if any, is to be preferred?

4.3. Alternative Forms of Commodity Tax: The Choice of Base

We classify the alternative forms of commodity taxation to be examined in terms of the restrictions on allowable arrangements—whether base restrictions, restrictions on rate structure, requirements for uniformity across commodities, or requirements for uniformity across individuals and over units.

The discussion can be conducted conveniently in terms of the diagrammatics of Figure 4.1. In this diagram, D_a and D_b represent the aggregate (market) demand curves for two private, partitionable goods, A and B. These demand curves are assumed to be linear for expositional convenience, and cost curves are horizontal to reflect constant average (and hence marginal) costs. Quantity units are defined so that the initial marginal cost (assumed equal to price) is unity.

Let us suppose that A and B represent the only potential tax bases that might be assigned to government. The individual's constitutional choice between them depends directly on the estimated needs for financing the quantity of public goods and services that he expects to desire over the sequence of budgetary periods during which the selected tax rule is to remain in force.

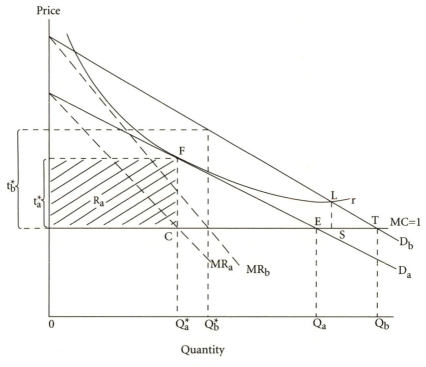

Figure 4.1

If government is assigned the authority to tax A, it will, under Leviathan assumptions, maximize the revenue it can obtain from taxes on this base. The power to tax commodity or good A is identical analytically to the assignment of a monopoly franchise for the sale of commodity A. As depicted in Figure 4.1, the revenue maximum occurs at Q_a^*, the quantity defined by the intersection between the marginal revenue curve, MR_a, and the marginal cost curve, MC. The revenue-maximizing tax rate is t_a^*; revenue collected is $t_a^* Q_a^*$, shown by the shaded area.

It is clear from the construction in Figure 4.1 that if the tax on commodity A is replaced by a tax on commodity B, the same amount of revenue could be obtained at a lower tax rate and a smaller excess burden. Let r be a rectangular hyperbola with the ordinate and the horizontal MC line as its axes, and let r pass through F. Every price-quantity combination along r, by construction, yields the same tax revenue ("monopoly profit") as at F. Since F is the point at which maximum tax revenue is obtainable from A, r must be tangent to D_a at F. Now, consider point L, at which r intersects with D_b (to the right of F).[5] At L, the same revenue that is obtained by the maximum revenue tax on A could be obtained by a tax of rate LS imposed on B. The welfare loss imposed by such a tax on B is LST, which is much smaller than the welfare loss FCE imposed by the tax on A. Hence, the traditional efficiency or welfare argument for the broader-based tax seems to emerge.

Under the assumptions about the behavior of government that we have made, however, it is clear that a tax rate of LS will not be imposed on commodity B. If government is granted access to base B, with no accompanying restriction on rates, this change will ensure that there will be an increase in the revenue that government will appropriate. Government will secure the maximum revenue obtainable from the tax on B. This revenue is $t_b^* Q_b^*$ in Figure 4.1, where Q_b^* is determined by the intersection of MR_b and MC, and t_b^* is the excess of demand price over MC at that quantity. It is clear that, under these conditions, the excess burden will be larger under the tax on B than the tax on A. Under the assumptions of proportional rate structure and linear

5. We ignore the intersection above and to the left of F, although its existence has been a source of some controversy in the literature on tax progression and leisure consumption. See Robin Barlow and Gordon R. Sparks, "A Note on Progression and Leisure," *American Economic Review*, 54 (June 1964), 372–77; and John G. Head, "A Note on Progression and Leisure: Comment," *American Economic Review*, 66 (March 1966), 172–79.

demand curves,[6] the excess burden induced by a tax exploited to its maximum revenue potential is exactly one-half the maximum revenue raised. A simple geometric proof of this proposition suffices at this point in the argument. All we need to note is that in the linear case, the marginal revenue curve lies exactly halfway between the demand curve and the vertical axis. In Figure 4.1, Q_a^* is exactly one-half Q_a. The area of the triangle CEF in Figure 4.1 is given by $\frac{1}{2}(t_a^* \cdot CE)$; and since CE equals Q_a^*, the welfare-loss triangle CEF is $\frac{1}{2}(t_a^* Q_a^*)$, or one-half of maximum revenue. Analogously, since Q_b^* is exactly one-half of Q_b, the welfare loss attributable to the maximum revenue tax on B is $\frac{1}{2} t_b^* \cdot (Q_b - Q_b^*)$ or $\frac{1}{2}(t_b^* Q_b^*)$. We can conclude therefore that the ratio of excess burdens induced by alternative taxes will be the same as the ratio of their maximum revenue yields: if tax B generates larger maximum revenue than tax A, then it will generate a concomitantly larger excess burden when maximum revenue yields are obtained.

An immediate corollary of this result is that if we compare two taxes with identical maximum revenue yields under a proportional rate structure, they will generate identical excess burdens (given the appropriate linearity assumptions). Consider, for example, a commodity-tax base, X, which, when used to generate maximum revenue, yields the same maximum revenue as does tax base Y. Any number of such tax bases may exist, but a simple direct comparison of any two of them will suffice to make the point. As before, let D_x and D_y depict the aggregate demand curves for these alternative tax-base commodities in Figure 4.2. The maximum revenue rates produce identical revenues. The solutions represent differing points along the rectangular hyperbola, r. Is either one of these taxes to be preferred on the grounds that it generates a lower excess burden? Since both generate the same maximum revenue, and since the welfare loss at maximum revenue rates is one-half of maximum revenue in both cases, *the excess burdens as well as the maximum revenues are identical*. In other words, in this construction if we compare proportional taxes that raise the same maximum revenue, there can be no

6. The linearity assumption is, of course, special. We should note, however, that this assumption is embedded in conventional measures of excess burden; by examining only first- and second-order terms in the relevant Taylor series expansion of the utility function, those measures of welfare loss are in fact only linear approximations. See note 7 below.

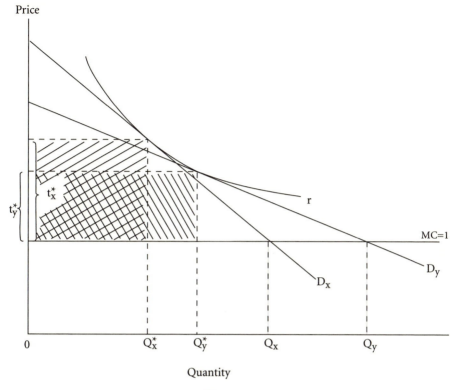

Figure 4.2

preference between them on excess burden grounds. Maximum revenue it-self becomes a sufficient indicator of excess burden, as conventionally mea-sured.[7]

7. Conventional measures of excess burden focus on the second term of a Taylor series expansion of utility functions. That is, if we can represent individual utility functions as

$$U = f(X_1, X_2, \ldots, X_n),$$

then

$$\Delta U = \sum_i \frac{\partial f}{\partial X_i} \Delta X_i + \frac{1}{2} \sum_i \sum_j \frac{\partial^2 f}{\partial X_i \, \partial X_j} \Delta X_i \, \Delta X_j,$$

which on manipulation can be shown to yield

$$\Delta U = \frac{1}{2} \sum_i \Delta P_i \, \Delta X_i.$$

A further corollary of this result is that if we compare two tax bases which are of identical magnitude pretax but for which elasticities of demand differ, the one with the lower elasticity of demand will give rise to the *larger* excess burden, because it gives rise to a larger maximum revenue. (Geometrically, this comparison could be depicted in a diagram similar in construction to Figure 3.3, with the demand curves of persons replaced by those for commodities.) This result is diametrically opposed to that which emerges from the conventional equi-revenue approach, which relates excess burden directly with elasticity.

If there can be no preference for broad-based taxes derived from excess burden comparisons (rather the contrary) within our Leviathan setting, the choice between broad- and narrow-based taxes—say, between a tax on A and a tax on B, as depicted in Figure 4.1—depends solely on the level of public-goods supply which the citizen expects to want. This anticipated desired level of public-goods supply depends in turn on both the predicted demand for public goods and on the total cost of providing them.

Consider total cost first. These costs are composed of three elements, as illustrated geometrically in Figure 4.3. First, there is the physical cost of production of G, depicted in marginal terms by MC_g (which again for convenience we assume to be constant). Second, there is the additional cost imposed by the Leviathan government's appropriation of some proportion, $1 - \alpha$, of tax revenue as pure surplus. If, out of each dollar of revenue, only 100α cents are expended on public goods, then the total revenue cost of $1's worth of G is $1/\alpha$ dollars. If government, for example, spends only one-half of each revenue dollar on providing G, then each dollar's worth of G will cost taxpayers $2 in tax revenue. This "$\alpha$ effect" raises the per unit cost of G to $1/\alpha\ MC_g$, as indicated in Figure 4.3. Third, there is the excess burden generated by the tax itself, which is also a genuine cost. As indicated above, given

---

[See Harberger, "Taxation, Resource Allocation and Welfare"; and Harold Hotelling, "The General Welfare in Relation to Problems of Taxation and of Railway and Utility Rates," *Econometrica*, 6 (July 1938), 242–69.] By taking higher terms of the Taylor series expansion, one can of course get more accurate measures of utility change. This is tantamount to allowing for differential curvature of demand (or marginal valuation) curves. So doing would permit a ranking of equi-maximum-revenue taxes according to total welfare loss but would involve measuring "excess burden" with a degree of refinement not used elsewhere in the literature and would in any case involve dealing with a high order of "smalls."

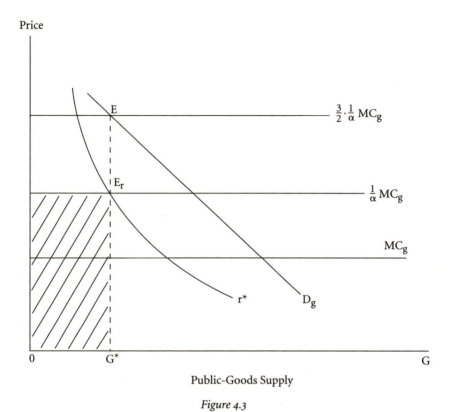

Public-Goods Supply

Figure 4.3

linear demand schedules and constant costs, and with proportional rates imposed at maximum revenue levels, this excess burden will be exactly one-half of (maximum) revenue. The aggregate cost per dollar's worth of G will then be $\frac{3}{2}$ $1/\alpha$ MC_g, depicted in Figure 4.3.

The desired level of G, given this aggregate cost, can now be determined by appeal to the typical citizen's constitutional predictions as to his demand for public goods. We should emphasize at this point that there is no necessary requirement here that all citizens have identical predicted demands for public goods (although in a strict veil-of-ignorance setting such an assumption would not be particularly implausible: to the extent that each individual is totally uncertain as to his future tastes and income level, we might expect that predicted demands for public expenditures on G would be roughly identical across individuals). It is sufficient here, however, to focus on the calculus of a single typical citizen. To consider the additional problems involved in deriving some constitutional agreement among citizens on the issue of appropriate tax allocations to Leviathan in the case where those citizens have differing predicted demands for G would complicate the discussion and divert us from our main purpose.

Let us depict the typical citizen's predicted demand for G by D_g in Figure 4.3. Where this demand curve cuts the aggregate marginal cost line, $\frac{3}{2}$ $1/\alpha$ MC_g, will determine the desired level of G, depicted by G^*. The level of *revenue* required to generate this output level, G^*, is $1/\alpha$ $MC \cdot G^*$, because $MC \cdot G^*$ is the physical cost of producing G^* and α is the proportion of revenue that Leviathan spends on G. This revenue level is depicted by the shaded rectangle in Figure 4.3. We can now, finally, construct a rectangular hyperbola through E_r, depicted by r^*, which depicts the desired level of (maximum) revenue.

The virtue of this diagrammatic treatment is that it permits us to show on a single diagram and in a neat and simple way the interrelationships among the citizen's demand for public goods; the cost of physically producing those public goods; the "exploitative" dimensions of Leviathan's surplus generation, as captured by the parameter, α; the excess burden generated by the tax system;[8] and the desired level of (maximum) revenue potential to which the constitution will permit Leviathan access.

Since our main interest here is with the constitutional selection of tax instruments, we focus directly on that issue. What we seek in the selection of the appropriate commodity-tax base is a base that will, when exploited to its maximum revenue potential, yield exactly that revenue which is required to generate G^* (i.e., a revenue level subtended by any rectangle under r^*). Suppose, for the purposes of argument, that the tax base A does this. In other words, suppose that the level of tax revenue indicated by r^* in Figure 4.3 is exactly the same as that indicated by r in Figure 4. 1. (Geometrically, this requires that if Figure 4.3 were superimposed on Figure 4.1 so that the abscissa in Figure 4.3 lay along the MC line in Figure 4.1 and so that the vertical axes were collinear, then r and r^* would be coincident.) Then, if tax base A is in use, it follows that any broadening of the tax base would be undesirable.

---

8. See David B. Johnson and Mark V. Pauly, "Excess Burden and the Voluntary Theory of Public Finance," *Economica*, 36 (August 1969), 269–76.

Such a broadening would lead to a higher level of tax revenues and of public-goods supply than the citizen-taxpayer desires, given the particular values of α and MC_g as shown in Figure 4.3. To select, for example, the tax base B would generate a maximum revenue level above that depicted by r^*, a corresponding level of G above G^*, and leave the citizen predicting excessive exploitation by government in postconstitutional periods, along with unnecessarily high welfare losses in the tax system. At the same time, any tax base that generates the same maximum revenue as can be derived from a tax on A is equally acceptable with A. Within that set of tax options which yield identical maximum revenue, the citizen-taxpayer is genuinely indifferent.

What this discussion shows can be encapsulated in two statements: first, greater broadness of coverage under commodity taxation is not unambiguously desirable and it is positively undesirable beyond some point; and second, excess burden varies directly and linearly with maximum revenue, so that taxes which have identical maximum revenue have identical excess burdens when maximum revenue rates are applied, and taxes with larger maximum revenue yield a larger excess burden when maximum revenue rates are used (and vice versa). Base limitation therefore emerges as a legitimate instrument in the design of tax constitution for a Leviathan government. The general thrust toward broader-based tax institutions, characteristic of the orthodox analysis, cannot be sustained within the alternative perspective on tax institutions that we postulate in this book.

4.4. Uniformity of Rates over Commodities

Let us now suppose that, maintaining the basic assumptions of the previous section, the maximum revenue realized from taxation of A or B is insufficient to provide the level of public-goods supply anticipated to be desired during the postconstitutional sequence. The question then arises as to how government might be granted authority to tax *both* A and B, in order to secure the required revenue. If we assume that specific rates for each commodity cannot be set in advance, essentially two tax-structure possibilities present themselves. Government may be constrained to set the *same* rate on both A and B, *or* it may be allowed to set the rates on commodity A and commodity B independently and separately. In other words, Leviathan may be allowed access to a "uniform" sales tax which includes A and B in the base; or it may be permitted to apply a set of discriminatory excises, with rates of its own choosing.

In the latter case, if we assume that A and B are two of a large number of commodities and neither complements or substitutes one for another, a change in the price of A does not directly affect the price of B, and vice versa. In this setting, it is clear that a revenue-maximizing Leviathan will set the tax rate on A at t_a^*, as depicted in Figure 4.4, and the tax rate on B at t_b^*.

If, by comparison, government is constrained to set a uniform rate for both commodities, it is necessary to aggregate the demand curves in order to depict its revenue-maximizing solution. Our construction in which quantity units for the two goods are normalized in the dollar's worth dimension facilitates the aggregating of heterogeneous commodities. We can, quite simply, add the demand curves for the two commodities horizontally, to get the curve D_{ab}, as shown in Figure 4.4. Given the rate-uniformity constraint, government will set the tax rate so as to generate the quantity determined by the

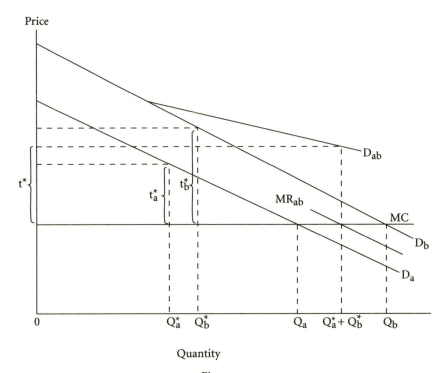

Figure 4.4

intersection between the marginal revenue curve relevant to the aggregated demand curve and the marginal cost curve. This solution is depicted in Figure 4.4 at quantity $\frac{1}{2}(Q_b + Q_a)$, with tax rate t^* imposed uniformly on each of the two commodities. Given the assumptions of linear demand and constant marginal cost curves, total quantity, over the two goods, remains constant as between rate uniformity and rate differentiation. This constancy result emerges from the simple geometrical configuration. Since Q_a^* (the quantity of *A* under discriminatory rates) is $\frac{1}{2}Q_a$, and Q_b^* (the quantity of *B* under discriminatory rates) is $\frac{1}{2}Q_b$, the aggregate quantity under the discriminatory solution is $\frac{1}{2}(Q_a + Q_b)$. But this quantity is identical to that which emerges in the nondiscriminatory solution. However, given that $t_b^* > t_a^*$, the quantity of *B* will be lower in the discriminatory solution than in the uniform-rate solution; conversely, the quantity of *A* will be higher in the discriminatory solution than in the uniform-rate solution. The revenue-maximizing uniform rate of tax, t^*, will lie between the two separate revenue-maximizing rates, t_a^* and t_b^*, in the discriminatory solution.

The maximum revenue yield to government is higher in the discriminatory than in the uniform-rate situation as long as the elasticities of demand for the two commodities differ and as long as positive revenues are obtained from both commodities in the uniform-rate solution. Under such conditions, by our earlier analysis, it follows that excess burden is also lower under the uniform-rate requirement than in the situation where differential revenue-maximizing rates may be set. These results are, of course, familiar and become obvious once one accepts the analogy between the granting of the power to tax a commodity and the granting of a monopoly franchise. The requirement for uniform rates of tax for separate commodities is precisely analogous to the prevention of discrimination in monopoly price over separate segments of a market.[9]

The connection between these aspects of our analysis and the optimal-tax literature here is interesting. Reinterpreted within the setting of our model, what the so-called "optimal-taxation" literature provides is a specific set of instructions to government as to how it might exploit its power to tax in the most effective way. The analysis provides precisely that tax-

9. See Joan Robinson, *The Economics of Imperfect Competition* (London: Macmillan, 1933), chap. 15.

price rule which would lead a monopolist to discriminate perfectly between markets.[10] In this context, the optimal-tax rules are *precisely* the maximum revenue–maximum profit rules. The analogy is evident here, but it has not, to our knowledge, been specifically noted.

The diagrammatic analysis we have employed is, to be sure, strictly partial—no allowance is made for the interaction between the demand for *A* and the price of *B*, and vice versa. It could therefore be claimed that it hardly bears on the optimal-tax literature, which typically adopts a general equilibrium framework. But the foregoing discussion can easily be extended to a general equilibrium setting; such an extension is provided in the appendix to this chapter.

We have, in this section, referred to differing rates of tax on differing commodities as "discrimination," partially to emphasize the analogy with discriminatory monopoly. This construction is made more tenable by our normalization of quantity units for separate commodities in the "dollar's worth" dimension. Nonetheless, we should acknowledge that economists conventionally do not apply the term "discrimination" with reference to relative tax treatment of observably different commodity bases. The language of this section can be modified to conform with conventional usage by referring only to uniform and nonuniform rates of tax.

There is an additional argument that may be adduced in support of conventional language here, an argument that has some relevance for the analysis of the following sections. As we know from orthodox price theory, a private monopoly firm may find it difficult to differentiate among customers or over units because of resale-retrading prospects. However, a monopoly firm that markets two separate and unrelated commodities would face little difficulty in setting different prices, even if quantity units are normalized in dollar-cost terms. In considering the differential rates of tax among commodities that governments may levy, we are analyzing a situation analogous to the monopoly firm in the second of these situations. By contrast, when we come to examine the prospects of tax-rate differentiation among persons or over units of goods, we look directly at the analogues to various forms of discriminatory monopoly.

10. Although not among consumers or over units of output; see below.

4.5. Uniformity of Rates over Individuals

It would in principle be possible for optimal-tax recommendations to extend to the discriminatory treatment of different individuals. The simple partial equilibrium diagrammatics in Figure 4.4 are applicable,[11] as was indeed indicated by our usage of essentially the same construction in Chapter 3 in Figure 3.3. By reinterpreting D_a and D_b in Figure 4.4 as the demand curves of two individuals for some taxable commodity X, and D_{ab} as the aggregate demand over the "market" comprised of these two persons, we can derive the following results:

1. Consistent with the optimal-tax approach, any given level of revenue, R, could be obtained with a smaller welfare loss by the appropriately discriminatory pattern of taxes—a relatively higher rate of tax on individual B than on A.
2. Equally and for precisely the same reasons, the maximum revenue potential increases when this pattern of discrimination is used.
3. If the maximum revenue potential is fully exploited, the welfare loss is concomitantly higher when discrimination among individuals is allowed.

As in the income-tax setting, therefore, the restriction that there be no discrimination among individuals on the basis of different tastes—one aspect of traditional horizontal equity norms—can be understood and justified in this setting as one limit on the revenue capabilities of Leviathan government.

We suggested that such possibilities for discrimination in rates among separate taxpayers exist "in principle" and that, if exploited, such discrimination would produce the comparative results indicated. The analysis requires the qualification noted at this point, however, because of the difficulty that even a monolithic and monopolistic Leviathan might confront in bridging the gap between "principle" and "practice." In this particular respect, the analysis applied to income taxation (Chapter 3) becomes significantly different from that applied to commodity taxation (Chapter 4). Individuals must earn income on their own; they cannot readily work out arrangements by

11. There is no interpersonal analogue to complementarity-substitutability relations between commodities.

which other persons earn income on their behalf. By contrast, individuals need not purchase commodities directly. They can consume commodities purchased for them by others. And any differentiation among persons in rates of commodity tax (and hence in purchase price) sets up strong incentives for such indirect "purchases" to be made. For ordinary commodities, especially those that are not consumed on the instant of purchase, differential tax rates among different persons may prove impossible to implement. In practice, the effective rate of commodity tax would tend to be the lowest rate imposed on any person in the community, with this person becoming the direct purchaser for everyone. Imposition of a tax on final consumption rather than purchase of commodities might allow for rate differentiation, but monitoring costs would likely become prohibitive, even for the monopoly government. In a sense, therefore, the analysis of rate differentiation here among persons is more of an intellectual exercise than a treatment of a relevant prospect. The exercise itself, however, has the advantage of extending the direct analogy between monopoly government and the monopoly firm in traditional price theory. The institutional barriers to effective discrimination are equivalent in the two cases.

4.6. Discrimination by Means of the Rate Structure

We may extend this analogy between the taxing power and the monopoly franchise even further. If the ability to tax X is identical with the power to sell X at monopoly prices, it is clear that the best of all possible situations for Leviathan would be a situation in which tax rates might be set to mirror the price structure of the perfectly discriminating monopolist. In both cases, the idealized objective is to appropriate the full consumer surplus of each and every consumer. For purposes of analysis, let us ignore the practical difficulties noted above and examine two questions:

1. In our model of constitutional choice, what are the implications of perfect discrimination both among individuals and over units of the taxed commodities within the purchase opportunities of a given individual?
2. What if discrimination *over units* is permitted but discrimination among individuals is not?

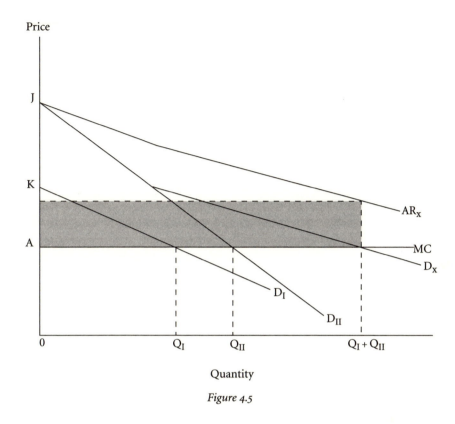

Figure 4.5

The "perfectly discriminatory" tax system. We consider initially a simple two-person community, in which government has power to tax some good, *X*, which we assume, as before, is produced under constant costs. The marginal evaluations of the two individuals for *X* are depicted in Figure 4.5 by D_I and D_{II}.[12] Under perfectly discriminatory taxes, each individual will face a different and regressive rate structure that traces out his or her marginal evaluation curve. The purchase-offer schedule will be designed to leave each individual with just enough consumer surplus to induce purchases up to the point where marginal evaluation equals marginal price, which will be set

12. As elsewhere, the demand curves and the marginal evaluation curves for *X* are taken to be identical—we abstract from income effects—strictly for analytic convenience.

equal to marginal cost. For example, the tax-rate structure for I will begin with a rate marginally below AK for the first unit of X, and the rate will fall linearly with increases in X consumption by I until the rate is zero at Q_I. Similarly, for II the tax-rate structure will begin with a rate marginally below AJ for the first unit of X that II buys, and the rate will decline linearly to zero at Q_{II}. Total revenue is given by the area under the aggregate demand curve for X, the shaded area determined from the aggregate "average-revenue" schedule depicted as AR_x in Figure 4.5. This revenue is obtained without the imposition of any *excess burden*.[13]

This relationship between rate discrimination and excess burden has implications that are worth exploring, even given the idealized confines of the model. To do so, we can ask the following question: If, under a uniform proportional tax on X, the level of revenue is precisely that desired, could we be certain that allowing discrimination by means of the rate structure would be undesirable? For any other form of discrimination so far considered, the answer would be an unambiguous affirmative: discrimination would increase maximum revenue, increase excess burden, and push the level of public expenditure beyond the desired level. In this case, where the discrimination involves differentiation in rates over separate quantities of commodities purchased, however, the conclusion is not definitive. The move from the uniform proportional rate to the perfectly discriminatory set of regressive rates would, in the linear case, exactly double the revenue collected from each individual and hence the total revenue derived. It would, however, increase the costs endured by each citizen-taxpayer by only one-third (again assuming a linear demand curve for the taxed commodity). These propositions can be demonstrated by appeal to Figure 4.6. In the uniform nondiscriminatory tax case, the revenue derived from X is the area $MNSW$, representing $\hat{t} \cdot Q'_x$. Under this tax regime, the individual enjoys the net consumer surplus depicted by triangle LMN. Consider the move to the discriminatory tax regime: the total revenue is here the full area of triangle LWE_x because all consumer surplus is appropriated by government in tax. Now, triangles LMN and NSE_x are congruent, because MN is equal to WS, which is in turn equal to SE_x (i.e.,

13. For an early analysis of the analogous construction depicting a private monopolist's profit-maximizing quantity discount offers, see James M. Buchanan, "The Theory of Monopolistic Quantity Discounts," *Review of Economic Studies*, 20 (1952), 199–208.

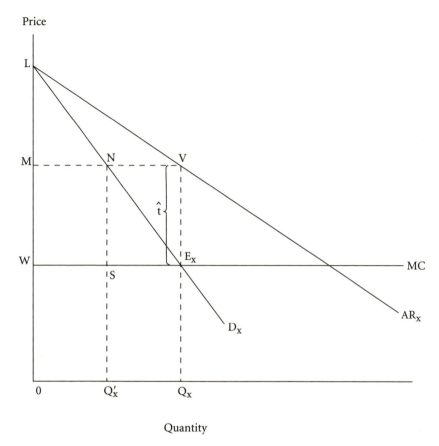

Figure 4.6

Q'_x is exactly half of Q_x), and *MN* and SE_x are parallel. Further, we know that NSE_x is exactly one-half the area of *MNSW*. Hence, LWE_x has twice the area of *MNSW*: revenue is twice as large in the perfectly discriminatory regime. And *LMN* has an area equal to one-third of MNE_xW. We can therefore conclude that, in the move from uniform to perfectly discriminatory taxation, total revenue (and the level of public-goods supply) doubles, while aggregate costs rise by one-third. There has clearly been a reduction in the per unit cost to the citizen of public-goods supply. We know that

$$G_d = \frac{\alpha R_d}{MC_g} \text{ so that } \frac{\alpha(2R_p)}{MC_g} = 2G_p, \tag{1}$$

where G is the level of public-goods supply, R is the level of revenue derived by government, and the subscripts d and p refer to the perfectly discriminating and uniform outcomes, respectively. Further,

$$C_d = \tfrac{4}{3}C_p, \tag{2}$$

where C is total cost to the citizen and equals the sum of excess burden and revenue.

Thus, the average cost, that is, the cost per unit of public good, which in this simple model is equal to marginal cost, varies in the two cases as follows:

$$\frac{C_d}{G_d} = \frac{\tfrac{4}{3}C_p}{2G_p} = \frac{2}{3}\left(\frac{C_p}{G_p}\right). \tag{3}$$

Perfect discrimination reduces the *per unit cost* of public-goods supply by one-third.

In short, perfect discrimination both increases the level of public-goods supply *and* reduces the per unit cost of public-goods supply. In order to determine whether the citizen-taxpayer would prefer the perfectly discriminating solution to the simple uniform outcome with the same tax base, we need to examine the value that he places on the additional units of public-goods supply he obtains. We can do this in a simple way by appeal to Figure 4.7. In this diagram, the revenue derived from tax base, X, under a uniform proportional rate structure is depicted by r_x, and the corresponding level of public-goods supply by G_x, where r_x and the horizontal line $(1/\alpha)MC_g$ intersect. The aggregate marginal cost, including excess burden, of this expenditure level is $\tfrac{3}{2}(1/\alpha)MC_g$ and the desired level of G, depicted by G^*, occurs where the citizen's-taxpayer's predicted demand for G, D_g, intersects this aggregate marginal-cost line. Now, let us suppose that X is an appropriate tax base, given a uniform proportional rate structure. Then, G_x and G^* will represent identical levels of public-goods supply; Figure 4.7 is drawn on this basis.

In this sense, the combination of tax base X with the simple proportional rate structure seems to represent a constitutionally optimal "fiscal rule." However, suppose that perfectly discriminatory taxation of X is now allowed. Revenue doubles, and public-goods output increases to $2G_x$, where $2r_x$ cuts $(1/\alpha)MC_g$. The relevant cost curve, however, is now lower than before: it is $(1/\alpha)MC_g$, not $\tfrac{3}{2}(1/\alpha)MC_g$, because the tax involves no excess burden. (We note that this represents a reduction in per unit costs of one-third, as derived above.) Because costs are lower, the level of G desired under the perfectly dis-

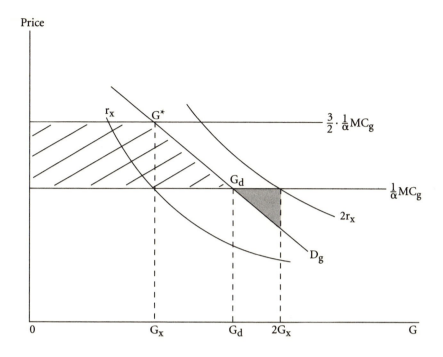

Public-Goods Supply

Figure 4.7

criminatory tax regime is correspondingly larger: it occurs where D_g cuts the new marginal cost curve, shown as G_d in Figure 4.7. Depending on the elasticity (or slope) of D_g, the point G_d may be to the right or the left of $2G_x$. In fact, G_d will be to the right of $2G_x$ if the point elasticity of demand evaluation at G^* has an absolute value greater than 3. For, if G_d and $2G_x$ were coincident, that elasticity, η, would be given by

$$\eta = -\frac{\Delta q}{q} \cdot \frac{p}{\Delta p}$$
$$= \frac{2G_x - G_x}{G_x} \cdot \frac{\frac{3}{2}(1/\alpha)MC_g}{\frac{1}{2}(1/\alpha)MC_g}$$
$$= 3.$$

However, even where G_d lies to the left of $2G_x$, as in Figure 4.7, the perfectly discriminating solution may still be preferred. The gain from the move to the perfectly discriminating solution is the shaded area to the left of D_g between $\frac{3}{2}(1/\alpha)MC_g$ and $(1/\alpha)MC_g$, and has to be compared with the area of the shaded triangle between G_d and $2G_x$ below $(1/\alpha)MC_g$, which is the loss from possibly excessive government spending. (It can, in fact, be shown that the perfectly discriminating solution will be preferred if the point elasticity of demand at G^* is greater than $\frac{3}{4}$.)

Care must be taken in the analysis throughout to avoid confusion between the taxpayer's anticipated demand for G, the public good, and his anticipated demand for tax-base commodities, A, B, or X in our discussion, and depicted in Figures 4.1, 4.2, 4.4, 4.5, 4.7, and 4.8. Only in Figures 4.3 and 4.7 and the associated discussion are demand schedules for the public good depicted. In the discussion immediately above, the perfectly discriminatory solution serves to eliminate all potential consumer's surplus in the purchase-use of the tax-base commodity, X. But, by lowering the effective cost-price for the public good, G, through the elimination of all excess burden in taxing X, consumer's surplus involved in the "purchase-use" of G is increased. And, given plausible values of relative elasticity coefficients, it is conceivable that the taxpayer-consumer may prefer the discriminatory tax solution to the nondiscriminatory one.

At this point, we note an important difference between the model of the monopoly firm in price theory and our model of Leviathan as tax gatherer. In the former, the effective value of the analogue of α is zero—that is, the consumer is not conceived as being a beneficiary of any part of the profits that the monopolist secures, and hence no value is placed by the consumer on any addition to such profits. The consumer would never voluntarily give up the net surplus that a shift from simple to discriminating monopoly would involve. In the Leviathan model, by contrast, the taxpayer does place some positive value on increments to monopoly tax revenues, because some proportion, α, of them is spent on things (public goods) that the taxpayer values; and the parameter α must take a positive value if any taxing power is to be granted to government at all.

It is interesting to note, however, that beyond the requirement that α be positive, its value plays no direct role in the foregoing analytics at all: everything hinges on the elasticity of the demand curve for public goods. In some ways, this is a slightly surprising result because it seems to imply that the value of the increment to revenue that the move from proportional to perfectly discriminatory taxation generates is independent of the proportion of that revenue expended on public goods. However, this apparent anomaly is explained by the fact that the parameter α exercises a similar influence on both the value of the incremental units of G *and* the units originally allowed for under the proportional tax structure alternative. To the extent that α does exercise an influence on this calculation, it does so indirectly and in a slightly surprising direction. The smaller α is, *ceteris paribus,* the higher the price and hence the smaller the quantity of G within the neighborhood of which the extension of public-goods supply occurs. It seems reasonable to presume that, as in the case of a linear demand curve, the elasticity of demand will be higher in this range. In this sense, the smaller the proportion of revenue spent on public goods, the greater the likelihood that the citizen will desire the extension of revenue that the shift from a proportional to a perfectly discriminatory rate structure makes possible.

The results of this section contrast strikingly with those which emerged under other forms of discrimination examined earlier. If there is discrimination among individuals or among commodities, but not over units (because, say, of a requirement that rate structures be proportional), excess burden is directly related to maximum revenue, and the comparison of alternative tax bases can be conducted in terms of maximum revenue comparisons alone. Once discrimination over units is allowed, however, excess burden issues obtrude. An increase in maximum revenue yield when the initial revenue yield is "appropriate" may indeed be desirable if that revenue increase results from a change in rate structure, from proportionality to regression.

Analogously, a reduction in revenue when revenue is "excessive," achieved by restrictions on the rate structure—requiring progression, perhaps, or outlawing regression—cannot be unambiguously designated as desirable.

A second aspect of these results merits emphasis. It is clear that, at the constitutional level, the individual would prefer a perfectly discriminatory tax regime to a proportional tax that generates the same revenue yield. Suppose, for example, in Figure 4.6, that there is some potential tax base, Y, the demand curve for which is identical with AR_x. The proportional tax on Y would achieve the same maximum revenue as the perfectly discriminatory tax on X, but would do so at 50 percent higher cost in terms of surplus forgone.

As in the earlier case with our discussion of possible discrimination in rates among taxpayers but not over quantities, the practical relevance of the whole analysis should not be overly emphasized. For the same reasons there mentioned, and others, effective rate discrimination over quantities may prove impossible to enforce for ordinary commodities. Even if interpersonal trades to implement indirect purchases could be prevented, the prospect for storage could allow single purchasers to take full advantage of the quantity discounts that the idealized differential rate structure would offer to the taxpayer. The possibility of any enforceable and effective differentiation over quantities purchased would be limited to nonstorable commodities.

Uniformity among persons, discrimination over units of commodity. To complete the discussion of this section, it is interesting to examine briefly the case in which there is uniformity of treatment as among individuals, but where regression in the rate structure is allowed. We might conceptualize this setting as one in which constitutional-legal rules dictate uniformity of treatment among persons, but where differentiation in rates of tax over units is allowed as long as all persons face the same "offer schedule." What rate structure will generate maximum revenue under these conditions? To answer this question, consider Figure 4.8. The simple two-person setting is again used, with D_I and D_{II} being the demand curves of individuals I and II for commodity X. Under the constraint that I and II must be treated identically (i.e., they must face the same rate structure), it is clearly possible for II to be treated "as if" his demand curve for X is D_I; it is equally clearly impossible for I to be treated as if his demand curve were D_{II}, because D_I lies inside D_{II} throughout. The revenue to be obtained from a single perfectly discriminating rate structure based on D_I is given by the area between the new curve R_I and MC; R_I is constructed so that the vertical distance between R_I and MC at any output is twice the vertical distance between D_I and MC. The revenue to be obtained from a single perfectly discriminating rate structure based on D_{II} is the area under D_{II} above MC. A rate structure geared to discriminate ideally along D_{II} would, of course, have the effect of eliminating the first person (I) from the market completely. The revenue-maximizing Leviathan will, if limited to these two options, choose between these solutions on the basis of revenue yield.

However, government will not in general find it revenue maximizing to focus on one or the other demand curve entirely. What is relevant here is the

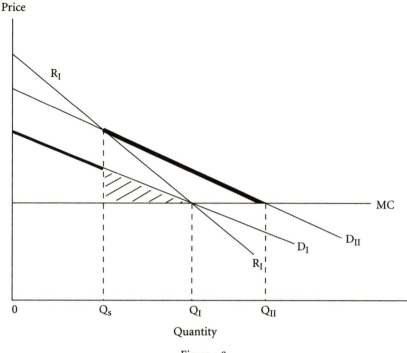

Figure 4.8

upper "envelope" combining the R_I and D_{II} curves. Up to the quantity level Q_s, where R_I and D_{II} intersect, more revenue is obtained by pricing according to D_I; beyond that point, revenue will increase if there is a switch to D_{II} and government levies a tax rate that just induces II to purchase additional units of X. For instance, consider the output unit immediately beyond Q_s. If government levied taxes according to D_I, the marginal revenue would be R_I, which is less than D_{II} in this range. The rate structure is, then, that depicted by the heavy line in Figure 4.8. It follows D_I to Q_s and D_{II} thereafter. It is therefore "regressive" over the ranges zero to Q_s and Q_s to Q_{II}, but there will be a sudden discontinuous jump in rates at Q_s.

It is of some interest to compare the welfare loss in terms of excess burden per dollar of revenue in this solution with that in the various other discriminatory solutions previously examined, over commodities or individuals. We can show easily that the excess burden is indeed smaller here. For it will be recalled that, under maximum revenue assumptions, in all the cases where discrimination over quantities to individuals is not allowed, excess burden is exactly one-half of maximum revenue. In the case under examination here, however, such discrimination is all that is allowed. For individual I the excess burden is the shaded area under D_I between Q_s and Q_I (Figure 4.8). Because R_I lies above D_I but below D_{II} over this range, this excess burden is less than one-half of the revenue raised from II over that range (from Q_s to Q_I); since more revenue than this is raised *in toto,* excess burden must *a fortiori* be less than one-half of revenue over the entire range zero to Q_{II}. And there is no excess burden on individual II since he purchases the same quantity under the tax structure postulated and under the no-tax market solution. The general conclusion, therefore, is that, under maximum revenue assumptions, the possibility of discrimination over units of the taxed good by means of the appropriately "regressive"[14] rate structure provides a means of achieving revenue "more efficiently" (i.e., at smaller welfare loss per dollar of revenue raised) than does the completely nondiscriminatory alternative. Discrimination among goods and individuals in the absence of discrimination over units of output does not exhibit this property. Furthermore, this "efficiency" advantage of discrimination within the rate structure confronting each person does not depend on the presence or absence of other forms of discrimination.

It seems, on this basis, that the same conclusions hold here as with the perfectly discriminating regressive rate structure examined above. A uniform proportional tax may be dominated in the constitutional calculus by a tax that gains the same maximum revenue by means of an appropriately chosen rate structure that declines over units but is uniform among persons, applied to a smaller base. The desired level of revenue will be larger in the latter case, because total costs of public goods are lower due to the lower excess burden. It is possible that a tax which raises "too much" revenue under a uniform proportional rate will raise "too little" under a uniform "regressive rate" structure, even though revenue in the second case will be larger than in the former.

---

14. Note that the rate structure is violently progressive in the neighborhood of Q_s, but regressive elsewhere.

4.7. Summary

To an extent, this chapter has involved tying up many "loose ends" in comparative tax analysis and in particular application to commodity taxation. The comparative framework, which has allowed us to examine the explicit Leviathan model of our own construction in juxtaposition with the implicit benevolent despot of the conventional tax theory, necessarily introduces considerable complexity into the analysis, perhaps more than seems warranted for any straightforward presentation of the basic points. Comparisons with tax orthodoxy aside, the analysis of commodity taxation under our Leviathan assumptions becomes an extension of essentially the same logical construction developed with reference to income taxation in Chapter 3. The normative argument for tax-base restriction or limitation and against tax-base comprehensiveness is identical in the two separate fiscal institutions. The implicit orthodox argument for idealized rate differentiation among income sources is less familiar than the similar argument for idealized rate differentiation among differing commodity bases, largely because equity issues are allowed to enter more directly into the income-tax analysis. Nonetheless, the dramatic change in normative results produced by a shift to a government model of Leviathan applies equally to the two cases. The requirement for uniform treatment among persons in the income tax as well as the requirement for uniform rates of commodity taxation become instruments for limiting governmental fiscal appetites, instruments that may become relatively "efficient" when examined from the individual taxpayer's genuine constitutional perspective.

The comparative analysis of the chapter has its own by-product advantages. It enables us to show how the equi-revenue setting of orthodox tax theory can be transformed into a useful analytical device even in a Leviathan model of government. When two tax instruments, exploited to produce maximum revenues, provide government with equal revenue yields, the traditional excess burden norms come into their own. In this context, however, the analysis suggests that there is a direct relationship between maximum revenue and excess burden. Under standard assumptions of linearity, equal maximum revenue taxation will generate equal excess burdens. Allowing departures from this linearity assumption would, of course, modify this precise relationship. But such complexity would do nothing to undermine the basic thrust of our analysis here.

Like Chapter 3, the discussion of Chapter 4 may be interpreted as a series of exercises in applied price theory. As noted previously, the assignment of a power to levy tax on a commodity base is fully analogous to the award of a monopoly franchise in the sale of a good. Price theory proceeds from the analysis of simple monopoly to that monopoly which finds it possible and profitable to engage in varying degrees of price discrimination as among markets, persons, and over quantities. As this chapter's discussion has indicated, essentially the same logical catalogue can be applied to the taxing power, with essentially the same results if properly interpreted.

Appendix

The purpose of this appendix is to extend the analysis of Section 4.4 to a simplified general equilibrium approach somewhat more in keeping with the modern optimal-tax literature. Consider, for example, one of the simpler and more familiar discussions, that provided by Harberger.[15] The tax rule derived by Harberger is designed for minimizing the welfare loss of a system of excises, given a revenue constraint, in a three-good setting in which one of the goods (leisure presumably) is tax-free. Let X_1, X_2, and X_3 be the three goods, following Harberger's formulation, and suppose X_3 to be tax-free leisure. Then the change in X_1 and X_2 in response to taxes t_1 and t_2, respectively, is given by

$$\Delta X_1 = \frac{\partial X_1}{\partial p_1} t_1 + \frac{\partial X_1}{\partial p_2} t_2, \tag{1}$$

$$\Delta X_2 = \frac{\partial X_2}{\partial p_1} t_1 + \frac{\partial X_2}{\partial p_2} t_2, \tag{2}$$

where the units of X_1 and X_2 are chosen so that the initial prices are unity. Using the expression for the welfare loss as

$$W = \tfrac{1}{2} \sum_i t_i \, \Delta X_i, \tag{3}$$

---

15. Harberger, "Taxation, Resource Allocation and Welfare," sec. 4.3.

we obtain

$$W = \tfrac{1}{2}(S_{11}t_1^2 + 2S_{12}t_2 + S_{22}t_2^2), \tag{4}$$

where

$$S_{ij} = \frac{\partial X_i}{\partial p_j} \left(= \frac{\partial X_j}{\partial p_i} \right)$$

is the Hicksian substitution effect.

In the Harberger case, W is minimized with respect to t_1 and t_2, given a revenue constraint. Harberger does not allow for the effect of changes in the tax base on revenue, but this can be done without changing the nature of his solution. For we seek to minimize

$$M = W - \lambda(R - K), \tag{5}$$

where

$$R = t_1(X_1^0 - \Delta X_1) + t_2(X_2^0 - \Delta X_2). \tag{6}$$

This becomes

$$
\begin{aligned}
M &= \tfrac{1}{2}t_1 \, \Delta X_1 + \lambda t_1 \, \Delta X_1 + \tfrac{1}{2}t_2 \, \Delta X_2 \\
&\quad + \lambda t_2 \, \Delta X_2 - \lambda(t_1 \, X_1^0 + t_2 X_2^0 - K) \\
&= (\tfrac{1}{2} + \lambda)(S_{11}t_1^2 + 2S_{12}t_1 t_2 + S_{22}t_2^2) \\
&\quad - \lambda(t_1 X_1^0 + t_2 X_2^0 - K).
\end{aligned} \tag{7}
$$

The minimization exercise yields a set of equations

$$S_{11}t_1 + S_{12}t_2 = \frac{\lambda}{1 + 2\lambda} \, X_1^0, \tag{8}$$

$$S_{12}t_1 + S_{22}t_2 = \frac{\lambda}{1 + 2\lambda} \, X_2^0, \tag{9}$$

which solve to yield the optimal-tax structure,

$$\frac{t_1^*}{t_2^*} = \frac{X_1^0 S_{22} - X_2^0 S_{12}}{X_2^0 S_{11} - X_1^0 S_{12}}. \tag{10}$$

(Harberger manipulates this to get

$$\frac{t_1^*}{t_2^*} = \frac{\eta_{21} + \eta_{12} + \eta_{23}}{\eta_{21} + \eta_{12} + \eta_{13}}, \tag{11}$$

where η_{ij} is the elasticity of demand for the ith good with respect to the jth price.)

For our purposes, however, we note that R is given by

$$R = t_1 X_1^0 - t_1(S_{11}t_1 + S_{12}t_2) + t_2 X_2^0 - t_2(S_{12}t_1 + S_{22}t_2)$$

or

$$R = t_1 X_1^0 + t_2 X_2^0 - (S_{11}t_1^2 + 2S_{12}t_1 t_2 + S_{22}t_2^2). \tag{12}$$

So to maximize R with respect to t_1 and t_2 yields two equations:

$$S_{11}t_1 + S_{12}t_2 = \tfrac{1}{2}X_1^0, \tag{13}$$
$$S_{12}t_1 + S_{22}t_2 = \tfrac{1}{2}X_2^0, \tag{14}$$

which have the solution

$$\frac{t_1^*}{t_2^*} = \frac{X_1^0 S_{22} - X_2^0 S_{12}}{X_2^0 S_{11} - X_1^0 S_{12}}, \tag{15}$$

which is precisely identical to Harberger's tax rule, (10) above.

We note further that the left-hand side of (13) is ΔX_1^* from (1), and the left-hand side of (14) is ΔX_2^* from (2). So we have

$$\Delta X_1^* = \tfrac{1}{2}X_1^0 = X_1^0 - \Delta X_1^*, \tag{16}$$
$$\Delta X_2^* = \tfrac{1}{2}X_2^0 = X_2^0 - \Delta X_2^*, \tag{17}$$

and multiplying (16) by t_1^*, (17) by t_2^*, and adding, we have

$$t_1^* \Delta X_1^* + t_2^* \Delta X_2^* = t_1^*(X_1^0 - \Delta X_1^*) + t_2^*(X_2^0 - \Delta X_2^*)$$

or

$$W^* = \tfrac{1}{2}R^* \tag{18}$$

from (3) and (6).

We can on this basis conclude that optimal-tax rules and maximum revenue rules are indeed identical, even in this simple general equilibrium setting; and further, that under maximum revenue assumptions, total revenue remains exactly twice the welfare loss, just as in the partial equilibrium case, even where discrimination between goods is permitted and general equilibrium effects allowed for.

5. Taxation through Time
Income Taxes, Capital Taxes, and Public Debt

Indeed, the abuse or misuse of the coercive power is so constant a risk that there are in pagan, Christian, and anti-Christian philosophies strong tendencies toward limitation and distrust of the state even where practice tends to exalt it.

—W. A. Orton, *The Economic Role of the State*, p. 64

In the analyses of Chapters 3 and 4, the activities of a revenue-maximizing government were examined in highly simplified single-period settings. In this chapter, we shall modify this single-period aspect of the model in order to introduce several interrelated issues that involve a temporal dimension.

One of the issues that emerges directly concerns the taxation of capital or wealth. In any multiperiod setting, individuals may save (create capital) and dissave (consume capital) in order to allocate consumption appropriately over their anticipated life cycle. They may, of course, also save in order to transmit capital values to heirs. The accumulation and maintenance of capital offers a potential source of tax revenue. We need to examine the implications of making this source available to government, and in particular we must analyze the characteristics of the capital levy as opposed to the income tax in our Leviathan model.

A second issue that emerges concerns public debt. Governments, as well as individuals, may have the inclination to borrow, and they may or may not be assigned the capacity to do so. How do constitutional constraints on the government's borrowing and lending powers complement—or more generally interact with—restrictions on the power to tax?

Questions about capital taxes and public debt must include consideration of more than just the *size* of the revenue source. In the single-period setting, and assuming the disposition of revenues, the α in the earlier models, to be exogenously fixed, the only criterion in the constitutional calculus is the *level* of public-goods supply that a particular tax base and/or rate structure is expected to generate. By assumption or analytical convention, the base-rate structure, once chosen, is presumed to generate the same level of revenue, and hence public-goods supply, in any period. In an explicit multiperiod setting, the additional problem of generating an appropriate *time stream* of public spending must be considered.

A third issue concerns the temporal characteristics of government itself. In a multiperiod setting we must allow for the possibility that governments themselves may change their identity and nature. In this connection, it is relevant to ask what happens if government assumes Leviathan characteristics only occasionally. How, for example, does this possibility influence the individual as he behaves toward the fisc within a succession of budgetary periods? How does the taxpayer adjust his plans in reaction to a *threat* of a revenue-maximizing Leviathan, even in the current absence of such a regime? And taking such predictions all into account, how does the shift from continuous to sporadic Leviathan—what we here term "probabilistic Leviathan"—influence the individual's *constitutional* calculus? The inclusive set of constitutional rules or arrangements may well include constraints on government's fiscal behavior that are not expected to be binding during "normal" periods, but which are designed to come into play only when governmental fiscal activity exceeds certain bounds. Such contingency rules become central in an analysis of a probabilistic Leviathan, and these rules may be viewed as offering protection against fiscal abuse rather than constraints on ordinary exercises of the taxing power. Restrictions on the government's power to tax capital and to borrow may take on special significance as *contingency* rules, even when they would have no particular status under continuous Leviathan assumptions.

Our aim in this chapter is to examine these interrelated issues. Before we proceed, however, it may be useful once again to review the public-finance orthodoxy briefly, for the purpose of emphasizing the distinctions between this orthodoxy and our own approach in application to the issues noted. Following this review in Section 5.1, we examine income and capital taxes in the perpetual or continuous Leviathan setting of the preceding chapters.

5.1. Income Taxes, Capital Taxes, and Public Debt in Orthodox Public Finance

In the traditional public-finance literature, it has long been recognized that a tax on the income from an asset is equivalent to a tax on the asset's capital value. A tax of one type can readily be converted into its equivalent as a tax of the other type. A tax of 1 percent levied on the capital value of an asset yielding 10 percent per annum is equivalent to a tax on current income from the asset of 10 percent. And as Ricardo argued, essentially the same "equivalence" logic can be applied to show that the public debt issue is identical with either of the two taxes: a specific public debt liability, implying future tax commitments to service and redeem the debt, can be converted into its equivalent as a current tax on either capital or income.[1]

Our initial concern here is not, however, with the "equivalence" logic.[2] For the purposes of this discussion, we can assume that the taxpayer is subjectively indifferent among the various alternatives on an equivalent net liability basis. But indifference among equi-revenue present-value liabilities at a specified point in time does not imply indifference on the part of a potential taxpayer as among the several fiscal arrangements at some constitutional level. In constitutional perspective, the present values of the liabilities under the several instruments are not specified, and the tax-fiscal arrangements may vary enormously in their revenue potential and significance. Crucial for the citizen's constitutional choice are not his own predicted attitudes toward equivalent liability instruments within a single period, but rather the differ-

---

1. It can, of course, be argued that the full discounting of future tax liabilities that is required for full Ricardian equivalence is psychologically and empirically unrealistic, and hence that policy analysis should not be based on it. See James M. Buchanan, "Barro on the Ricardian Equivalence Theorem," *Journal of Political Economy*, 83 (April 1976), 337–42.

2. For our criticism of this basic theorem, see Geoffrey Brennan and James M. Buchanan, "The Logic of the Ricardian Equivalence Theorem," *Finanzarchiv*, Heft 38/1 (1980), 4–16.

ent possible governmental responses that emerge under access to the various revenue-raising instruments, and in particular with respect to capital taxes and debt. The distinction between the normative implications of the orthodox public-finance analysis and our own approach is critical at this point, and further discussion seems warranted. Public-finance orthodoxy includes the demonstration or proof that, within the assumptions of a rational behavior model, a tax on an income flow is equivalent to a tax on the value of the capital asset yielding the income flow. Further, by an extension of the same logic, especially if the distribution of net liabilities can be assumed away, a somewhat more extreme model of rational behavior allows for a demonstration that the tax on income or capital is also equivalent to an issue of public debt. In a single postconstitutional period, the individual taxpayer "should be," therefore, indifferent among these fiscal instruments, provided only that the rates are adjusted so as to make his net liability identical under each instrument. Given this indifference, which emerges from a postulate of rational behavior on the part of the taxpayer, the alternative fiscal instruments produce identical behavioral responses. The implication is that, on the economist's criterion of efficiency, the three alternatives are perfect substitutes.

We should not, however, lose sight of the implicit assumptions that underlie this familiar logic. The revenue requirements of government are presumed to be settled somehow independently of the taxing process. Here, as elsewhere, the orthodox analysis implicitly commences with: "Given any revenue requirement." Such an approach totally neglects the possible feedback effects that fiscal institutions may exert on the setting of revenue requirements in the first place. And, of course, these feedback effects become central to our whole constitutional analysis. The difference here does not depend on the Leviathan model of government at all. Whether we model government as a continuing Leviathan, as a probabilistic Leviathan, or as a median-voter-dominated majoritarian democracy, differing fiscal or revenue-raising instruments may exert differing effects on the amounts of revenue that governments will seek to raise. Once these effects are recognized, the equi-revenue or equi-liability setting for the orthodox analysis simply becomes irrelevant in any genuine choice among fiscal arrangements at the constitutional level.

In this chapter, we shall retain—except where otherwise stated—the central ingredients of the Leviathan model as outlined in preceding chapters. That is, we assume that government will seek to maximize revenue, but is constrained—by virtue of other elements in the fiscal constitution—to spend some proportion of that revenue on public goods genuinely desired by the citizenry. Purely electoral constraints are, however, taken to be ineffective.

5.2. The Timing of Rate Announcement

In the single-period or instantaneous models discussed in Chapters 3 and 4, it was not meaningful to introduce announcement effects. Implicitly, we presumed that tax rates were announced at the start of the period and that taxpayers made behavioral adjustments in full knowledge of prevailing tax arrangements. Once we introduce a multiperiod setting, however, announcement effects become important and must be explicitly discussed before we examine particular taxes.

Initially, let us consider a simple two-period model in which a Leviathan or revenue-maximizing government is operative in both periods, and in which the government is assigned the authority to impose a capital levy. The two-period model here is a simple extension of one version of the model outlined in Chapter 3. The behavior of only one taxpayer-citizen is examined, and Leviathan is constrained by the restriction that all tax rates are to be proportional. Characteristics of the model are specified in the following way: the individual lives for two periods only; in period 1, he expends effort to derive income from labor, income that he can either consume in that period or save; in period 2, he consumes any income "saved" from the previous period's income, plus any interest these savings have earned, but does not derive any labor income. (To counter possible objections to the "realism" of some of the corner solutions to be discussed, we can assume also that the individual can subsist without receiving either labor or interest income. We may, if we want, assume that subsistence levels are guaranteed by governmental provision of relief payments, payments computed in the α share of total revenues collected.)

The in-period behavioral adjustments in this simple intertemporal model can be depicted diagramatically in Figure 5.1. Period 1 labor income is measured along the ordinate. $0A$ represents the maximum level of consumption, including leisure, that is feasible or possible in period 1. If none of this in-

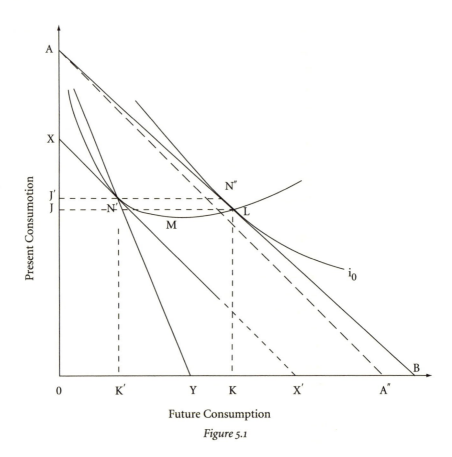

Figure 5.1

come is taken in leisure, and all of it should be saved, the maximum feasible consumption of $0B$ could be attained in period 2; $0B$ is larger than $0A$ to the extent that the interest rate on saving is positive. The rate of interest is given by $A''B/0A''$, where A'' is the abscissa terminal of the 45° line drawn from A. In the absence of tax, the citizen would allocate consumption intertemporally to attain the equilibrium position shown by the point L. He would consume $0J$ in period 1, save AJ and consume $0K$ in period 2.

Into this extremely simplified model, we now introduce a capital levy. The effects clearly depend on the extent to which the taxpayer, at the time of his consumption-saving choice, anticipates such a tax. Initially consider the case of extreme ignorance, and suppose that the taxpayer makes his saving decision without taking any account of the possibility of tax at all. He will then behave as he would in the complete absence of tax. That is, he will save *AJ* in period 1 for an expected consumption of *0K* in period 2. Hence, *AJ* would represent his capital stock at the end of period 1. In this case, and remaining within the limits of the two-period setting defined, a Leviathan government will maximize its revenue collection by appropriating all the capital. In the absence of explicit restrictions to the contrary, it will always pay Leviathan to impose a completely confiscatory capital levy. Regardless of the size of the capital stock, Leviathan does best by appropriating it all. More than this, where the taxpayer does not anticipate any capital levy, Leviathan may do even better by somehow inducing the taxpayer to increase saving in period 1 above that which would be chosen in absence of tax. In Figure 5.1, Leviathan might achieve this goal by preannouncing a tax rate on capital just sufficient to induce the taxpayer to move to the minimum of the price-consumption curve *AN'L*, shown by *M* in Figure 5.1. After the taxpayer makes the predicted behavioral adjustment, Leviathan would then levy a confiscatory tax that would acquire all of the capital as revenue. If the price-consumption curve should have its minimum beyond *L* to the right, beyond the no-tax equilibrium position, Leviathan might actually subsidize accumulation.

Especially in a model where Leviathan is perpetual, however, it is unreasonable to endow the taxpayer with such naive expectations. It is surely more reasonable to move to the opposite extreme and assume that the taxpayer will recognize Leviathan's interests in confiscating whatever capital might be accumulated. In this expectational setting, the citizen will consume all his income in period 1; he will save nothing, and a Leviathan that is limited to a capital levy will obtain no revenue at all. In this case, point *A* represents the highest level of utility the taxpayer can achieve.[3]

Under these conditions, in fact, Leviathan and the taxpayer are locked

---

3. We set aside at this stage any limits on taxpayer behavior caused by the recognition that some proportion of revenue is spent on public goods which would otherwise not be provided. This is entirely reasonable if we bear in mind that the taxpayer in question is one among many, each of whom will rationally "free-ride" by avoiding taxes.

into a genuine dilemma-type situation.[4] *Both* could be made better off than at A—the "independent adjustment equilibrium"—but only if a relevant binding agreement can be entered into. For this reason, it is rational for Leviathan to bind itself, even if no explicit constitutional restrictions are imposed by the citizenry. In choosing among all possible rules, Leviathan will select the revenue-maximizing rule—that rule which enables it to "preannounce" the revenue-maximizing tax rate on capital. In this way, Leviathan selects a rate so as to generate taxpayer equilibrium at N' in Figure 5.1, where a line parallel to AB is tangent to the price-consumption curve $AN'L$. This rate on capital is $BY/0B$ and leaves the taxpayer consuming $0J'$ in period 1 and saving AJ' for consumption in period 2. From this saving, the tax taken is $N'N''$ (equal to $X'B$) leaving the taxpayer with a net consumption in period 2 of $0K'$. However, it is quite clear that mere preannouncement of the rate $BY/0B$ is not enough—the taxpayer must believe that this tax rate will in fact apply, and he will only have such faith if the preannouncement is genuinely binding. If it is not binding, the taxpayer may recognize it as such, and retreat to position A prior to the imposition of the tax in expectation of Leviathan's rational strategy of imposing a confiscatory capital levy.

In a sense, the same analysis could be applied to the income tax, and Figure 5.1 could be reinterpreted to apply to the taxpayer's choice between leisure and income-producing effort. As the analysis in Chapter 3 (particularly that illustrated in Figure 3.1) demonstrated, there will be a definitive revenue-maximizing rate of tax, given preannouncement, that enables the taxpayer to respond optimally to the tax. The preannouncement of the tax rate was, in Chapter 3, more or less assumed to be inherent in the fiscal structure. The

4. The game may be depicted as follows:

Taxpayer's strategy	Leviathan's strategy	
	Confiscatory levy	Nonconfiscatory levy
Save something	[5,20]	[15,10]
Consume everything	[10,0]	[10,0]

where the taxpayer's payoff is the first-mentioned in the pair and Leviathan's payoff is the second-mentioned. Since the confiscatory levy is dominant for Leviathan, the taxpayer consumes everything.

multiperiod setting under consideration here allows us to raise the meaningful and highly relevant question as to whether the government should be granted power to set tax rates to apply to the income already earned, that is in the period *just completed,* as distinct from the power to set tax rates on income to be earned in the period subsequent to announcement. Would a perpetual or continuous Leviathan prefer to have the former authority? What we have succeeded in showing with our analysis of the capital levy is that, in the perpetual Leviathan case, the ability to set tax rates *ex post* might be desired neither by the citizen-taxpayer nor by government. And this result applies equally to all taxes, including the income tax, provided only that taxpayers in their in-period behavioral adjustments are expected to anticipate Leviathan's rational taxing strategy.

It should be emphasized, however, that certain aspects of the discussion on this point are restricted by the simple two-period nature of the model. For one thing, the simple "dominant strategy" character of the dilemma situation in which Leviathan and the taxpayer are placed becomes moderated as we extend the model to include many periods. Even in the absence of any binding agreement and in the presence of some positive saving by the taxpayer, a Leviathan government may refrain from imposing a confiscatory tax over some sequence of periods. It might do better over some initial sequence of periods by encouraging the taxpayer to save something, to accumulate capital, thereby enlarging the revenue base. If the "game" is finite, of course, Leviathan would impose the confiscatory levy during the final period, but with a continuing Leviathan an infinite sequence may be a more appropriate characteristic of the model than a finite one. Modeled in an infinite sequence, whether Leviathan would forbear to impose the confiscatory rate over some periods will depend on such things as its own rate of discount and its predictions of the individual taxpayer's attitude toward risk. If Leviathan's discount rate is very high, it may still be rational to appropriate all capital as soon as it appears. In the same way, if the taxpayer is highly risk averse, he will tend to prefer the certainty of a dollar's current consumption to some probability of more future consumption or confiscation. In this case, Leviathan would find it difficult to encourage the taxpayer to save by merely refraining from the capital levy over some sequence of periods. However, it seems unlikely that a zero saving–confiscatory tax solution would prevail indefinitely: scope for implicit collusion over successive "plays" of the game seems likely to secure at least some of the mutual gains. Nevertheless, a more explicit constitutional restriction relating to preannouncement with enforceability will be preferred by *both* parties, except in those situations where the taxpayer can be consistently fooled.

An important aspect of the discussion to this point has been the assumption of perpetual or continuing Leviathan. In the one-period models of Chapters 3 and 4, the assumption of a revenue-maximizing Leviathan required no direct consideration of the prospects for perpetuation of fiscal powers. As we move to a multiperiod setting, however, a new issue more or less naturally emerges. How will the constitutional calculus of the potential taxpayer-beneficiary be affected if he predicts that a true revenue-maximizing Leviathan will show up only in the occasional time period? In other periods, a government more closely modeled as a "benevolent despot" may be predicted. Alternatively, nonfiscal constitutional constraints (including electoral rules) may be expected to be operational part of the time. The possibility of Leviathan in any period will, nonetheless, imply that the potential taxpayer's constitutional decision must incorporate such possibility.

In this setting, which we can call that of the "probabilistic Leviathan," two departures from the previous analysis emerge. The first is that it can no longer be in Leviathan's interest to have preannouncement of tax rates. The dilemma situation between the taxpayer and Leviathan discussed earlier depends on the mutual expectation that the latter will continue in existence over some sequence of periods. The second is that, even if preannouncement of taxes is somehow required, the nature of capital is such that significant current or in-period adjustment is not feasible. A distinction arises here between capital taxation and income taxation that is not relevant in the perpetual Leviathan case.

The first of these differences is easily explained. The results of introducing a probabilistic Leviathan are twofold. First, the taxpayer cannot predict with certainty what the tax rate in any period will be. He cannot anticipate that revenue-maximizing tax rates will be imposed, whether these be estimated in simple one-period terms, as in Chapters 3 and 4, or in complex present values, as introduced in this chapter. Any sequence that allows for non-Leviathan government, even probabilistically, becomes less definitive. Second, the occasional Leviathan does not bear the full future period cost of current-period reductions in the tax base.

Consider, for example, an income tax in an environment where Leviathan is operative with probability 1 in 10 and where postbehavioral announcement of tax rates is permitted. When and if it comes into effective power, even for one period, Leviathan can collect *all* income earned in a single period by announcing a rate of 100 percent *after* the income has been earned (i.e., after the relevant leisure-effort choices have been made). In the multiperiod perpetual or continuing Leviathan setting, this fiscal behavior would not, of course, be rational because the individual would respond by supplying *no* tax base in all future periods. Assume that the taxpayer expects the non-Leviathan government to impose a tax rate of 10 percent, but he expects a Leviathan government to impose wholly confiscatory rates of 100 percent, announced *after* income-leisure choices are made. In the probabilistic setting indicated, the risk-neutral taxpayer will respond to the threat of Leviathan in accordance with his expected tax rate—which is $[0.9(10) + 0.1(100)]$, or 19 percent. If p, the probability of a Leviathan-like fiscal authority, is one-tenth, then the taxpayer, in maximizing his expected utility, in each period will supply the amount of taxable base that he would supply if he faced a certain tax rate of 19 percent in each period. In this case, Leviathan would clearly prefer the possibility of *ex post* announcement. Correspondingly, the citizen-taxpayer would prefer a constitutional requirement that income-tax rates be preannounced before he makes behavioral adjustments. In the latter case, the taxpayer would always know at the start of each period whether Leviathan is operative or not, and with appropriate planning, he could presumably arrange to transfer leisure intertemporally so that he would earn relatively little income in those periods when Leviathan comes into being.

The advantages of preannouncement to the taxpayer are less dramatic, however, in the case of the capital levy than they are with the income tax. If he is given enough advance notice, the individual can presumably dissave drastically; he can "eat up his capital" and eventually deplete his entire stock of value. But the essence of the distinction between capital (a stock) and income (a flow) implies that whereas a strictly current tax (i.e., one not announced *ex post*) on income permits behavioral adjustments in leisure-effort choices to occur, a current tax on capital does *not* permit comparably efficacious adjustment because the capital that becomes the base of the tax is already in existence. Capital does not primarily emerge out of any decisions made currently. The size of the tax base is determined by past decisions on the accumulation of savings and what has been done is not readily undone. Hence, any tax on capital is, by the nature of capital itself, *ex post*, unless, of course, the tax is to be imposed only on *new* capital formation subsequent to the announcement. A distinction between capital and income taxation thereby emerges in the probabilistic Leviathan setting, a distinction that is much less striking when a Leviathan government exists continuously. Capital taxation has the effect of permitting the occasional revenue-maximizing government to extend its appetites so as to "enjoy" the fruits of many periods. Income taxation does not have this effect, or at least it does so only to the extent that a tax on interest income is an indirect form of a tax on capital.

Two implications for the individual's constitutional calculus emerge from a recognition of the points made in this section:

1. The citizen-taxpayer should insist on a constitutional requirement that all tax rates be preannounced, and that such preannouncements be binding. At least in the probabilistic Leviathan setting, one could not expect such restrictions to be self-imposed even where taxpayers take full account of the Leviathan possibility.
2. The potential taxpayer should exhibit a constitutional preference for income taxation—and a corresponding antipathy to capital taxation—based on the belief that when Leviathan is probabilistic rather than perpetual, in-period adjustment to avoid exploitative taxation is more feasible under income taxation.

5.3. Income and Capital Taxes under Perpetual Leviathan

We have, in the foregoing section, already indicated one major difference between income and capital taxes in the probabilistic Leviathan setting. In this section, we shall compare income and capital taxes more directly, with a consideration of both the level and timing of revenues. To do this, we return initially to the simple two-period model outlined in the beginning of Section 5.2, in which Leviathan is assumed to be operative in both periods. The essential features of this highly restricted model are:

1. All rate structures must be proportional.
2. We examine the behavior of only one (representative) taxpayer-citizen.

3. In period 1, labor income is earned and "current" consumption may occur. In period 2, no labor income is derived, but interest is earned on
   savings from the first period. And, of course, "future" consumption may
   occur.
4. All tax rates are announced in advance.

The capital tax. We discussed this case in Section 5.2. Using the diagrammatics introduced in Figure 5.1, we know that the equilibrium that will emerge
under these assumptions involves the maximum revenue capital levy. The
position of the taxpayer is depicted by N'. Present or first-period consumption is $0J'$; future or second-period consumption is $0K'$. Leviathan obtains a
total revenue of $N'N''$, all of it in period 2.

The income tax. For the purposes of discussion, we assume that leisure-effort
trade-offs are such that the revenue-maximizing rate that can be imposed on
labor income is 50 percent. And for ease of analysis, we can assume that this
revenue-maximizing rate depends solely on the present value of all future
and current consumption. This assumption implies that whatever tax is imposed on future consumption, the revenue-maximizing rate on first-period
income remains the same. With total labor income being $0A$, maximum current consumption is thus given in Figure 5.2 by $0A'$. The line $A'Q$ indicates
the 45° line from A'. The line $A'B'$ traces the locus of present and future consumption opportunities, given the tax of $A'A$ in period 1. The maximum future consumption, $0B'$, exceeds $0A'$ ($0Q$) by an amount QB' which represents positive interest returns.

An income tax of the standard type includes interest as well as labor income in the tax base.[5] An expenditure tax of the type recommended by Mill,
Kaldor, Fisher, and more recently by Andrews and Feldstein does not do so.
Hence, such a tax does not distort individual choices between present and
future consumption. In discussing the "income" tax, therefore, it is necessary to distinguish among (1) a tax on labor income only, (2) a tax on consumption only, and (3) a tax on labor *and* interest incomes (i.e., consumption *and* saving). In this discussion, we assume initially that tax-rate changes
between the two periods are not permitted.

---

5. So, too, would a tax on income measured in the Haig-Simons manner, sometimes
referred to as the "net-accretions" conception or definition of income.

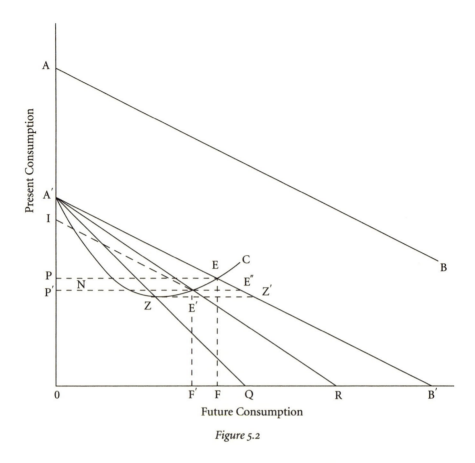

Figure 5.2

Both (1) and (2) lead to a posttax equilibrium at E (Figure 5.2), at which the consumer consumes $0P$ in period 1 and $0F$ in period 2. However, the tax on labor income secures all of government revenue, $A'A$, in period 1; this result stems from the simple fact that no labor income is earned in the second period, by assumption of the model. This tax on labor income can be contrasted with a tax on consumption expenditures. Both these taxes are neutral intertemporally—that is, both leave the relative price of future, as against present, consumption unaffected. Both lead to equilibrium at E. But in the case of the consumption tax, tax collections are spread over the two periods in the same proportions as aggregate consumption is. For this reason, the time sequence of revenue collections is different in the consumption tax case: instead of receiving all revenue in period 1, as under the labor income tax, a proportion $0P/0A'$ will be received in period 1 and the remaining $PA'/0A'$ will be received in period 2. Aggregate revenue will, however, be the same in present discounted terms.

Let us now consider the tax on "total income" which involves both a tax of 50 percent on labor income in period 1, *and* also a tax of 50 percent on interest income in period 2. This tax yields an equilibrium at E', which is determined where $A'R$ cuts the price consumption curve from A', where R is such that it falls midway between Q and B'. At E', government revenue is $E'E''$ in period 2, over and above the amount AA' collected in period 1.

It is worth emphasizing here that, in the absence of explicit constitutional restrictions to the contrary, it would always be in Leviathan's interest to *increase* the income-tax rate in period 2. It would be perfectly consistent with preannouncement restrictions, for example, to apply a rate of 50 percent in period 1 along with a rate of 100 percent on interest income in period 2. Leviathan would still appropriate $A'A$ in revenue in period 1 but could, in this manner, obtain $Z'Z$ as revenue in period 2, as the taxpayer-citizen adjusts his savings behavior to yield equilibrium at Z, where interest returns are zero. Only if Leviathan is explicitly restricted by some requirement of intertemporal uniformity in tax rates would this prospect be precluded. It is, therefore, worth noting that intertemporal uniformity in rates of income tax does limit revenue potential, except in the special case where the revenue-maximizing rates on labor and interest income are the same.

If these revenue-maximizing rates are different, however, the imposition of uniformity requirements may lead Leviathan to impose an "excessive" tax on current labor income in order to approach more closely the desired rate on interest income. The effects here do not seem likely to be large. As the tax rate on labor income increases beyond the revenue-maximizing limits, first-period revenue falls. And because of the increased tax on future consumption, there is a substitution effect toward current consumption. The increased rate of tax on future consumption must generate sufficient revenue to offset both effects and seems likely to do so only over a limited range.

For purposes of simplifying the analysis here, we have introduced the simple two-period model in which labor income is earned exclusively in one period and interest income in the other. A possible uniformity requirement involves the elimination of intertemporal differences in rates of tax. In a more general setting, a uniformity requirement might involve the prohibition of rate differentials as among separate sources of income, even if these sources yield returns in the same period. The effects of the uniformity requirement would remain the same as those discussed for the more simplified setting.

The income tax and the capital levy. In this subsection, we shall analyze the effects of allowing Leviathan to have access to a capital levy over and above a tax on income. For the income tax, we continue to use the assumptions adopted in the previous subsection. Leisure-effort choices are assumed to depend on the present value of income over the time sequence. From this assumption it follows that a tax on capital that is preannounced could have no influence on the revenue-maximizing rate of tax on labor income in period 1. In this context, the best that Leviathan can do is to levy the revenue-maximizing income-tax rate, in period 1, and then to select the revenue-maximizing capital levy that would generate a final equilibrium such as depicted by N in Figure 5.3. (As noted, we limit analysis to tax rates that are appropriately preannounced.) The income tax reduces maximum current consumption to $0A'$, and the locus of possible equilibria is shown by the price-consumption curve drawn from A'. The maximum revenue from the capital levy and/or the income tax on interest is achieved at N, where a line SS', parallel to $A'B'$, is tangent to the price-consumption curve. Present- or first-period consumption by the individual is $0P_T$, future- or second-period consumption is $0F_T$, and total governmental revenue in present discounted value is AS. Of this intake, $A'A$ accrues from the income tax in period 1; and $S'B'$ accrues in period 2 from the capital levy and income tax combined. The present value of $S'B'$ is $A'S$. This total revenue of $A'S$ (or $S'B'$) in period 2 can be raised by exclusive reliance on the capital levy, with no income tax on interest income. Or it can be raised from the tax on interest income equivalent in rate to the tax on labor income plus some capital levy. In this latter case, the share of period 2 revenue attributable to the interest income tax, given maintenance of the 50 percent income-tax rate on both labor and interest income, is $E'E''$, with $S'B'$ minus $E'E''$ assignable to the capital levy. The revenue-maximizing capital levy will clearly involve a smaller rate in the presence of the tax on interest income than in its absence.

There is, of course, some tax on interest income that would obliterate the revenue potential of the capital levy entirely: the rate would be MB'/QB'

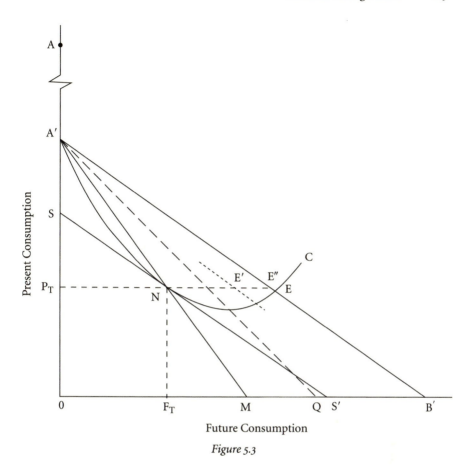

Future Consumption

Figure 5.3

(Figure 5.3) and would be well in excess of 100 percent as depicted. Generally, one might assume that rates of tax on interest in excess of 100 percent are infeasible. Taxpayers could simply substitute money balances for interest-bearing assets. In the presence of inflation, however, money is itself depreciating in value over time. Real tax rates on income from all assets in excess of 100 percent become feasible, and have indeed been operative over recent periods in many Western economies. Inflation becomes a form of capital taxation in itself, but it also makes possible rates of tax on interest-bearing assets that may approximate the maximum revenue capital levy equivalent. Of course, this result depends on the fact that the accumulation of consumption goods is costly, but the issue here involves an aspect of inflation that is worth special attention.[6]

We can conveniently bring the discussion of this section together in Table 5.1. In this table we show, in the context of our simplified two-period model and for each of the tax arrangements discussed, (1) the revenue collected in each period, and (2) the total revenue discounted to present-value terms. Whether this total discounted revenue figure is meaningful or relevant is an issue postponed for discussion in the following section. The rubrics refer, of course, to those in Figures 5.1, 5.2, and 5.3. As Table 5.1 reveals, these various tax arrangements differ both in terms of the total value of revenue raised and in terms of the time stream of the revenue receipts. Of particular interest, in the light of equivalence theorems that inhabit orthodox analysis, is the distinction here between capital taxation and income taxation.

5.4 Leviathan's Time Preference

One interesting question that arises out of the tax comparisons summarized in Table 5.1 concerns the extent to which Leviathan's revenue-collecting strategy may depend on the timing of tax receipts, as well as on the maximum revenue in present-value terms. Initially, we restrict our attention to the two-period model with the perfect taxpayer foresight previously employed. In such a setting, the Leviathan fiscal authority will always choose that tax arrangement which maximizes the present value of its tax receipts provided it is not constrained in its ability to lend, and if it is assumed it can do so at the market rate of return.

The "best" arrangement for a revenue-maximizing Leviathan is that in which it has access to both the income tax and the capital levy. It would, of course, impose both at the maximum revenue rate, and it would obtain $A'A$ in period 1 plus $B'S'$ in period 2. This is the arrangement that maximizes the present value of total revenue. Because of the presumed power to lend at will, Leviathan's revenue-raising and consumption activities become completely separable. The present value of total revenue is maximized, and then by

---

6. It is also an aspect that most conventional "indexing" schemes for income-tax rates ignore. The simple rate-adjustment process as practiced in Canada and Australia cannot handle this problem.

Table 5.1. Timing and level of revenues under alternative tax arrangements

Tax arrangements	Revenue in period 1	Revenue in period 2	Total present value
Capital levy	—	$N'N''$ (Fig. 5.1)	AX (Fig. 5.1)
Income tax (labor and interest) (uniform rate)	$A'A$ (Fig. 5.2)	$E'E''$ (Fig. 5.2)	AI (Fig. 5.2)
Income tax (labor only)	$A'A$ (Fig. 5.2)	—	$A'A$ (Fig. 5.2)
Consumption tax[a]	$0P$ (Fig. 5.2)	$0F$ (Fig. 5.2)	$A'A$ (Fig. 5.2)
Income tax plus capital levy	$A'A$ (Fig. 5.3)	$B'S'$ (Fig. 5.3)	AS (Fig. 5.3)

[a]On the assumption that the revenue-maximizing rate is 50 percent, so that $0A' = A'A$.

lending at the market rate of interest, the resultant surplus[7] is allocated intertemporally in accordance with Leviathan's utility function. We may depict Leviathan's consumption possibilities in Figure 5.4 by the line IK.[8]

The assumptions of our model, in which all labor income is earned in period 1, necessarily allocate the major portion of Leviathan's consumption prospects in period 1 if no lending is attempted. (We shall examine the matter of borrowing in more detail below.) Here, we assume that Leviathan's time preference indicates a desire to postpone some consumption to period 2. We need to ask the question concerning the effect of possible restrictions on Leviathan's capacity to lend (invest) at market rates. Suppose, first, that Leviathan is not allowed to lend on the open market; government is not allowed to purchase income-earning assets. However, government might still retain a capacity to *hoard;* in this case, the consumption possibilities are reduced to IQ in Figure 5.4, where IQ has a slope of unity. In such a setting, will it be possible for Leviathan to allocate his desired consumption intertemporally more effectively by not maximizing present value of tax revenues? There seem to be two instruments which *might* facilitate this result. Leviathan may find it to his interest to reduce the rate of tax on income and

7. Surplus is a proportion $(1 - \alpha)$ of (maximum) revenue, where α is the proportion of revenues collected that must be spent on public goods.
8. Both axes reflect maximum revenue in each period scaled down by the factor $1 - \alpha$.

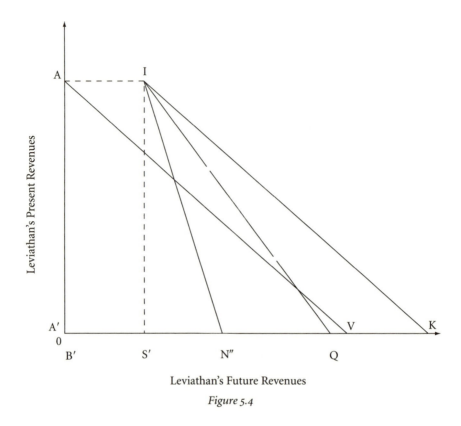

Figure 5.4

to collect more revenue under the capital levy in period 2 as individuals save more in period 1. The second method would be to use the consumption-expenditure tax.

Consider the first of these possible adjustments. As the rate of tax on labor income is reduced, individuals will save more; this ensures that the maximum revenue capital levy will collect more. Revenue is forgone in period 1, but more revenue is collected in period 2. Whether or not Leviathan will find it advantageous to make this shift depends critically on the rate of trade-off faced. As the tax rate is reduced on first-period income, however, only some share of the extra dividend will be saved by taxpayers. Under normal conditions, the rate of return on the extra savings, along with the initial capital, could not produce a period 2 capital levy prospect for Leviathan that would exceed that which he could have available by the desired share of first-period collections simply hoarded for second-period use. In the geometry of Figure

5.4, the prospects for Leviathan that might be generated by forgoing income-tax revenue in period 1 and substituting capital-tax revenue in period 2 are shown by IN'', which lies entirely within IQ, the latter being the opportunities under hoarding.

Let us now consider the possible intertemporal trade-off that is offered by the consumption-expenditure tax. As the summary Table 5.1 indicates, Leviathan would never rely on this revenue-raising instrument if the objective is to maximize present value of revenue over a time sequence. However, if intertemporal adjustment in revenue use is restricted, and, specifically, if hoarding but not lending is possible, resort to less-than-optimal fiscal instruments may be considered. Since the tax on consumption expenditure wholly eliminates saving from tax, individuals would be predicted to shift more of their own consumption to period 2. In so doing, of course, they carry over, at the same time, more revenue potential for exploitation by Leviathan. If the additional saving generated by a shift to consumption taxation should be relatively great, such a prospect may be effective for a Leviathan whose utility function is weighted toward period 2 use of revenues. Under normal circumstances, however, in this as in the income-tax case, Leviathan, if given the opportunity to hoard revenues once collected, will still find it advantageous to arrange tax structures so as to maximize the present value of revenues independently of Leviathan's own time preference.[9]

We may impose yet more restrictive conditions on Leviathan's intertemporal adjustment opportunities. If government is denied the power to hoard as well as to invest at some positive return, resort to non-present-value maximization would seem more likely to be desirable. This situation is not nearly as bizarre as it might seem at first glance. In particular, many lower-level

9. Under the consumption-tax arrangement, the locus of *potential* equilibria in Figure 5.2 is $A'B'$, so that the locus of potential revenue receipts is AB *minus* $A'B'$, or $A'B'$ (since the maximum revenue consumption rate is 50 percent). Thus, the consumption-tax revenue combination lies somewhere along the line AV in Figure 5.4, and this will lie *inside* IQ, unless the maximum revenue under the capital tax ($B'S'$ in Figure 5.3) is less than interest on $A'A$, depicted as QK in Figure 5.4. It *is* conceivable that $B'Q$ in Figure 5.2 exceeds $B'S'$ in Figure 5.3, but it is not by any means necessary and indeed seems somewhat unlikely. We have drawn it this way in Figure 5.3. In any case, it is clear that for this to be a utility-maximizing possibility for Leviathan, the taxpayer must save a great deal, so that the superior efficiency of the individual as a saver offsets the revenue loss due to the removal of the income–capital tax combination.

agencies and bureaus operate on a no-carryover basis. Funds made available to such units can be neither invested nor hoarded. If the Leviathan model is interpreted, not as some centralized decision-making monolith, but instead as a useful "as if" model for the very complex set of interdependent arrangements that describe modern governments, the no investment–no hoarding model becomes much more plausible.

In this setting, where neither the investing nor the hoarding of revenue collections is possible, Leviathan must, of course, use revenues gathered in each period. From this perspective, access to *both* the income tax and the capital levy will clearly dominate reliance on either of these taxes on its own. The relevant alternative for Leviathan's consideration would be a tax on consumption expenditure. Would such a tax prove more desirable than some combination of the income tax and the capital levy? By comparison with the income tax, the consumption tax will encourage the taxpayer to save more in period 1, and to plan on consuming more in period 2. If Leviathan's intertemporal preferences, along with the taxpayer's consumption-saving behavior, fall within specific configurations, it is possible that the consumption tax will be utilized, even when the income-tax–capital-levy combination is available. Under most plausible circumstances, this sort of fiscal arrangement on the part of Leviathan is not likely to emerge. And, of course, any such possible departure from present-value maximization of revenues depends critically on an assumption that neither investment nor hoarding is possible.

The possible departures from present-value maximization on the part of Leviathan that we have examined in preceding paragraphs are made to seem more important than they are by the simplified two-period model we have introduced. In a more general model, of course, some taxpayers will be earning income from labor in every period. Once this point is recognized, it seems almost impossible to construct a scenario that would suggest that Leviathan's interest would dictate departure from those tax arrangements that are predicted to maximize the present value of revenues at each point in time.

Questions such as those discussed in this section arise only if we remain in the perpetual or continuing Leviathan model. If we consider the behavior of the revenue-maximizing government that only occasionally emerges and remains in power for only a single period, rational behavior will, of course, dictate maximum revenue extraction within that period.

5.5. The Time Preference of the Taxpayer-Citizen with Respect to Public Spending

We have already taken account of the taxpayer's time preferences as he adjusts between present and future consumption in the face of alternative tax arrangements. We noted that such adjustments will affect the time pattern of governmental revenue collections. Time preference will enter into the citizen's constitutional calculus in another and different fashion when he recognizes the relationship between the time pattern of revenue receipts and the time pattern of the public spending that those revenues facilitate. Throughout the analysis, we have continued to assume that a proportion of the revenue collected by Leviathan (designated by α in the initial model in Chapter 3) must be expended on public goods. Therefore, the timing of public-goods expenditure will reflect the timing of revenue receipts. Recognizing this relationship, the individual taxpayer-citizen at the constitutional stage may prefer to allocate to Leviathan greater taxing powers than otherwise might be the case, if by doing so a preferred time stream of public-goods benefits can somehow be ensured.

For the purpose of isolating the relevant dimensions of taxpayer choice in this regard, we may reconstruct Table 5.1 to include the taxpayer's consumption of public and private goods in each of the two periods of the simplified model. The results are shown in Table 5.2.

If we assume that all public goods generate consumption benefits in the same period in which they are provided, one attribute of Table 5.2 warrants particular notice. The consumption-expenditure tax allocates public expenditures over the two periods in precisely the same proportion as the individual allocates his private expenditures. Of course, the desired intertemporal pattern of public-goods consumption may differ from the desired pattern for private goods. But there should at least be some presumption that the two desired temporal patterns will tend to be roughly the same. If this presumption is accepted, an a priori case for consumption taxation is established, by comparison with the alternatives set out in Table 5.2.

As previously noted, the striking intertemporal patterns of revenues associated with the income and labor income taxes is partly imposed by the simplifying assumptions of our two-period model. As we extend the analysis to many periods, and to many taxpayers, and allow labor income to be earned

Table 5.2. Levels and timing of public-goods and private-goods consumption
under alternative tax arrangements

Tax arrangements	Private-goods consumption in period 1	Public-goods consumption in period 1	Private goods in period 2	Public goods in period 2
Capital levy	$0J'$	—	$0K'$	$\alpha N'N''$
	(Fig. 5.1)		(Fig. 5.1)	(Fig. 5.1)
Income tax (labor and interest)	$0P'$	$\alpha A'A$	$0F'$	$\alpha E'E''$
	(Fig. 5.2)	(Fig. 5.2)	(Fig. 5.2)	(Fig. 5.2)
Income tax (labor only)	$0P$	$\alpha A'A$	$0F$	—
	(Fig. 5.2)	(Fig. 5.2)	(Fig. 5.2)	
Consumption tax	$0P$	$\alpha 0P$	$0F$	$\alpha 0F$
	(Fig. 5.2)	(Fig. 5.2)	(Fig. 5.2)	(Fig. 5.2)
Income tax plus capital levy[a]	$0P_T$	$\alpha A'A$	$0F_T$	$\alpha B'S'$
	(Fig. 5.3)	(Fig. 5.3)	(Fig. 5.3)	(Fig. 5.3)

[a]Assuming that these are used to generate maximum revenue.

in all periods, the intertemporal lumpiness of income-tax revenues disappears.
Nevertheless, to the extent that the time pattern of aggregate income and aggregate consumption diverge, there does seem to be something to be said for
the consumption base along the lines indicated in the analysis.

If public goods are assumed to be durable, so that they generate benefits
over both periods, there may be some preference for expenditure earlier rather
than later. In order to obtain the appropriate time stream of benefits, the taxpayer may prefer larger revenues in earlier periods. There does not, however,
seem to be any a priori reason for believing that public consumption goods
are more durable than private goods.

5.6. The Power to Borrow

In the earlier section on Leviathan's time preference, we examined restrictions on government's ability to lend and hoard as a means of influencing its
choice between alternative tax instruments. At that point, we deferred discussion of the power to borrow. The reason for separate treatment of government borrowing is that while this instrument may, of course, provide a
means for Leviathan to allocate desired revenue use intertemporally, its ma-

jor importance stems from the fact that public debt offers an additional revenue source in its own right.

A government's power to borrow (to issue debt) is a power to create current assets which carry an obligation for governments in future periods to pay to the holders of those assets (government bonds) designated sums, presumably to be financed from the tax revenues collected in those future periods. For purposes of meaningful analysis, we shall assume that debt obligations must be honored. A government observed, or even expected, to default could not readily market debt instruments.

The total amount that a government can borrow is or may be constrained in three ways: (1) by the ability of the government to service and redeem the debt—that is, the future revenue capacity assigned to government defined by its constitutionally allowable taxing powers; (2) by the relative preferences of individuals as between government bonds and other assets; and (3) by the general extent to which individuals wish to postpone current consumption (and acquire assets). These possible constraints may be separately discussed.

In the first place, the power to create bonds is futile unless the government also has power to tax. The power to borrow in itself assigns to government no power that is not already embodied in the assigned revenue instruments to which it has access. What the power to borrow permits government to do, within the limits imposed by the other constraints mentioned, is to appropriate *now*, in some current period, rather than later, the capitalized value of the future revenue streams. Under "perpetual Leviathan" the chief significance of such borrowing power is its effect on the time stream of public spending rather than the aggregate level. The situation becomes dramatically different under probabilistic Leviathan assumptions. Here, the power to borrow implies that the revenue-maximizing government, finding itself in office and not anticipating to remain, may, by means of borrowing, appropriate to itself the full value of tax revenues in *all* future periods, including those in which such a Leviathan is no longer operative. In other words, the power to borrow effectively transforms the "probabilistic Leviathan" into "perpetual Leviathan" from the viewpoint of the potential taxpayer at the constitutional stage—or at least does so up to the point at which the two other constraints mentioned become operative.

We should note, however, that the time-stream effects of borrowing—under perpetual Leviathan—may indeed be desired, under certain conditions.

A recurrent theme in classical (i.e., pre-Keynesian) public finance is the idea of "extraordinary expense" (e.g., wars) and the extraordinary revenue devices that might be restricted to the financing of expenses of this type. Here, constitutional provision limiting government access to potentially large and multiperiod revenue sources might take the form of restricting the use of such sources to periods of fiscal "emergency." The precise definition of such emergency situations is, of course, highly problematic. One would hardly wish to grant Leviathan ready access to enormous fiscal powers by the simple expedient of declaring a state of emergency. Nor would one wish government to have positive incentives to create emergency situations with an eye to their revenue implications. For these reasons, borrowing may be precluded altogether: the legitimacy of its use under the "extraordinary expense" rubric may be simply too dangerous.

Limits to governmental power to borrow, and hence to lay claim to future revenue streams, may also be set by "supply" characteristics of assets markets. If the marginal return on investment declines over quantity, government will find it necessary to pay higher and higher rates on its bonds as it increasingly displaces private investment opportunities. Future government revenue may be exhausted before all private assets are replaced by bonds.[10]

Finally, limits are set on the ability of government to sell bonds by the maximum level of the community's capital formation. In Figure 5.5, the maximal capital accumulation for the representative individual depicted is given by AM' —the level of savings when the price-consumption curve reaches its minimum at M. Whatever the level of future tax revenues, government cannot acquire more from this person than that level of savings in the current period. But can the governmental Leviathan, finding itself in power for a single period, extract this maximum from the individual as long as we continue to assume that bond purchases are voluntary?

The answer to this question depends critically upon the reaction of the individual concerning the future-period taxation that current-period debt issue purchase implies. If the individual fully discounts the future-period liability that any current-period debt issue embodies, he will recognize that he can escape at least some portion of this liability, in present-value terms, by

10. Leviathan may be able to compel individuals to buy bonds, or by use of tax or other concessions induce them to do so. We do not examine coerced purchase here.

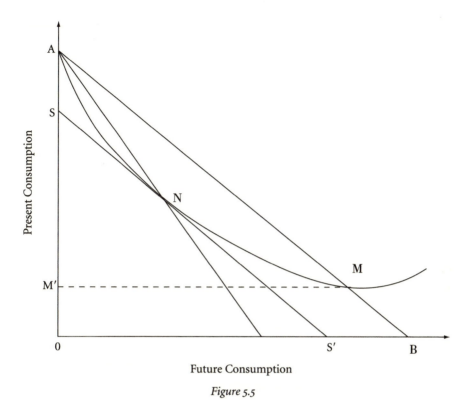

Figure 5.5

consuming more in the initial period. In this setting, public debt issue becomes equivalent to the capital levy in our two-period model previously discussed. The maximum revenue that can be secured from the sale of bonds in
period 1 is the amount measured by *AS* in Figure 5.5.

However, much more revenue may be secured by debt issue if the individual does not discount future tax liabilities and modify his consumption-
saving behavior accordingly. If the individual whose choice calculus is depicted in Figure 5.5 acts solely in response to the apparently attractive offers
of interest returns on bonds, he can be induced to purchase bonds in the
maximal limit indicated by the distance *AM'*, the limit at which saving from
current-period income is maximized.

When we consider government borrowing, it is also necessary to distinguish between internal and external sources of funds. Such a distinction is
not necessary in the treatment of alternative tax arrangements, since govern-

ment's power to tax externally is prima facie implausible, at least directly.[11] But borrowing involves a voluntary exchange between government and bond purchasers (lenders), and there is no apparent constraint against the sale of bonds to foreigners. This prospect of external debt has important implications for the maximum amount of revenue that Leviathan might raise in a single period, regardless of the possible individual anticipation of future tax liability embodied in such debt. In this case, there is an important distinction between allowing government to have access to internal and external borrowing. If Leviathan can sell debt instruments *externally*, there is no way that the individual can make offsetting behavioral adjustments even if he fully anticipates the future-period tax liabilities. And if no such anticipation occurs, the maximal saving does not limit debt issue as in the internal debt case.

How much can Leviathan borrow in such circumstances? The limits here are those imposed by the full capitalized value of future-period tax revenues. The governmental Leviathan, finding itself in office, can levy revenue-maximizing current-period taxes and, in addition, can appropriate the present value of all future tax revenues. This finding suggests that the total "burden of debt" will potentially be much larger under external than under internal debt, simply because more debt will be issued in the former case. Constitutional constraints on the ability to borrow externally would, then, tend to be more restrictive than constraints on the ability to borrow internally. But in both cases, the power to borrow implies the assignment to Leviathan government of the power to gratify revenue appetites over the indefinite future, when that Leviathan government is no longer operative. One would, therefore, expect that restrictions on the power to borrow would be particularly severe.

5.7. Conclusions

The highly abstract and simplified analytical models introduced in Chapters 3 and 4 as well as in this chapter have been constructed to demonstrate the dramatic differences in the normative implications for taxation that emerge as between the orthodox model of the benevolent despot and our model of

---

11. See the discussion in Chapter 9 on possible tax exportation within a constitutional choice perspective.

government as a revenue-maximizing Leviathan. The analysis in Chapters 3 and 4 was limited to a single-period or instantaneous model. Under the assumption that a designated proportion of all revenue collections is expended on public goods and services desired by citizens-taxpayers, the analysis demonstrated that Leviathan's revenue-raising proclivities might be efficiently constrained by some appropriate selection of tax bases and tax rates. The analysis of this chapter has extended essentially the same model to a multi-period sequence.

The distinction between the taxation of income or expenditure on the one hand and the taxation of capital (along with the issue of public debt) on the other becomes especially important in such an intertemporal fiscal structure. If a revenue-maximizing government, whether such an entity be envisaged permanently or only probabilistically, is predicted, the constitutional calculus of the potential taxpayer-beneficiary would probably incorporate severe restrictions on both capital levies and on public debt, except in times of dire fiscal emergencies as described by forces exogenous to the political process. To allow unrestricted access to either capital taxation or to public-debt issue ensures that a revenue-maximizing government may appropriate future revenue potential for current-period usage, a result that the potential taxpayer could hardly be expected to prefer.

The analysis does not necessarily suggest that the consumption tax will dominate the income tax in the rational constitutional calculus of the potential taxpayer. As we have noted, under some conditions, the consumption tax will tend to ensure a more even supply of public goods over time. Further, restriction of the tax base to consumption outlays will reduce the revenue potential of Leviathan, an objective that may in itself be desirable if the income tax is predicted to generate an overly large sum under revenue maximization. That is, saving becomes one possible nontaxable option that may be allowed to taxpayers. A by-product advantage of the consumption base, of course, lies in the additional saving, and additional economic growth, that is generated. Our analysis does not, however, bear directly on this aspect of fiscal choice.

As in the more simplified analysis of Chapters 3 and 4, the results here reinforce what appear to be widely held taxpayer attitudes concerning governmental fiscal powers. Capital levies are viewed with alarm by the ordinary citizen-taxpayer, and we observe debt limitation on the fiscal powers of many modern states. Our analysis here offers the theoretical basis for what may have often been interpreted to be such "gut" reactions to alternative fiscal arrangements.

An important conclusion that emerges directly from the analysis of this chapter concerns the effects of preannouncement of taxes. At the constitutional stage of decision, the potential taxpayer will prefer that governments be required to announce tax rates before the appropriate behavioral adjustments take place. This generalization of the legal precept against *ex post facto* legislation becomes especially significant under capital taxation, although it is by no means absent from income-tax considerations.

As regards public borrowing, the analysis tends to reinforce classical precepts that limit governmental resort to this revenue-raising instrument to periods of demonstrable fiscal emergency, when extraordinary expenses must somehow be financed. Even in such emergencies, however, constitutional restrictions against external as opposed to internal borrowing may remain in force. As the analysis has demonstrated, resort to external borrowing allows government to appropriate the full value of future revenues. Even if the citizen-taxpayer, at the constitutional stage of decision, projects only the possibility that a revenue-maximizing Leviathan may emerge, rational choice should dictate a preference for quite severe constraints on governmental power either to levy taxes on capital or to create public debt.

6. Money Creation and Taxation

There is no subtler, no surer means of overturning the existing basis of society than to debauch the currency.

—John Maynard Keynes, *The Economic Consequences of the Peace*, p. 236

Money creation can be and frequently has been used by government as a device for raising revenue. In this chapter, we wish to examine money creation as a revenue instrument, broadly conceived, from within our constitutional perspective, and with our characteristically monopolistic assumptions about the behavior of government. In some ways, this involves a simple extension of the analysis of the taxation of wealth undertaken in Chapter 5. We have, in particular, consistently noted the analogy between assigning some tax base, X, to government and assigning to government a monopoly franchise in the provision of X. At one level, we could simply reverse the analogy and assert that assigning to government a monopoly franchise in the creation of money is equivalent to permitting government to levy a tax on money holdings. Since money holdings are a subset of aggregate wealth, the relevance of our earlier discussion of wealth taxation is clear.

There is, however, enough that is unusual about money creation to justify a somewhat more detailed discussion. The analysis of money issue in the context of our basic perspective on politics turns out to be both intrinsically interesting and potentially significant in an empirical sense. The peculiarities of inflation as a revenue device will emerge in the ensuing discussion. There is, however, one aspect of money creation that sets it apart from anything we have discussed so far and which merits mention at the outset.

Previously when we have discussed the power to tax as analogous to a corresponding monopoly franchise, we have done so on the assumption that the sole function of the arrangement is to raise revenue. There has been no implication that in the absence of the exercise of the taxing power, the competitive market structure could not or would not provide the tax-base goods in a tolerably efficient and acceptable manner. There is no plausible argument that the supply and provision of goods that might be potential tax bases need be socialized. With money creation the case is not so clear. Monetary theorists engage in a long and continuing debate over whether competition in the supply of monetary instruments would be reasonably efficient or even whether competitive organization is at all feasible. The justification for the government's possession of a monopoly franchise in the creation of money normally found in the literature is not based primarily on the implications for revenue raising: the revenue implications emerge as an incidental feature, to the extent that they are treated explicitly at all.

We do not ourselves wish to take sides in the debate over the possible efficacy of a free market in money. What we do wish to point out are the revenue implications of assigning to government a monopoly franchise in money creation, implications that emerge emphatically in our Leviathan model of politics. Our analysis concentrates on predictions as to how such a monopoly franchise will be exploited. Even if the market provision of money should be grossly inefficient in the standard economic sense, the costs of the predicted government alternative are relevant in any constitutional choice between possible institutional settings. And even if the market alternative should be rejected after careful institutional comparison, predictions about likely outcomes when government is assigned the power to create money remain crucial in setting the terms of the constitutional restrictions that the rational citizen-taxpayer might desire to impose on government in the exercise of that power.

Our argument in this chapter is organized in several stages. In Section 6.1, we develop some simple propositions about the revenue significance of the power to create money. In Section 6.2, we turn to the discussion of inflation specifically. We do so by appeal to an analogy between money and a durable physical asset, "land." Our aim in this section is to point up the crucial role of expectations in determining the revenue significance of inflation and the monopoly money franchise. In Section 6.3 we consider the question of inflation and money creation more directly, using the analogy of Section 6.2. Section 6.4 attempts to indicate the sorts of expectations of government action that the citizen-taxpayer might be expected to hold. In Section 6.5, we contrast the tax on money balances with other forms of wealth taxation, and in Section 6.6, we attempt to indicate where our discussion diverges from the orthodoxy, and why. Section 6.7 offers some comments about the timing of revenue streams under alternative monetary constitutions. The relation between inflation and income-tax revenues is considered briefly in Section 6.8. We conclude in Section 6.9 with a broad methodological comment on the connection between existing literature on the "monetary constitution" and our own exercise of establishing an analytical basis for a "fiscal constitution."

6.1. The Power to Create Money

Despite the widespread reference to inflation as a means of raising revenue, inflation is not the only aspect of government's power to create money that has revenue significance. Even under a zero-inflation regime, the granting to government of a monopoly franchise in the creation of fiat money is worth something because this franchise carries with it the power to create at essentially zero cost an asset upon which individuals place economic value. In what follows, we offer a brief discussion of the nature of money in some very simple settings in order to establish elementary propositions about the revenue significance of the money-creation monopoly. This discussion also serves to set the analytic stage for the ensuing, and more detailed, discussion of inflation as a tax. Initially, however, we abstract from inflation entirely. We also abstract from the host of questions that have occupied the attention of monetary theorists relating to the issue of how money might emerge in a barter economy. We simply assume, for the purposes of our argument, that the government is to be assigned its monopoly franchise in money creation *ab initio*. We shall restrict the analysis to an economy that is stationary; there is no growth and the basic parameters (wants, resources, technology) are assumed to be unchanging through time. The basic analysis could, of course, be readily extended to allow for economic growth and, hence, for increasing demands for money. For simplicity and economy in exposition, we shall forgo this extension here. As elsewhere in our book to this point, we assume the economy to be closed. In this setting, the government can, if authorized to create money, ignore any constraints that are imposed on its behavior by the presence of competing monies.[1]

We consider initially a simple two-period model. In period 1, a set of transactions among individuals occurs in which a set of buyers, B, exchange cash for a set of goods initially in the possession of a group of sellers, S. In period 2, these sellers, S, must be able to exchange that cash for goods which they value, since the cash has no intrinsic value. If this were not so, the sellers would not accept cash for goods in period 1. The creation of money then requires that in the second period the money-creating authority must be in a position to replace cash with goods or their equivalent.[2] If the money-creating authority is the government, how can this be done? There are two means:

1. The government can return to individuals the resources it acquired from them in return for cash at the beginning of period 1. Those individuals would have forgone interest on their money stocks in return for the transaction services of money. Government would have obtained an interest-free loan of an amount of assets equal to the money stock—which is worth $r \cdot M$, where r is the rate of interest and M is the real value of the money stock.[3]

---

1. It is evident that any "opening" of the economy tends to place limits on the power of government to create money, quite apart from constitutionally imposed constraints. The revenue-maximizing rate of inflation could be expected to be lower in the presence of competing monies, simply because domestic monopoly power is reduced. See F. A. Hayek, *The Denationalization of Money: An Analysis of the Theory and Practice of Concurrent Currencies* (London: Institute of Economic Affairs, 1976).

2. For a discussion of the necessity of repurchase or its equivalent in a wholly different analytical context, see Boris P. Pesek and Thomas R. Saving, *Money, Wealth and Economic Theory* (London: Macmillan, 1967).

3. It would also be possible to imagine a situation in which government printed only "period 1 monies"—that is, money that explicitly is legal tender only for a specified period. The capital value of such a money stock would presumably be the value of the transaction services it provides over the period of its legality. In the case of the example cited here, this period 1 value would presumably be rM. There are some interesting aspects to a regime of annual monies, not the least of which is that it seems to deprive government of any possible benefits from inflation. However, money as we know it is a durable asset—a stock, not an annual flow of transactions services—and all our discussion here is predicated on that fact.

2. The government can permit the cash to be "paid" in lieu of taxes. In this case, the government forgoes (part of) the real goods and services that it would otherwise have obtained in period 2, because it accepts cash in lieu of those real tax resources in that period.

It seems clear, from either perspective, that money is rather like a form of debt. Money creation permits the government to reallocate the fruits of its taxing power intertemporally: government can by virtue of its money-creation (and taxing) powers shift the period 2 tax revenues to period 1. In addition, however, because it needs to pay no interest on its implicit loan, government obtains from its power to create money the equivalent of the interest on the money stock. Government could invest the resources it obtains in return for cash in period 1, and "repay" an amount equal to the same absolute value of those resources in period 2, keeping the interest.

The power to create money therefore assigns to government the market value of the transactions services of money for revenue purposes. In this simple model, that power is contingent on the government's preparedness to accept money as payment of tax liabilities, or equivalently on government's preparedness not to use up the resource base that money creation initially provides. Here and throughout the subsequent discussion, we neglect the deposit banking: government fiat issue is the only money.

Let us now extend this model by removing the simplifying assumption of two periods. In the case with infinite time horizons, the value of the money stock to government is the present value of the infinite stream of transactions services it provides to citizens. In other words, the value to government of a perpetual interest-free debt is equal to the principal—the real value of the money stock itself, in this case. If government obtains $r \cdot M$ per period forever, the capitalized value of this is $1/r \cdot rM$, or M.

It is quite clear therefore that, even in the absence of inflation, the power to create money is of revenue significance. The question we must ask here, however, relates to whether a Leviathan government could be expected to be content with the zero-inflation regime. What pattern of inflation (or deflation) might we predict Leviathan to choose? And what is the significance of this for the assignment of an unconstrained money-creation authority to government?

In order to answer these questions, we need to focus on inflation per se.

In our discussion, we aim to do several things. First, we seek to establish the connection between inflation and the tax on money balances. Second, on the basis of this connection, we shall be able to reiterate the main conclusions of Chapter 5 concerning wealth taxes in specific application to inflation.

6.2. Inflation and the Taxation of Money Balances: A "Land" Analogy

To establish the connection between inflation and the taxation of money balances, and to illustrate the crucial role of expectations, we find it helpful to introduce an analogy. We shift attention to "land," assumed here to be an infinitely durable resource.[4] Suppose that government monopolizes the supply of this land, defined in normalized homogeneous units, but that the total supply is more than sufficient to meet the needs of the population. These conditions ensure that some units of land would remain unoccupied even if land were made freely available. The efficiency-generating price would, of course, be zero.

Consider, now, a sequence of periods. Suppose that, in period 1, the monopoly government decides to sell some amount of land, in a setting in which no land has been sold. There are two elements that will enter into the price which the market is prepared to pay for the quantity of land offered for sale: the rental value of that land given the quantity released; and individuals' expectations about the level of land supply, and hence the market value of land, in future periods. Consider Figure 6.1. In this diagram, we depict the annual marginal value product per unit of land on the vertical axis, and the quantity of land measured in homogeneous physical units (acres) on the horizontal axis. The MVP curve illustrates the way in which this annual marginal value product declines as the quantity of land in use increases. It indicates the price per acre that emerges in a market with free competition among buyers for an annual lease on the services of land, given the quantity of land released. For example, at quantity Q_1 the price of an annual lease of 1 acre of

---

4. We do not imply here that the "land" resource as defined in this model has a real-world counterpart. Our purpose is to isolate those features of a resource that may assist in explaining the money-creation power.

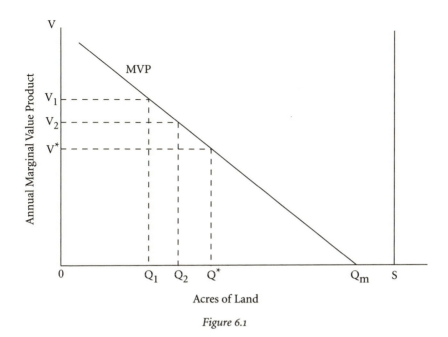

Figure 6.1

land is V_1. The aggregate supply of land is given by $0S$, and is by construction such that MVP is zero at or before the quantity of land in use reaches $0S$.

In our model, however, purchasers do not acquire annual leases but rather buy the right to permanent use. If the quantity of land Q_1 is released for sale in period 1 and if Q_1 is believed to be the quantity of land that will prevail indefinitely (i.e., if this is believed to be the only sale of land there will ever be), then the price per acre will be the capitalized value, L_1 (depicted in Figure 6.2), of the annual marginal value products; that is,

$$L_1 = \frac{V_1}{r}, \tag{1}$$

where r is the real rate of return on alternative assets. Suppose, however, that buyer expectations turn out to be wrong—that the government releases an additional $(Q_2 - Q_1)$ units onto the market in period 2, making the aggregate supply Q_2 units. Suppose further that purchasers once again believe this release of land to be the last. Then the new price for land, L_2, will be the present value of the annual marginal value products obtained when Q_2 acres of land are in use; that is,

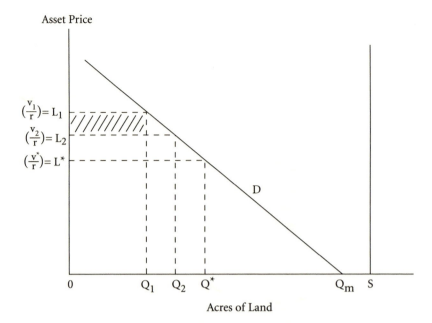

Figure 6.2

$$L_2 = \frac{V_2}{r}. \tag{2}$$

The decline in land prices from L_1 to L_2 inflicts capital losses onto period 1 purchasers. In this setting, the release of additional units of land for sale acts as a wealth tax on all period 1 purchasers.

Given that all buyers expect the quantity in each period to be that which will prevail forever, we can show the price per unit of land in Figure 6.2 as V/r with V determined from Figure 6.1. The curve D shows how the price per acre of land changes as the quantity in use changes, and is the same as the MVP curve with the vertical axis denominated in prices, L, for a perpetual flow of annual rentals, V, or V/r. In Figure 6.2, the loss to period 1 purchasers can be depicted as the shaded area $(L_1 - L_2)Q_1$: this is the additional revenue that government has obtained from being able to "fool" period 1 purchasers.

Of course, if the precise timing of the release of land for sale is known beforehand, each "generation" of buyers will pay for rights to ownership of land only the capitalized value of the future rental streams that the land makes possible. Hence, "generation 1" buyers would be prepared to pay for each unit of land a price, P_1, which is

$$P_1 = V_1 + \frac{V_2}{1 + r} + \ldots + \frac{V_n}{(1 + r)^{n-1}} + \ldots, \tag{3}$$

where V_i is the marginal value product of land in period i and is a function of the aggregate supply of land, Q_i, in use in period i.

In this case, where the time pattern of release of land for sale is fully known by all purchasers, no capital losses will be sustained by any buyer: each buyer will earn a normal rate of return on land. Obversely, the government cannot obtain additional revenue from unanticipated land sales. In this case of perfect expectations, what would be the government's (monopolist's) revenue-maximizing strategy?

Since the time pattern of release is known, the revenue-maximizing arrangement is to maximize the rental value of the land stock in each period. This maximum is depicted in Figure 6.1 as V^*, prevailing when the supply of land is Q^*, and is derived from MVP in exactly the same way as we derived the maximum revenue solution in the single-period cases analyzed in Chapters 3 and 4 (with the special consideration that here "marginal cost" is zero). Geometrically, with MVP linear, Q^* is half Q_m. This revenue maximum depends of course on our assumptions that the total quantity of land is more than sufficient to satiate all demands, and that the resource is infinitely durable. The government will release the entire revenue-maximizing supply, Q^*, all in the first period. To fail to release any part of that quantity in period 1 would involve an unnecessary sacrifice of revenue in that period.

This revenue-maximizing solution, analogous to the single-period case, depends crucially on the assumption that the future course of land release is completely and accurately predicted by purchasers. But precisely as with the capital tax discussed in Chapter 5, the purchasers of land in this example can only be secure in their predictions about government's future release of land for sale if government undertakes a binding commitment that purchasers consider to be effectively constraining. If individuals do not really believe that any sale of land will be the final one as long as any land is held by government, they may not purchase land at any price. In this case, we are back in the dilemma-type situation discussed in Chapter 5; both individuals and Leviathan can be made better off by a mutually binding agreement. In the land example, a visible destruction of some part of the total supply might suffice.

Suppose, however, that individuals are not fully "rational" in this expectational sense and that they simply predict that the supply of land in each period will prevail indefinitely without any guarantee to that effect. What is the government's revenue-maximizing strategy in this imperfect expectational setting? Here, government can obtain the full surplus to be derived from land. By adding an additional unit of land in each period, a set of prices for land will be traced out which follows D in Figure 6.2 exactly—aggregate government revenue will be the area under D.[5]

6.3. Inflation and the Taxation of Money Balances

Comparison of money and the land analogy. In some ways, money is similar to the land in our simple example, but in other ways it is profoundly different. It is similar in the sense that the time profile of supply determines the "price" in each period: all future releases onto the market will be taken into account in determining current prices. To the extent that individuals' expectations about those future releases are in error, individuals will bear capital losses and government can increase its revenue acquisitions from sale above

---

5. This assumes that the additional price obtained over the range up to Q^* compensates government for the interest it forgoes in postponing the receipt of revenue from the sale of extra units. For example, in period 1, Leviathan could either release Q_1 units at price L_1, aiming to release an extra $(Q_2 - Q_1)$ units next period, or could release all Q_2 units at price L_2. In the former case, it obtains

$$L_1 Q_1 + \frac{(Q_2 - Q_1)L_2}{1 + r} \tag{1'}$$

in period 1 values, because it has to wait until period 2 to obtain the revenue from the extra $(Q_2 - Q_1)$ units. In the latter case it obtains

$$Q_2 L_2 \tag{2'}$$

in period 1 values. The former will exceed the latter only if

$$Q_1(L_1 - L_2) > r(L_2 Q_2 - L_1 Q_1). \tag{3'}$$

In the range above L^*, the right-hand side of $(3')$ is positive and may exceed the left-hand side. If so, Leviathan will move instantly to (L^*, Q^*) and proceed to add successive units beyond Q^*. In this range, the right-hand side of $(3')$ is negative, so that $(3')$ always holds.

the "maximum revenue yield," L^*Q^*. In much the same way, the demand for money depends on expectations about the future quantity of money that government may release. If those expectations are wrong, the government might obtain revenue significantly in excess of the maximum revenue yield when expectations about the future course of the money supply are completely accurate.

It will be useful to try to conceptualize the problem so as to make it as closely analogous as possible to the simpler land example introduced above. We can depict, in Figure 6.3, a "demand curve" for real money balances, D_m. Care must be taken, however, in defining the units to be measured, along both the abscissa and the ordinate. Along the abscissa, we measure the quan-

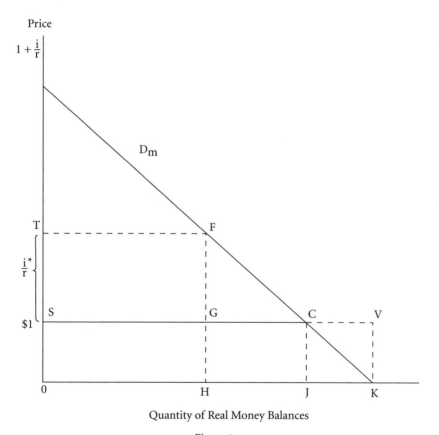

Quantity of Real Money Balances

Figure 6.3

tity of real money balances, but it is useful to define these in units of initial period dollars, M_0. Along the ordinate, we want to measure the "prices," or current capitalized costs, that individuals face in holding differing quantities of real balances, so measured, in perpetuity.

In this conceptualization, the demand curve for real money balances in Figure 6.3 becomes analogous to that for land in Figure 6.2. But there is an extremely important distinction between land and money that emerges here. As noted earlier, with land the supply or stock is measured in units of physical quantity directly (in acres, square miles, or square feet). The number of such physical units expected to be in productive use determines the prices that persons are prepared to pay for rights to permanent usage. The monopoly supplier can determine this price, or value, by changing the physical quantity offered for sale.

Money is dramatically different in this respect. It matters not at all whether money is denominated in dollars, dimes, or cents. The quantity of the nominal units of money, the parameter over which government may be allowed to exercise direct control, does not determine directly the value persons place on any given stock. The monopoly issuer of nominal money can determine the value that persons place on any given regime offering monetary services only by varying the rate of inflation—the rate of increase in the stock of nominal units. In a stationary or no-growth economy, the zero-inflation regime would yield to government an initial-period capital value, defined in units of initial-period money, M_0, precisely equal to the number of units created in that period. The price per unit placed on this money stock, and hence on the permanent "rights" to the quantity of real money balances indicated by the appropriate point along the demand curve, would be, quite simply, $1. In this noninflationary regime, therefore, the capitalized value of the monopoly franchise to government is measured either by the area $0JCS$ or by the distance $0J$ in Figure 6.3.

In an inflationary regime, however, measurement of the capitalized value of a unit of real money balances becomes considerably more complex. In order to maintain a unit of real money balances in perpetuity, a person must reckon on suffering a current capitalized "cost" that is *larger* than the number of initial-period dollars held in the form of monetary assets. Hence, the "price" for a unit of real money balances, defined in M_0, must exceed $1. Obversely, the value of the monopoly franchise to government must be larger per unit of real money balances under regimes with positive than with zero rates of inflation.

The "price" of a unit of real money balances, defined as a dollar's worth of M_0, to be maintained in perpetuity may be computed more precisely as follows:

1. The current or initial-period portion of the "price," which is simply the initial-period $1 held in the form of monetary assets; plus
2. The present value of the increments to the initial allocation of resources to money balances that will be required in order to maintain the same real (and desired) stock of real balances. (Since no increments need be added in the noninflationary regime, this second term becomes zero; hence, as noted above, the capital value of a dollar's worth of real balances in perpetuity is $1.)

In a regime with a preannounced and permanent positive inflation rate, i, invariant as among periods, there must be an increment in resource requirements in each period. To get a current capitalized value, these increments must, of course, be appropriately discounted. The aggregate cost of these increments in present-value terms is given by

$$\frac{i}{1 + (i + r)} + \frac{i(1 + i)}{[1 + (i + r)]^2} + \ldots$$
$$+ \frac{i(1 + i)^{n-1}}{[1 + (i + r)]^n} + \ldots = \frac{i}{r}. \quad (4)$$

Hence, the "price" for a dollar's worth of real money balances, in M_0 dollars, is

$$1 + \frac{i}{r} \text{ or } \frac{r + i}{r}.$$

The revenue-maximizing government will select that rate, i^*, which given the demand for money, D_m, will maximize

$$\left(1 + \frac{i}{r}\right) \cdot M \quad (5)$$

because money is costless to produce.[6] This maximum is obtained when

$$\frac{d(1 + i/r)M}{di} = 0 \qquad (6)$$

or when

$$\frac{dM}{M} \cdot \frac{(r + i)/r}{di} = -1. \qquad (7)$$

a familiar condition requiring that the price elasticity of the D_m curve in Figure 6.3 be unity. Note that this problem is again almost equivalent to that confronting the land monopolist discussed above. The one difference is that the value placed on any stock of real money balances can only be altered by changing i, rather than some independently measurable physical quantity.

With linear demand curves, the revenue-maximizing solution will be determined at that quantity of real money balances where marginal revenue equals marginal cost (in this case, zero), indicated by H in Figure 6.3. Note that the quantity of real money balances in this solution will always be precisely *one-half* that quantity which would be dictated by an "optimum" regime, where the negative rate of inflation must offset the positive real rate of interest.[7]

Quite apart from considerations relating to revenue-maximizing government, the formulation here is helpful in any assessment of the genuine op-

---

6. The same capitalized price can be determined by asking the question: What is the present capitalized value of the revenue that the government obtains under an inflation rate, i, if the real money stock held each period is $\overline{M}$? Now

$$\overline{M} = \frac{M_0}{p_0} = \frac{M_1}{p_1} = \ldots = \frac{M_n}{p_n} = \ldots$$

and is measured in some real *numéraire*. The real revenue that government obtains in each period is rM by virtue of interest on M that it does not have to pay, plus iM by virtue of deflating the real liability that money represents. This revenue stream is in terms of some real *numéraire* and must be capitalized by the real rate of return to yield to

$$\left(\frac{r + i}{r}\right)\overline{M}.$$

7. This solution is emphasized by Milton Friedman, "The Optimum Quantity of Money," in *The Optimum Quantity of Money and Other Essays* (Chicago: Aldine-Atherton, 1969), pp. 1–50.

portunity costs of any regime of permanent and continuing inflation. By utilizing the formula $M_0 (1 + i/r)$, and by selecting values for i and for r, we can define the capitalized costs for a unit of real money balances under differing regimes. Consider, for example, an i of 10 percent, with an r of 2 percent, chosen as plausibly descriptive for the United States in 1980. In this case, the capitalized cost of a dollar's worth of real balances, defined in the M_0 *numéraire*, is \$6. This says, quite simply but dramatically, that the cost of maintaining a unit of resource value in the form of monetary assets in a continuing regime described by these parameters is *six times* the cost of maintaining a unit in a noninflationary regime. Even if the positive rate of inflation only matches the real rate of interest, the cost of maintaining real money balances doubles over that incurred in the zero-inflationary setting.

The foregoing analysis is applicable only to those settings where the government is presumed able to select one from among a set of alternative permanent inflationary regimes with rates of inflation stable through time, a selection that both individuals and the government treat as binding. In our land example, we noted that the government monopolist could guarantee against further exploitation by destroying a part of the total stock. Even in the absence of this sort of demonstrated protection, however, additional releases of land for sale, beyond the revenue-maximizing quantity offered in the initial period, would drive the incremental gains to government toward zero. Money is also quite different from land in this respect. Government can add to the nominal stock of money without limit and without necessarily driving the value of additional increments to zero. For example, if the population systematically believes that each current addition to the money stock is the last that will ever be made, the real revenue that the government can obtain approaches $0JCS$ (Figure 6.3) *in each period.* By an appropriately large increase in the number of units of nominal money, the government can reduce the value of all previously existent units to insignificance. On each occasion all individuals believe the increase in the money stock to be a once-and-for-all denumeration of the currency; but such a "once-and-for-all" denumeration occurs each period. Of course, no such set of expectations is in the least plausible, but the point remains that with an analogous set of expectations the same outcome could not emerge in the land case.

The crucial question in all this is clearly the delineation of a set of expectations that is plausible. What would it be reasonable for the taxpayer—money holder to believe about government monetary strategy? What expectations are "rational" in this setting? The answer clearly depends on the maximand which the taxpayer–money holder attributes to government, and the severity of the constraints (electoral and otherwise) which he believes to apply—that is, on the particular "public-choice" model which implicitly informs taxpayer–money holder–citizen actions. In keeping with our discussion elsewhere in this book, we wish to explore the implications of one particular model of "public choice"—the Leviathan model—which we believe to have considerable relevance, both potential and actual, to the real political world.

6.4. Inflationary Expectations under Leviathan

In order to explore more fully the question of what expectations concerning inflation individuals might rationally adopt under Leviathan government,[8] we shall examine three simple cases:

1. A three-period model, with permanent Leviathan.

8. Our analysis in this chapter has both points of similarity and points of difference with the "rational-expectations" models that have been developed in modern macroeconomic theory. (See Thomas Sargent and Neil Wallace, "Rational Expectations and the Theory of Economic Policy," *Journal of Monetary Economics*, 2 (April 1976), 169–83; and R. E. Lucas, "Econometric Testing of the Natural Rate Hypothesis," in O. Eckstein, ed., *The Econometrics of Price Determination Conference* (Washington, D.C.: Board of Governors of the Federal Reserve System, 1972). Like economic orthodoxy generally, these models do not contain a specific objective function for government, although implicitly, government is considered to be interested in promoting the standard macroeconomic policy goals. The models concentrate attention on the prospect that the individual will be able to act on the same information that is available to government; hence, government cannot independently influence behavior in a way that is not subsequently validated. Government cannot "fool the people." Our revenue-maximizing Leviathan does have a specific maximand, and the fully "rational" citizen-taxpayer may know what this is, but such knowledge cannot eliminate the strategic aspects of the interaction between the individual and government, as our analysis indicates. For example, if the individual predicts that Leviathan will adopt the revenue-maximizing permanent rate of inflation and acts on this prediction, Leviathan will find it to its own interest to inflate beyond such limits. To our knowledge, the only specific critique of the rational-expectations literature that concentrates on these strategic aspects is that by Gerald P. O'Driscoll and Andrew Schotter, who do not, however, model government in Leviathan terms. See Andrew Schotter and Gerald O'Driscoll, "Why Rational Expectations May Be Impossible: An Application of Newcomb's Paradox," Discussion Paper, Center for Applied Economics, New York University, November 1978.

2. An infinite-time-horizon model, with permanent Leviathan.
3. An infinite-time-horizon model, with probabilistic Leviathan.

In each case, the assumption is made that fiat money is acceptable by the government in payment of taxes so that the implicit resource base of the money stock is validated. We also assume that other taxes exist of such magnitude as to ensure that liabilities more than absorb the payback requirements of fiat money issue.

Permanent Leviathan: the three-period case. Suppose in period 1 that the government releases an initial money stock of 100 units and that taxpayers believe that no increase in the supply of money will occur in the second period. They will then exchange for that money stock a certain quantity of real goods and services—$100's worth at period 1 prices. When period 2 comes, the revenue-maximizing government has a clear incentive to inflate to the maximal extent possible. If, for example, it increases the money stock to 1000 units, and individuals believe that no further inflation will occur, there will simply be a denumeration of the currency so that new prices are 10 times the old ones. By this period 2 inflation, the government obtains a further quantity of real goods and services equal to nine-tenths of the quantity that it obtained initially. In the third period (and final period in this model), the government simply allows individuals to use cash to pay off their tax liabilities at second-period prices—a real payment of $100's worth at period 1 prices, or $1000's worth in period 2 prices. The government has gained *additional* revenue here equal to nine-tenths of the value of the money stock (when inflation is expected to be zero). What has happened is that the initial "loan" of real resources made by individuals to government when they accepted money (interest-free debt) is effectively denumerated in money terms. Those individuals can in period 3 only "buy back" tax relief at *period 3* prices. Inflation enables government to organize for itself a capital gain worth virtually the full amount of the real value of initial money stock. We should note that this incentive toward maximum inflation is independent of individuals' inflationary expectations. If citizens believe that a tenfold increase in the money stock will occur, they will be prepared to hold money only up to the point where the capital losses due to the inflation are compensated by the transactions virtues of money. Period 1 prices (i.e., the relative values of goods and money) will be such as to be equal to period 2 prices minus the marginal

Table 6.1.

Taxpayer	Government	
	(1) *Maximum inflation*	(2) *Restraint*
(1) Hold cash	$[-a, +c]$	$[+a, +b]\ c > b$
(2) Zero money balances	$[0,0]$	$[0,0]$

benefits of holding money per se. Whatever initial price level obtains, however, it is always in Leviathan's interests to inflate to the maximum possible extent.

Recognizing that maximum inflation—independent of inflationary expectations and hence of initial prices—is the dominant strategy for Leviathan, *the rational citizen will not hold any cash balances at all.* The taxpayer-government interrelation is precisely identical to that which occurs with a tax on wealth,[9] and can be depicted in the game matrix as shown in Table 6.1. The taxpayer will recognize that if he holds cash, the government will maximize the rate of inflation, hence imposing a cost larger than that consequent upon holding no cash balances at all. The predicted outcome is the lower row, with zero payoffs to both parties, whereas both could secure positive payoffs in the upper right-hand cell.

Permanent Leviathan: unbounded time horizons. Games of the sort depicted above are, as is well known, more likely to have socially superior solutions when played over long periods, particularly if there is no end point. Even in the absence of an explicit monetary constitution, government may rationally refrain from inflicting maximum inflation in every period in the expectation that individuals may be induced to hold positive cash balances. Since a necessary condition for holding positive cash balances is that citizens believe that government will not maximally inflate, it is in government's interest to establish an environment in which citizens hold those beliefs. To do this, Leviathan needs to play a strategy of restraint.

9. See Chapter 5, note 3.

It is, however, clear that any outcome of this type, in which individuals hold positive cash balances and Leviathan exercises voluntary restraint in new money creation, is inherently precarious. If such an "equilibrium" can be achieved, it seems reasonable to suggest that it may also be achievable *after* implicit agreement has broken down. In that case, the cost to Leviathan of departing from the "equilibrium" is determined by the number of periods (noninfinite) in which individuals will aim to hold zero money balances, until confidence in government restraint is reestablished. Periodic departure from the policy of restraint may therefore be in Leviathan's interests.[10]

A very simple form of the playing of such a game is described in a short note by Harry Johnson.[11] In Johnson's discussion, he assumes (Cournot-like) that citizens believe that government will in each period inflate at the rate applying in the previous period. In this rather simplistic case, he shows that it is rational for Leviathan to depart from a stable inflationary equilibrium and "play" alternately high and low rates of inflation. In other words, the constant rate of inflation strategy is dominated by the policy of alternate high inflation and low inflation.

As Johnson himself observes, the expectations imputed to citizens in this model seem highly questionable. But it is of the essence that, in situations of this type, expectations are difficult to model. A small increase in inflation rates may lead individual money holders to unload cash very quickly, if it leads citizens to believe that larger inflation rates are imminent. Alternatively, quite substantial variations in the money stock may lead to little change in real money balances or inflation rates. The adjustment of desired

10. For a discussion of this point that has some similarity to our treatment, see Larry A. Sjaastad, "Why Stable Inflations Fail: An Essay in Political Economy," in *Inflation in the World Economy*, ed. Michael Parkin and George Zis (Manchester, England: Manchester University Press, 1976), pp. 73–86.

We should note that a shift from a high rate to a low rate of inflation may, for a short period, increase rather than decrease government's revenue-raising potential in money creation. If the shift causes persons to expect higher values of the money unit, they will seek to increase money balances. Government may, temporarily, gain more from the increased money creation dictated by a response to this demand than it loses by the initial shutdown or slowdown of the presses. On this point, see Gordon Tullock, "Can You Fool All of the People All of the Time?" *Journal of Money, Credit and Banking*, 4 (May 1972), 426–30.

11. Harry G. Johnson, "A Note on the Dishonest Government and the Inflation Tax," *Journal of Monetary Economics*, 3 (July 1977), 375–77.

real money balances (and therefore prices) to changes in the money stock seem impossible to predict here, but seem likely to be extremely volatile. Needless to say, in this setting, the "revenue-maximizing inflation rate" as derived in a world of perfect foresight is totally inapplicable—and indeed must be under anything other than a fixed predetermined monetary rule, because it is only with such a rule that perfect foresight is possible. In much the same way, the extent of revenue that may be obtained from the money-creation power must remain somewhat doubtful. The level of money balances individuals would be prepared to hold in the absence of a given money rule is presumably quite different from that which they would hold in the world of perfect foresight. Whatever the influence on revenue potential, it seems clear that the welfare costs in terms of surplus forgone will be much higher in the absence of a fixed money rule. As we have shown in Chapter 5 in relation to wealth taxes more generally, if governments have discretion over effective rates welfare losses seem certain to be higher than in the case where tax rates are known with certainty *ex ante.*

Probabilistic Leviathan. In what ways would the foregoing model be altered if governments only assume Leviathan attributes occasionally? One of the interesting features of the perpetual Leviathan model is that it seems likely that government would *not* be motivated to act so as to maximize aggregate revenue in each period. Leviathan-like attributes will not always be in evidence. This is because the cost in revenue forgone in future periods exceeds the benefit in current revenue obtained—at least over some range.

With a Leviathan government operative in fact only occasionally, these prospects of lost revenue in future periods are hardly relevant. These costs will not be borne by the revenue-maximizing government itself. Hence, when and if such a revenue-maximizing government does come into power, it could be expected to inflate to the maximum extent possible. As long as notes have value, it will continue to print them.

In one sense, this model introduces an additional element of volatility into taxpayer-citizen expectations. If a government is recognized to have Leviathan-like properties, a very rapid inflation may ensue as individuals try to dump cash on the market—and this sort of inflation could be substantially independent of any increase in the money stock as such. The modest built-in constraints in the perpetual Leviathan model are not operative in this situation, and taxpayers-citizens will recognize this fact. Even the risk of massive exploitation through inflation will not necessarily be sufficient to prevent individuals from holding any cash at all. But such risk will rationally be taken into account in determining the desired quantities of real money balances. It is interesting to note here that the taxpayer-citizen may gain virtually nothing from the relative frequency of "good" government. If government has the power to create money, the citizen who holds cash remains open to exploitation by the occasional revenue-maximizing Leviathan who may obtain office, and the costs of potential exploitation may not be much different from those that would be incurred under a continuous revenue-maximizing Leviathan.

6.5. Inflation, Wealth Taxation, and the Durability of Money

Since we have, in the foregoing analysis, provided what is essentially an application of our earlier discussion of wealth taxation, it may be useful here to indicate one sense in which the taxation of money balances differs from the taxation of most other assets. Suppose, for example, that at time t_1 government announces a future increase in the money stock, say at time t_3, of some magnitude, say x percent. In what way would this be different from a tax on whiskey stocks, or some other physical asset, at an equivalent rate, with identical advance warning? The answer is that it would be different in that, whereas whiskey can be drunk, and physical capital can depreciate, money has no intrinsic value and does not physically decay. The only possible response to the anticipated inflation for the money holder is to trade money for other things. The original nominal money stock remains, and prices adjust totally to allow for its anticipated depreciated value. The extent of the advanced warning of the increase in the money stock is therefore immaterial in a way that it is not in the case of most other capital assets.

In the standard literature, this absence of adjustment prospects is a desirable feature of a tax. Real money balances will adjust subsequent to the announcement of the future inflation; but, since someone in the community must continue to hold all of the nominal money units in existence, there is no net "escape" or "evasion" from the burden of the inflation tax. In this highly restricted sense, the welfare loss is minimal. But precisely because of this feature, note that the money-creation power may offer greater scope for fiscal exploitation of the taxpayer than that offered by the standard form of wealth tax.

6.6. The Orthodox Discussion of Inflation as a Tax

It may be useful at this point to contrast our own discussion of inflation as a tax with the prevailing orthodoxy—that essentially follows the approach taken in Martin Bailey's influential 1956 article.[12] A brief review of that paper seems appropriate here. The central element in the Bailey discussion is a diagram similar to that of our Figure 6.3. However, whereas our construction embodies capitalized values for permanently available units of real money balances, Bailey's basic diagram is constructed in a single-period or time-rate dimension. Bailey's objective is to measure the welfare cost of inflation in a manner "which is fully analogous to the welfare cost or 'excess burden' of an excise tax on a commodity."[13] He does this by considering an increase in the rate of inflation from zero to i^*, so as to produce a shift from S to T in Figure 6.3 where individuals expect the inflation rate i^* to prevail over the indefinite future. Bailey measures the resultant welfare loss as area FGC, and by appeal to certain of Cagan's results on European hyperinflations, he attempts to indicate the magnitude of the welfare loss per dollar of revenue raised from inflation at various levels. He also attempts to identify plausible maximum revenue rates of inflation for certain countries.

Subsequent criticism has succeeded in refining the Bailey analysis. As Tower[14] points out, Bailey implicitly assumes that a zero-inflation regime is optimal, and he calculates welfare losses by reference to the zero-inflation "price," r in his model, $1 in our construction. For example, Bailey measures the welfare loss involved in the move from an inflation rate of zero to i^* as FCG, rather than FHK, the correct measure. This zero-inflation base has im-

---

12. See Martin Bailey, "The Welfare Cost of Inflationary Finance," *Journal of Political Economy*, 64 (April 1956), 93–110; P. Cagan, "The Monetary Dynamics of Hyperinflation," in Milton Friedman, ed., *Studies in the Quantity Theory of Money* (Chicago: University of Chicago Press, 1956), pp. 25–117; and Edward Tower, "More on the Welfare Cost of Inflationary Finance," *Journal of Money, Credit and Banking*, 9 (November 1971), 850–60.

13. Bailey, "The Welfare Cost of Inflationary Finance," pp. 93–94.

14. Tower, "More on the Welfare Cost of Inflationary Finance."

plications also for Bailey's calculations of revenue-maximizing inflation rates. He derives the revenue-maximizing inflation rate as that rate which maximizes the revenue increment over and above the zero-inflation rate, rather than that rate which maximizes the total present value of the money-creation power.[15]

So much for a sketch of the prevailing theory of inflation as a tax. Our differences with this orthodoxy should be obvious. As we have been at pains to point out in the previous discussion, there is a fundamental distinction between the world in which a fixed monetary constitution (a money rule, perhaps) prevails, and the world in which there is no such constraint on government's monetary behavior.

Given plausible assumptions about the behavior (or possible behavior) of government, it is only in the former world that the rational citizen's monetary expectations are stable. When government has discretion to determine the money supply, the citizen's expectations must be highly volatile. Any slight departure from the status quo may with equal plausibility be interpreted either as a minor anomaly or as evidence that major recourse to the printing press for revenue purposes is in the offing. The rational citizen's response is, however, quite different according to which interpretation he adopts. The basic point is that, in the absence of a genuinely binding monetary constitution, any monetary equilibrium must be inherently precarious.

If the relevance and importance of this expectational difficulty is accepted, several conclusions follow. First, the Bailey model, essentially translated into our own construction in Figure 6.3, is only applicable in the strict sense to a world in which a binding monetary constitution is operative. The model can be used to determine the welfare implications of one monetary rule rather than another: one for example that involves a predicted inflation rate of i_0 rather than i^*. But it cannot be used to examine the welfare implications of

---

15. Geometrically, we could derive the Bailey "revenue-maximizing rule" by taking the rate at which D_m is tangential to a rectangular hyperbola that has as its vertical and horizontal axes the ordinate and zero-inflation or \$1 line, respectively, in Figure 6.3. The true revenue-maximizing rate is determined where D_m is tangential to a rectangular hyperbola that has as its vertical and horizontal axes the ordinate and abscissa, respectively, in Figure 6.3. The latter rate must lie below Bailey's, since the latter hyperbola lies everywhere below the former.

an increase in inflation rates in-period, because such an increase is only possible when a binding monetary constitution is not in being. In the same way, the Bailey model, like our own, can be used to define that monetary rule from among the set of all possible rules that would maximize to government the present discounted value of the real money stock. Such a calculus might be relevant if government were required to select a binding rule and stick to it. But the basic Bailey model cannot be used to specify the revenue-maximizing monetary strategy of a government when no such money rule prevails, where no such precommitment need be made. One of the interesting anomalies of the Bailey analysis is the fact that in European hyperinflations to which he draws attention, actual rates of inflation were in many cases grossly in excess of those which seemed revenue maximizing in terms of the parameters of his model. Why governments might choose to inflate beyond revenue-maximizing limits becomes the obvious question. Were government decision makers malevolent, stupid, or irrational? One obvious answer is that they need have been none of these. They may, in fact, have been aiming to maximize revenue. Bailey's calculations of revenue-maximizing strategy may have been inappropriate to the setting in which those governments were operating. The derivation of a revenue-maximizing monetary *rule* is irrelevant to the understanding of revenue-maximizing monetary *strategy* when no binding rule prevails. More generally, the "monetary-rule" analytics are, and can be, only marginally relevant to explaining what we observe in a world where no such rule prevails—and this particularly in relation to hyperinflationary situations. Equally, these "monetary-rule" analytics are of little use in deriving the welfare costs of inflationary finance in a setting where the monetary authority is not effectively constrained.

It can be seen therefore that our discussion and the orthodox inflation-as-a-tax discussion are addressed to different issues. We have been concerned to specify the implications of assigning to government constitutional authority to create money in the same way we have discussed the implications of assigning government the power to raise revenue from other sources, in Chapters 3 through 5. We have specifically examined this issue in a setting in which government has discretion to determine the use of its assigned money-creation power. The orthodox inflation-as-a-tax discussion, however, implicitly assumes that such discretion is precluded by some additional constitutional constraint that imposes a money rule, and seeks to derive the welfare implications of alternative money rules in this setting. Insofar as credibly binding money rules are not in practice operative, this orthodox discussion is dubious as a guide either to positive explanation of what we observe or to normative policy conclusions.

6.7. The Monetary Constitution

The Leviathan exploitation of the revenue potential of the money-creation power is a possibility that will be among those to be reckoned with in the constitutional deliberations of the citizen when he considers the possible efficacy of granting independent powers of money creation to government. As the analysis is intended to suggest, it is difficult, if not impossible, to construct an argument that could offer coherent logical support for such a delegation of power in any open-ended sense. Equally, the analysis suggests that *constitutional rules* for money creation may be among the alternatives considered in any efficient set of fiscal-monetary arrangements. If, on the one hand, conventional tax instruments are chosen that will generate an approximately efficient level of public-goods supply when exploited to their maximum revenue potential, the citizen will wish to guard against additional revenue raising through money creation. Government franchise in money creation may be constitutionally prohibited. Alternatively, the individual may deny government access to standard tax arrangements sufficient to finance desired public expenditure levels and instead allow government access to the inflationary financing option. Whereas with most taxes the assignment of the *base* is sufficient, however, it seems likely here that rate limitations will also be desirable, probably even to Leviathan itself. In this sense, the monetary constitution, embodying some set of rules relating to the extent of monetary expansion, is necessarily more restrictive than the fiscal limitations we have been discussing heretofore—both base *and* (maximum) rate limits are involved.

A constitutionally selected and enforced rate of inflation that would provide government with funds sufficient to finance an estimated desired quantity of public goods would not run into the confidence dilemma previously discussed. But this difference emerges precisely because the rate of inflation is chosen constitutionally, as a rule to be enforced on government, rather than an announcement of intent by government. In this context of a constitutionally selected institution for financing governmental outlays, inflation does become a simple tax on money balances, and, as such, it might be considered along with other taxes on capital stocks, which would also have to be designed to embody constitutionally designated rates to prove at all acceptable.

Our purpose in this book is not to discuss properties of an optimal or desired monetary constitution, which may or may not include a constitutionally designated rate of inflation as a viable alternative for consideration. Our more limited purpose here has been to consider, even if briefly, inflation as a tax and to determine the prospects of reconciling this sort of fiscal instrument with the choice calculus of the citizen who models government in Leviathan terms.

However, in the light of our earlier discussion of wealth taxes more generally, there is one aspect of the "monetary constitution" that Bailey's analysis and indeed all the relevant literature seems to have overlooked and that is important in the setting outlined here. Bailey's analysis and the subsequent literature focus solely on the welfare losses attributable to different rates of inflation. But it is clear that inflation—of the steady, totally preannounced, and legally binding type—not only distorts asset choices and not only determines the magnitude of government revenues; it also determines the timing of the revenue stream which the money-creation power makes possible.

For example, assuming a stationary economy, a zero-inflation monetary constitution implies that the full revenue value of the money-creation power under this constraint, $0JCS$ in Figure 6.3, accrues in the initial period when the money supply is introduced. By contrast, the less constrained monetary constitution embodying a positive fixed inflation rate of i^* increases the total present value of the money-creating power to the capitalized value $0HFT$ in Figure 6.3. But only a portion of this present value can be secured by government in period 1. The additional value accrues in equal annual increments, as inflation proceeds, and the present value of those increments in real terms is the area $SGFT$. Analogously, the "optimal" rate of inflation in the Friedman analysis involves an initial value of the money stock of $0SVK$ but annual interest payments which in present-value terms are exactly equal to that initial value.

If the money-creation power is to be used for financing desired public goods and services under a Leviathan government or the possibility of one, this timing pattern is clearly of some account in its own right. To provide the desired time stream of public goods, one presumably requires continuous spending. Under a continuous benevolent government, we might conceive of a situation in which the "sale" of money in the initial period serves to establish a sinking fund, the interest from which is used to finance ongoing spending. Once one allows the possibility of revenue-maximizing Leviathan, however, this possibility seems unlikely to be feasible: any sinking fund would surely not survive beyond the period in which Leviathan is in office. Since inflation involves spreading revenue over time, the problem of lumpiness in the time stream of revenues becomes less severe under a monetary rule with a positive inflation rate. For example, as the constitutionally specified rate of inflation rises from zero to i^* in Figure 6.3, the initial real value of the money stock in period 1 falls from $0SCJ$ to $0HGS$, but the present value of the revenue attributable to future inflation rises from zero to $SGFT$. To equalize the revenue stream in every period would require an inflation rate of 100 percent: the proportionate increase in the nominal money stock in every period would be the same.

Consequently, the timing characteristics of the revenue flows become more desirable as the constitutionally appointed rate of inflation increases, over the range up to 100 percent. On the other hand, welfare losses increase and beyond some point the aggregate revenue may decline as the rate of inflation embodied in the monetary rule rises. Some trade-off here is presumably required. What seems clear is that the Friedman "optimal" money rule may not be optimal, even in the restricted limits of the model used, once these timing problems are confronted. Negative or zero inflation rates may not be preferred: moderately high rates of inflation may be.

One implication here is that there is no way that the power to create money can be divested of its revenue implications by a money rule alone. This may be viewed as a persuasive argument for relying on possibly imperfect market alternatives, and denying government the power to create money under any circumstances at all.

6.8. Inflation and Income Tax Revenue

Throughout this chapter, we have focused on the direct effects of money creation as a revenue device in its own right. We have ignored the possible indirect effects of inflation on revenue arising from its intersection with income taxation, a topic that is probably more familiar to mainstream public-finance specialists than those we have dealt with here. These indirect effects are of two types. The first and most obvious is that inflation, in the absence of any countervailing measures, increases real rates of progressive income taxation by pushing taxpayers into higher tax brackets.

To the extent that these apparently gratuitous effects of inflation are less conspicuous than explicit tax-rate increases, it follows that inflation presents government with a discreet and unobtrusive means of raising additional revenue. Such a possibility hardly fits neatly into our analytic framework. We have not introduced "fiscal illusion" at any other point: the entire discussion so far has proceeded in the bright glare of full taxpayer rationality. Leviathan is unashamedly exploitative, and taxpayers are completely aware of this. The revenue-maximizing rates for a given degree of progression will be arrived at, and beyond some point at least, increases in those rates can only reduce revenue. Discussion of this problem properly belongs to an analysis of fiscal illusion, and we have not included any such analysis in this book for obvious reasons of economy.[16]

The second aspect of the interaction between inflation and income taxation does not depend on progression at all, but rather on the extent to which income taxation, by virtue of taxing property income as well as labor income, involves an element of wealth taxation. As mentioned in Chapter 5, the extent of this tax on wealth can be increased by increasing the rate of inflation, given that nominal property returns are taxed. For example, if the rate of inflation is 9 percent and the real rate of return 3 percent, a nominal income tax rate of 25 percent becomes equivalent to an effective rate of 100 percent on property income. By setting the rate of inflation at the required level, it becomes possible for a single income tax to obtain maximum revenue both from labor income and from wealth without any overt discrimination, even though the demand elasticities between leisure and effort on the one hand, and between present and future consumption on the other, are

16. For a more lengthy treatment of this topic by one of the authors, see James M. Buchanan, *Public Finance in Democratic Process* (Chapel Hill: University of North Carolina Press, 1967), chap. 10.

quite different. This possibility would not of course be present if the "income tax" were levied solely on consumption expenditure.

6.9. Monetary Rules and Tax Rules

Two separate features emerge in a consideration of monetary rules that warrant more discussion, even if that discussion is brief. The first involves the notion of "efficiency" or "optimality" in monetary rules; the second involves the underlying presuppositions about the workings of government. These features combine to suggest that, at least in some respects, the monetary-rule discussion provides a plausible lead-in or bridge to our basic model of analysis.

As the analysis of this chapter has indicated, the welfare economics of "inflation as a tax" almost necessarily draws attention to the *rate* of inflation through a sequence of periods. It would be analytically meaningless to refer to an "optimal" rate of inflation in a strict one-period model. "Optimality" or "efficiency" in the monetary context, therefore, must refer to a policy that embodies some multiperiod dimension.

In present-value computations, such as those embodied in the construction of Figure 6.2, the multiperiod dimensionality of the model necessarily emerges. One of the reasons for the ambiguities in the application of the Bailey-type analysis may stem from the single-period or flow model, which may have obscured the fact that the model's relevance is limited to alternative permanent regimes. The multiperiod setting is in sharp contrast to the single-period setting assumed for most of the equi-revenue models for determining "optimality" in the allocation of tax shares. In a real sense, the discussion of monetary rules must be quasi-*constitutional* simply because a "rule" by its nature must remain operative over an indefinite future.

The definition of the optimal monetary rule or the optimal rate of inflation that has emerged from the welfare analysis of inflation as a tax is, however, somewhat bizarre when looked at in comparison with familiar tax norms. As enunciated most clearly by Friedman, and, as noted above, in the standard model, the "optimal" rate of inflation is the negative offset of the positive real rate of interest. If the real rate of interest in the economy is 2 percent, the "optimal" monetary rule involves deflation at 2 percent per period. The logical basis for such an attribution of optimality lies in the zero (or near-zero) cost of creating nominal money. To prevent persons from economizing uneconomically on the use of money, it is necessary that money be made available at its genuine marginal cost, defined in opportunity-cost terms as the risk-free rate of yield on assets in the economy. Only if money itself is made to yield a positive return will such efficiency in individual portfolio adjustment be ensured. To implement such a monetary rule, however, government will necessarily be required to generate budgetary surpluses sufficient to allow for the reduction in the money stock period by period.

In this setting, there is no excess burden, no efficiency loss, from the monetary sector. The full value of the "money-users' surplus," the value of money for transactions purposes, is captured by the users themselves. No part of this value is captured by *government:* government is not allowed to secure any of the rent that is implicit in possession of money-creating power.

This notion of "optimality" seems straightforward enough until it is placed alongside the standard tax analysis. In commodity taxation, for example, an equivalent "theorem" could readily be derived, and proved, to the effect that the "optimal" rate of tax for any commodity is *zero.* In such a case, no excess burden is generated; efficiency losses are zero; and the full rent of commodity production, under competitive conditions, accrues to consumers. And since the result can apply to any commodity taken in isolation, it must also apply to every commodity and, indeed, to any and all conceivable bases of tax. But it would mean very little to say that optimality in taxation involves zero rates on all potential bases.[17]

Since, by presumption of the whole analysis, government must collect some revenues, we are necessarily in a regime where some excess burden must be anticipated. Once this situation is recognized, the implicit tax on money balances that any departure from the so-called optimal monetary rule introduces is to be compared with taxes on other possible bases, and some overall optimality in taxation may then be defined. All of this follows directly

17. See Edmund S. Phelps, "Inflation in the Theory of Public Finance," *Swedish Journal of Economics,* 75 (March 1973), 67–82; and Jeremy J. Siegel, "A Note on Optimal Taxation and the Optimal Rate of Inflation," *Journal of Monetary Economics,* 4 (April 1978), 297–305.

from within the frame of orthodox tax analysis; this critique does not in any way depend on either our constitutional or our Leviathan perspective.

From the latter perspective, the rational selection of some monetary rule is not determinate a priori, at least not independently of the effects of taxing alternative bases and of the demands for governmentally provided services. The optimal tax on money balances cannot be determined in isolation any more than could an optimal tax on beer.

A second feature of the monetary-rule discussion concerns the implicit assumptions made about the workings of the political process. Many economists have lived with the contradiction that government can, in some way, be "trusted" to allocate tax shares benevolently in accordance with criteria for efficiency and equity, but that the same government cannot be comparably trusted to keep monetary creation within desired limits. These economists have tended to support monetary rules, as if these are to be constitutionally enforced, while they neglect tax rules and may even oppose any introduction of such constraints.[18] The anomaly here may stem from the observed rates of inflation, which seem to be out of line with any model of "responsible benevolence" on the part of government and its arms and agencies. By contrast, increases in the levels of taxation beyond desired limits are less readily observable, and these intrude less directly on the consciousness of citizens.

Nonetheless, the familiar tendency to model government behavior nonbenevolently with respect to monetary policy actions does seem to offer a plausible bridge to an acceptance of the generalization of such a model offered in this book, and specifically the extension to tax actions by government. To the extent that the rules side in the "rules versus discretionary authority" debate in monetary policy circles wins adherents, the prospects for serious examination of "constitutional tax rules" in lieu of "discretionary tax policy" surely must improve.

18. The position of Arthur Burns is in sharp contrast with that suggested here. At an American Enterprise Institute conference in mid-1979, Burns indicated support for tax or fiscal rules while holding fast to his familiar opposition to monetary rules.

7. The Disposition of Public Revenues

Public services are never performed better than when their reward comes only in consequence of their being performed, and is proportional to the diligence in performing them.

—Adam Smith, *The Wealth of Nations*, p. 678

In the analyses of Chapters 3 through 6, we have been concerned primarily with ways in which the constitutional selection of tax institutions might be used to limit the overall *level* of governmental activity, the withdrawal of resources from the private sector of the economy. In order to concentrate on this aspect of constitutional fiscal choice, we assumed that the *disposition* of governmentally collected revenues was set exogenously, that is, independent of the tax system itself. By "disposition" here we refer to the mix between that share of revenues collected that is devoted directly to the production or provision of goods and services valued by taxpayers-consumers and that share directed to the provision of perquisites (pecuniary and nonpecuniary) to the politicians-bureaucrats. The *disposition* of revenues, as defined, is clearly an important element in the efficiency of the fiscal system, an element that is not necessarily less important than the *level* of revenues, previously analyzed.[1] In this chapter, we shall focus primarily on the disposition-of-revenues issue.

We published a preliminary version of this chapter as "Tax Instruments as Constraints on the Disposition of Public Revenues," *Journal of Public Economics*, 9 (June 1978), 301–18.

1. A third element determining the overall efficiency of the public expenditure, over and beyond both the *level* and the *disposition*, is the *composition* of budgetary outlay as among separate components. We do not discuss this element explicitly, although our analysis does have implications that are relevant.

The setting for analysis is the same as that introduced in preceding chapters. We are examining the choice calculus of an individual at the constitutional stage where he is confronted with a selection of tax or fiscal instruments that are to be applied throughout a sequence of periods. At this stage, the individual is presumed to be unable to predict what his own economic position will be during the relevant sequence. We presume, further, that the only controls upon the Leviathan-like proclivities of government are those that might be imposed constitutionally. Voters-taxpayers are essentially powerless to affect government's fiscal activities in postconstitutional political settings.

Previous discussion has demonstrated how the potential taxpayer-beneficiary may seek to build constraints into the effective tax constitution that will limit the total revenue demands of government. But how may the potential taxpayer-beneficiary, at the same time, ensure that the revenues collected will be devoted to the financing of those goods and services that he values? Once given the taxing power, what is to prevent Leviathan from utilizing revenue to further its own particular purposes? At one period in history, monarchs used substantial revenues to equip and maintain lavishly appointed courts;[2] in more recent times, excessive staff, high salaries, numerous perquisites, and congenial working conditions have characterized governmental establishments.

A variety of mechanisms may, of course, be conceived which might prevent undue diversion of revenues from the intended purpose of providing public services. In this chapter, however, we want to concentrate on those enforcement mechanisms that may be built into the tax structure itself. The particular virtue of tax constraints, as opposed to most of the obvious alternatives, is that they build into the very structure of Leviathan's coercive power an automatic interest in wielding such power for the "common good": the incentives are arranged so that the natural appetites of Leviathan are mobilized to ensure that, to a substantial degree, revenues are used as taxpayers desire

---

2. "It was found, on one occasion, that nearly half the money that had been voted for the Dutch war had gone to the 'corporal pleasures' of the most religious and gracious king—see *Pepys's Diaries*, A.D. 1666, Sept. 23 and Oct. 10." Footnote in "Edinburgh Review and the 'Greatest Happiness Principle,' " *Westminster Review*, 22 (October 1829). Reprinted in *Utilitarian Logic and Politics*, ed. Jack Lively and John Rees (Oxford: Clarendon Press, 1978), p. 184. The author of the *Westminster Review* essay is presumably not known.

them to be used. The fiscal constitution becomes, in this basic sense, self-enforcing. The central feature in such a constitution is a particular form of earmarking, which the analysis of this chapter will demonstrate.

7.1. The Model

Because the focus of analysis is somewhat different from that in preceding chapters, it will be useful to restate our basic model. The quantity of the public good (or public-goods bundle), G, provided by the monopoly government (Leviathan) is defined as

$$G = \alpha R, \tag{1}$$

where, as before, R is total tax revenue collected and α is the share or proportion of that revenue devoted to outlay on the public good, G. In earlier chapters, we examined limits on R that might be exerted by appropriately chosen constitutional restrictions on tax bases and rate structures, with the value of α assumed to be exogenously fixed. In such a context, it was appropriate to assign a revenue-maximizing objective to Leviathan (or value-maximizing in the case of inflationary finance). This objective function for a Leviathan government was invariant as between a Niskanen-type bureaucracy model, in which the value of α is effectively unity, by virtue of constraints inherent in the political process,[3] and a "pure surplus" model, in which the maximand is the excess of revenues collected over outlays on the public good. The fixity of α implies revenue maximizing as a rational course of action in either case. [In the "pure surplus" model, the maximand becomes $(1 - \alpha)R$, which for given α, is maximized simultaneously with R.]

The restrictive effects of assuming α to be fixed should be clear. It is evident that the value of α may depend on the tax institutions selected, and it is this relationship that we address directly in this chapter. Let us suppose that we envisage the constitutional process as one that establishes a "mon-

---

3. In a Niskanen model, Leviathan achieves its surrogate equivalent of "surplus" by producing excessive quantities of G. See William Niskanen, *Bureaucracy and Representative Government* (Chicago: Aldine-Atherton, 1971). The model has been subjected to criticism precisely because it fails to allow for any diversion of revenues away from the financing of genuine public goods. See Jean-Luc Migué and Gérard Bélanger, "Toward a General Theory of Managerial Discretion," *Public Choice*, 17 (Spring 1974), 27–42.

archy," under which a "king" may be treated as a utility maximizer in the standard manner. Both the monarchy and the king here are, of course, artifacts constructed solely for convenience in exposition. The king becomes a shorthand expression for the appropriately chosen collection of politicians and bureaucrats whose behavior generates outcomes in postconstitutional political settings, or even the decisive majority in a context of revolving coalitions where that majority exploits the minority. In any case, this collection acts "as if" it were a utility-maximizing entity, or king.

We ascribe to this behavioral unit the maximand, Y_k, where

$$Y_k = R - G \tag{2}$$
$$Y_k = (1 - \alpha)R. \tag{3}$$

Given (3), the king will aim to maximize R and to minimize α (i.e., to set α at zero) if R and α are unrelated. If, however, α can, in some way, be positively related to R, the maximization of Y_k may not involve the minimization of α. Recognition of this facet of the king's maximization problem provides the setting for the potential taxpayer-beneficiary's constitutional strategy in choosing tax instruments to assign to the king in the first place.

Before explaining this strategy in some depth, it is necessary to specify carefully the relationship of the king to other members of the political community. If the goods and services expected to be provided by government, G, are genuinely "public" in the nonexcludable sense, and, further, if the king shares in the benefits along with others, α may not be reduced to zero, even if its value remains wholly within the control of the king. That is, if the king's utility function, U_k, contains an argument for G as well as for privately divisible goods that may be enjoyed exclusively, a strict maximizing calculus would imply some provision of G, and hence some value for α, assuming the absence of lumpiness. Largely for purposes of simplifying our discussion here, we shall initially assume that the king is wholly external to the other members of the community in the sense that he does not secure any positive benefits from the provision of G, even though the latter may be described as a collective-consumption good for all other persons. A somewhat more complex model which allows the king to be among the sharers of public-goods benefits and/or which allows for G as a direct argument in the king's own utility function is presented in Section 7.4. In Sections 7.2 and 7.3, we shall assume that the king does not benefit from public-goods supply and that the surplus that accrues to the king is pure loss to the society. Both assumptions can be considerably weakened without the central results being lost—but initially it is convenient to deal with the more extreme case.

7.2. Public-Goods Supply under a Pure Surplus Maximizer: Geometric Analysis

The characteristic feature of our Leviathan model is that, in the absence of any constraints that force him to act differently, the king will set α at zero. That is, he will provide none of the public good, G, valued by citizens. He will simply maximize tax revenues, R, and he will utilize all of these for the funding of his own privately consumed goods and services. The question to be posed is as follows: Is there any way in which tax institutions may be selected, at the constitutional stage, so that α will not be set at zero—so that at least some G will be provided?

By our Leviathan-like assumptions about political process in post-constitutional periods, the potential taxpayers-beneficiaries have no direct control over the quantity of G provided by government. How can the king be induced to supply some positive quantity as a part of his own utility-maximizing behavior? Such inducement may be introduced if, by supplying G, total revenue collections are increased sufficiently to increase Y_k. That is, an increase in α, the proportion of revenue devoted to the financing of G, may, in certain cases, increase the value of $(1 - \alpha)R$, provided that there is a positive relationship between α and R.

Total revenues, R, are a function of the tax base and rate structure. In order to generate the required positive relationship between R and α, therefore, the base and rate structure, the essential determinants of R, must be variable and somehow related to the provision of G. This suggests that the tax base, whether it be an expenditure item or an item of income, must be *complementary* with the provision of G, as reflected in the independent behavioral adjustments of the taxpayers-beneficiaries.

The tax-base variable, B, may be arranged so that it is subject to some direct control by the taxpayers-beneficiaries. The public-goods variable, G, is, by our assumptions, under the direct control of government. Hence, we have a reaction-function sequence that may be illustrated in familiar diagrammatics. In Figure 7.1, we measure G along the abscissa and B along the ordi-

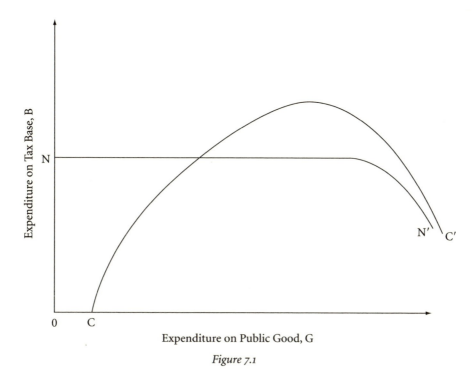

Figure 7.1

nate, both in dollar units. Consider now the curve NN', which is drawn to be horizontal over the range out to some production constraint. This represents the locus of equilibrium consumption levels of B as the quantity of G increases or, alternatively, the reaction curve (line of optima, ridge line) traced out by the utility-maximizing reaction of taxpayers-beneficiaries in "supplying" B for each possible level of G. Over the relevant range along NN', note that the "supply" of taxable base, B, is invariant with the provision of G. In such a situation, the government would have no incentive at all to use any tax revenues collected to provide a positive quantity of G. It can maximize R by levying the highest allowable tax rate on B, and then maximize Y_k by using all of the R to satisfy its own strictly private needs.

Contrast this situation with one in which B is highly complementary with G. The curve CC' in Figure 7.1 depicts this case. Note that here the amount of taxable base "supplied" by the taxpayers-beneficiaries increases with the amount of G provided by government, at least over a substantial relevant range. And as CC' in Figure 7.1 suggests, there may be situations where any revenue collection is impossible without some positive provision of the public good: individuals will simply not spend money on B unless there is some G to consume with it.

In order to determine how much G will be provided, it is necessary to specify the relationship between tax revenues and the tax base. For this purpose, we assume that the government is limited to a specific rate structure—which for ease of treatment we take to be proportional. This allows us, in Figure 7.2, to depict a relationship between the equilibrium amount of B consumed by individuals and the level of G, in the presence of the revenue-maximizing proportional tax rate, t^*, applied to the designated base, B. This is shown by QQ, which will in general differ from $C'C$ in Figure 7.1. The curve QQ traces out the behavioral adjustments of taxpayers-beneficiaries in generating taxable base under the imposition of the maximum revenue tax.

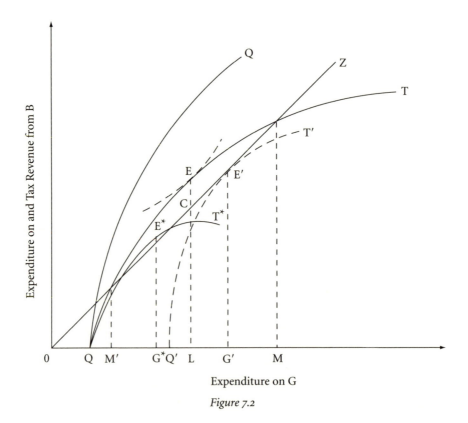

Figure 7.2

(QQ may lie above, below, or be coincident with CC' over any part of the relevant range, with the precise relationship being primarily dependent here on the income elasticity of demand for the base variable.) The curve QT in Figure 7.2 relates the tax collections derived from the revenue-maximizing tax on B to levels of G provision. For each level of G, the vertical distance from the abscissa to QT represents total tax revenue. The vertical distance between QT and QQ represents net-of-tax expenditures on B.

On the basis of the set of relationships indicated in Figure 7.2, what level of spending on G will the surplus-maximizing king opt for? Given that he is restricted to tax base B and a proportional rate structure, we can answer this question by constructing a 45° ray, $0Z$, from the origin. Since all variables are measured in dollar units, the location of a position on the 45° line implies that all revenues collected from the tax are required for spending on the provision of G. There is no net surplus. (Here, as elsewhere, we assume that government has no access to revenue-raising instruments other than those being analyzed.) Clearly, if B is the only tax source available, points to the left of M' are infeasible: the maximum revenue that can be raised from taxing B cannot, over this initial range, sustain the levels of G that are required to generate such revenues in the first place. Positions to the right of M' and below M are feasible in the sense that the levels of outlay on G required can be financed by levies on the designated tax base, B. If the relationships are as depicted in Figure 7.2, the king's surplus is maximized at E, where the "marginal cost" of producing more G is equal to the "marginal revenue" generated by that provision (where the slope of QT is unity). At this point, spending on G is measured by $0L$ (equal to LC), and total revenue collections are LE, with a maximum surplus of EC. The proportion of revenue spent on G, the α previously noted, is LC/LE. This illustration demonstrates that tax institutions—and specifically the selection of an appropriate tax base—may serve to ensure that the king (or, more generally, the monopoly government) will spend a share of tax revenues on financing valued output. He will do so to maximize his own utility, without any enforcing agency, in a setting where, if there were no such relation between the tax base and G, spending on G would be nil.

The surplus-maximizing solution for government or the king may, however, generate varying levels of G, depending on the tax base selected and on the precise shape of the complementary relationship between the base and the public good. Suppose, for example, that a tax base, B^*, is selected such that QT shifts to the shape shown by QT^* in Figure 7.2. Net surplus is max-imized at E^*. But G^* may not be the predicted efficient level of outlay on the valued public good; such a constitutional arrangement may succeed in rais-ing α only to ensure that an unduly restricted level of outlay be undertaken by government.

The construction does suggest, however, that, if there should exist an un-constrained choice among possible tax bases, with varying degrees of comple-mentarity between these and the public good, an optimum optimorum solu-tion might be imposed constitutionally. This would require that the tax base be selected such that, when the king levies the allowable revenue-maximizing proportional tax rate on this base, the only viable budgetary position requires that virtually all funds collected be spent on providing the good and, further, that these funds will purchase precisely the efficient quantity, as predicted at the constitutional level. Such a solution is shown at E', where G' is the pre-dicted efficient level of outlay on the public good, and where $Q'T'$ suggests that the position at E' is the only possible position for viable budgetary be-havior on the part of the government. In the limit, there is no surplus left over for exploitation by the revenue-maximizing, perquisite-seeking king. Under such constitutional "fine tuning" as this, the problem of ensuring the predicted efficient level of outlay is incorporated into the problem of ensur-ing that revenues collected will be disposed efficiently.

Possible criticism of the analysis at this point involves the unconstrained-choice assumption. Such fine tuning may not be possible, especially when it is recognized that the complementarity relationships for feasible tax-base us-age may be severely restricted in number, and, even among the feasible set, the relationships may be narrowly confined. Constrained optimization for the potential taxpayer-beneficiary will in general require trade-offs between allowing the king additional surplus, on the one hand, and accepting levels of public-goods outlay which differ from that desired.

Indeed, far from there being an unconstrained choice over tax base, each generating a different level of G and amount of king's surplus, we must face the possibility that there will be no tax base available that constrains the king to produce any G at all. To demonstrate some of the effective limits on the central proposition, consider Figure 7.3. If a tax base selected is too narrow in relation to the public good in question, a viable budgetary solution may prove impossible. For example, consider a situation like that depicted by the

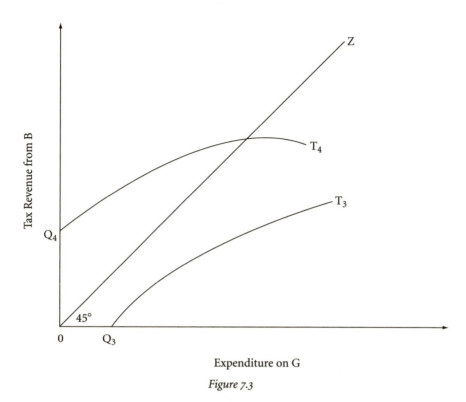

Expenditure on G

Figure 7.3

curve Q_3T_3 in Figure 7.3, which lies entirely below the 45° line. As an illustration, suppose that an attempt were made to finance highways exclusively by taxes on automobile air conditioners. It is probable that the revenue-maximizing tax on such a narrow base would generate far less revenue than would be required even to maintain a road network, much less construct it. A second possibility might be that the complementarity between a selected base and the public good might be insufficiently strong to offer any incentive for public-goods provision by the surplus-maximizing king. Consider a situation as depicted in the Q_4T_4 curve in Figure 7.3, which, as drawn, has a slope less than unity over its entire range. Unless otherwise constrained, and despite the complementarity between the tax base and the public good, the king will maximize his own surplus by providing none of the good, by keeping α at zero.

What is required for the disciplinary influence of selected tax-base constraints on governmental fiscal behavior in disposing of tax revenues is a tax base that exhibits a *strongly* complementary relationship with the public good *and* is sufficiently broad to finance its provision. It is not entirely obvious that such a tax base will be available for each of the public goods that the taxpayer-voter might demand. We can, however, think of some examples where the required relation does hold—and the highway–public road case is one such. In the absence of a road network, few automobiles would be privately purchased and used. In the presence of a road network, automobile usage is "supplied." Hence, a general constitutional requirement that roads be financed exclusively by taxes levied on automobiles (perhaps along with other privately purchased road-using inputs—gasoline, oil, tires, etc.) will ensure that the government, even in the model of the pure surplus-maximizing king, will spend some part of its tax revenues on road construction and maintenance.

7.3. The Surplus Maximizer: Algebraic Treatment

The basic relationships inherent in our central proposition, along with the limits within which these relationships must operate, may be more fully captured in a simple algebraic model.

In our discussion, the king is taken to maximize

$$Y_k = R^* - G, \tag{4}$$

where R^* is the maximum revenue that can be derived from the assigned tax base, B.

When the maximum revenue rate t^* is applied to base B, total expenditure on base B, gross of tax, is depicted by B^*. For example, in Figure 7.4, when D_1 is the demand curve for B, B^* is the area $ASTO$. We can, on this basis, specify revenue R^* as

$$R^* = a \cdot B^*, \tag{5}$$

where a is the proportion of gross of tax expenditure B^* represented by tax revenues.

The parameter a in (5) can be rewritten as

$$a = \frac{t^*}{1 + t^*}, \tag{6}$$

where t^* is the revenue-maximizing tax rate, expressed as a proportion of net-of-tax expenditure (as in Chapters 3 through 6).

Now, we have specified that the tax base is chosen so as to depend on the level of public outlay on the public good, G. So

$$B^* = B^*(G) \tag{7}$$

and

$$\frac{dB}{dG} > 0. \tag{8}$$

In general, the revenue-maximizing tax rate, t^*, and hence the parameter, a, will also depend on the level of public-goods supply. Consequently, we can rewrite (4) as

$$Y_k = a(G) \cdot B^*(G) - G. \tag{9}$$

We can now examine how Y_k, the government's maximand, responds to changes in expenditure on G. Consider

$$\frac{dY_k}{dG} = a\frac{dB^*}{dG} + B^*\frac{da}{dG} - 1. \tag{10}$$

If the selection of the tax base B is to exert a constraining effect on the government's disposition of revenues, then (10) must be greater than or equal to zero over the relevant range.

Complementarity between B and G in the relevant range implies that

$$\frac{dB^*}{dG} > 0, \tag{11}$$

but this is not sufficient, clearly, to ensure that (10) is positive. Since a is always less than 1 [see equation (6)], we would seem to require both that B^* be very responsive to changes in G and that da/dG also be positive. In fact, since B^* is potentially large, it does seem possible that the second term in (10) may predominate. Therefore, the sign of da/dG may be crucial.

In fact, under plausible assumptions, it seems as if da/dG will be positive. To see this, consider Figure 7.4. As the level of G rises, the demand curve for B depicted as D_1 in Figure 7.4 moves outward by virtue of the complementarity relation. Suppose that when there is a particular increase in G, it moves

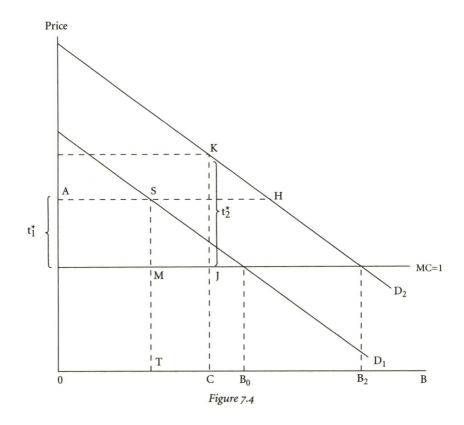

Figure 7.4

in a parallel fashion to take up the position D_2. The new revenue-maximizing equilibrium will be at $0C$, which is half of $0B_2$. The new revenue-maximizing tax rate, t_2^*, is the distance JK. We need to show that JK exceeds SM, that is, that the increase in G has led to an increase in the revenue-maximizing tax rate and hence in the parameter a. Now, TC is exactly half of B_0B_2 and hence exactly half of SH. It follows that K must lie on D_2 above and to the left of H, so that KJ must exceed SM; that is, $t_2^* > t_1^*$.

If $t_2^* > t_1^*$, then

$$\frac{t_2^*}{1 + t_2^*} > \frac{t_1^*}{1 + t_1^*},$$

and $da/dG > 0$. We can examine nonparallel shifts in D_1 in response to increases in G supply, but in all cases in which D_2 lies entirely above D_1, given our linearity assumptions, the revenue-maximizing tax rate will increase. Only in the special and somewhat implausible case in which D_1 and D_2 are coincident on the vertical axis will t^* not increase: in this special case, t^* and hence a remain invariant with respect to G (i.e., $da/dG = 0$). If this is accepted, then both the first and second terms in (10) will be nonnegative when B and G are complementary: there is therefore some presumption that increases in G may lead to increases in Y_k, and hence be desired by Leviathan.

Let us suppose, however, that condition (10) is not satisfied. Is there a simple way of increasing the likelihood that it may be met? It would be possible to relate government's (or the king's) receipt of revenue from *general* sources, unrelated to B, to the amount of revenue raised from the single source, tax base B, that is known to be tied to the provision of G. In such a case, R^* could be set as any multiple, β, of its value defined in (5). Hence, in lieu of (5), we have

$$R^* = (1 + \beta)a(G) \cdot B^*(G), \qquad (12)$$

where $\beta > 0$ and

$$\frac{dY_k}{dG} = (1 + \beta)a\frac{\partial B^*}{\partial G} + (1 + \beta)B^*\frac{\partial a}{\partial G} - 1. \qquad (13)$$

Clearly, if both $\partial B^*/\partial G$ and $\partial a/\partial G$ exceed zero, (13) exceeds (10) for $\beta > 0$, for a given value of G in the relevant range; and there exists some value for β which will guarantee that (13) is positive for positive values for G. Moreover, the higher the value of β, the larger the value of G for which (13) is zero.[4] Therefore, by increasing the value of β, we can both ensure that the king will want to provide some G, and increase the amount of G thereby obtained (at least up to the point where the complementarity relationship ceases).

While accepting this emendation analytically, it may be challenged on the grounds that it seems inconsistent with the underlying institutional assumptions. While one can imagine the possibility that the king's ability to raise general revenue might be tied to the revenue from base B, it does seem as if, once he has been allowed access to some more general tax source, he would use that source exclusively and spend all the revenue on private goods. In a

---

4. Given the second-order conditions implied by the shapes of CC' and NN' in Figure 7.1 (i.e., $\partial^2 B^*/\partial G^2 < 0$).

more realistic institutional setting, however, it may be possible to establish a bureau whose sole function is to raise revenue from some general source, under the constraint that it be handed over directly to other public-goods-supplying bureaus in direct relation to the latters' revenue-raising activities from the assigned complementarity tax bases.[5]

If even this seems implausible, roughly the same effect might in any case be achieved by assigning several tax bases to government, all of which are complements to the public good, G. Suppose that there should exist a whole set of potential bases, $B_1, B_2, \ldots, B_n$. Consider assigning both B_1 and B_2 for usage as possible tax bases to the surplus-maximizing king. In this case,

$$R^* = a_1 B_1^*(G) + a_2 B_2^*(G), \tag{14}$$

and

$$\frac{dY_k}{dG} = a_1 \frac{\partial B_1^*}{\partial G} + a_2 \frac{\partial B_2^*}{\partial G} + B_1^* \frac{\partial a_1}{\partial G} + B_2^* \frac{\partial a_2}{\partial G} - 1, \tag{15}$$

where

$$\frac{\partial B_1^*}{\partial G}, \frac{\partial B_2^*}{\partial G}, \frac{\partial a_1}{\partial G}, \frac{\partial a_2}{\partial G} > 0. \tag{16}$$

As before, (15) exceeds (10) for values of G in the relevant range, and the value of G for which (15) is zero (if it exists) exceeds the comparable value of G in (10). Hence, by adding bases to the government's taxing retinue, all of which are complements to G, we both increase the possibility that it will prove profitable to provide some public goods, some G, and increase the level of G that will be provided.[6]

---

5. There is an analogy of sorts between such an arrangement as that described here and the return of bloc grants or revenue shares to local units based on "fiscal-effort" criteria. The purpose in the two cases could, however, scarcely be more opposed. With the fiscal-effort criteria, the purpose is to ensure that local governments levy sufficiently high taxes on citizens. With our model, by contrast, the underlying purpose is to ensure that tax money is expended on public goods rather than on bureaucrats' perks.

6. Although their normative emphasis is quite different from that of this chapter, Atkinson and Stern introduce the complementarity between public goods and the tax base as a determinant of the allocatively optimal budget. See A. B. Atkinson and N. H. Stern, "Pigou, Taxation, and Public Goods," *Review of Economic Studies*, 41 (April 1974), 119–28.

7.4. The Nonsurplus Maximizer

Before turning to possible policy implications, it will be useful to modify the analysis in the direction of a more widely shared image of government. What effect will be exerted on rational constitutional choices among tax instruments if the model is changed so as to allow the institutions that supply public goods—be these kings, bureaucrats, politicians, or judges—to be somewhat less intractable than the earlier treatment makes them appear? The most selfish of kings or bureaucrats may supply some public goods, even from purely self-interested motivations, especially if they themselves secure shares in the nonexcludable benefits. Some law and order, some defense, some fireworks, will be supplied by a king for his own benefit; and the masses can then be expected to secure spillover benefits. Beyond this, political decision makers, even if unconstrained directly by the citizenry, may be honorable men and women motivated by a genuine sense of public duty; kings may care about their subjects.

We now want to allow for this, while retaining the assumption that the government will attempt to maximize revenues from any tax base or bases assigned to it. We want to examine a model in which some G will be provided due to the king's utility function. In Figure 7.5, assume that some arbitrarily chosen tax base yields a maximum revenue to the king of $0\overline{X}$. If the king is a pure surplus maximizer as previously analyzed, he will, of course, retain all of this revenue for personal usage. If, however, G is included as an argument in his utility function, he will want to provide some G. The king's preferences in this case may be represented in a set of indifference contours defined on B and G and exhibiting the standard properties. The rate at which a dollar's worth of revenues in the "king's" hands can be transformed into a dollar's worth of outlay on public goods is, of course, unity. Hence, the "price line" faced by the king is the $45°$ line drawn southeasterly from $\overline{X}$. Equilibrium is attained at H; the amount of revenue "given up" to provide the public good is $\overline{X}Z$; the amount of revenue retained as surplus is $0Z$, with the ratio $\overline{X}Z/0\overline{X}$ being the α previously discussed, although in this case its value is determined behaviorally rather than exogenously set, as previously assumed. This ratio is simply the king's average propensity to consume G out of revenues collected.

The curve $\alpha\alpha'$ in Figure 7.5 is the locus of equilibrium positions as the

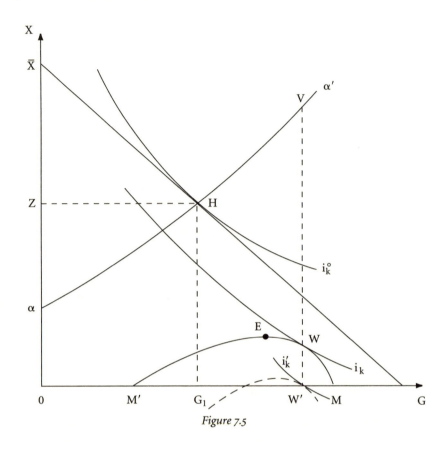

Figure 7.5

"king" is assigned more comprehensive bases for tax levies, all of which are independent of spending on G. (Note that an α of unity would imply that this curve lie along the abscissa.)

In the setting depicted in Figure 7.5, what is the effect of substituting a tax base that is complementary to G for the independent tax bases assumed in tracing out the $\alpha\alpha'$ curve? To answer this question, we may transform Figure 7.2 into Figure 7.5 by relating surplus to levels of G. Recall from Figure 7.2 that, at M', there is no net surplus, and that this rises to a maximum at E, while falling back to zero at M. We simply translate these results into Figure 7.5 with the same labeling. The curve $M'EM$ now represents the transformation possibilities facing the king. He will attain equilibrium at W, with W' being the total outlay on G made. Note that this solution involves more public goods and less surplus than the equilibrium at E reached in the surplus-maximizing model.

The dramatic difference between this complementary tax-base constraint and its absence can now be indicated by comparing the costs (in terms of surplus retained by the king) of securing the amount of G shown at W'. In the constrained model, these costs are measured by the vertical distance $W'W$. But, for the same G, these costs rise to $W'V$ in the unconstrained case. If the potential taxpayer-beneficiary is assumed to be confronted with an unlimited set of choice alternatives, he will conceptually be able to reduce the retained (wasted) surplus to zero in the limiting case, while ensuring that a predicted efficient level of outlay on public goods will be made. In Figure 7.5, if we assume that W' is the efficient level desired, a tax base may be selected that exhibits the complementarity properties required to generate a curve like the dashed one drawn through W'. Note that, in contrast to the comparable curve in the surplus-maximizing model, this curve can lie above zero along a part of its range. Surplus is reduced to zero (assuming the required properties of the king's utility function) because the king places an independent marginal valuation on G.

7.5. Toward a Tax Policy

The analysis of this chapter indirectly supplies an efficiency argument for a particular form of behaviorally induced earmarking. There need be no constraint that explicitly directs government to use tax revenues for specific spending functions. Instead, the nature of the tax bases, in themselves, ensures that government will be induced to utilize revenues for the spending desired. The normative implication is that each activity of government, each budgetary component, should have assigned to it a specified tax instrument, or set of instruments, designed not merely to ensure a level of revenue adequate to and appropriate for a predicted desirable level of the activity, but more particularly to introduce complementarity between the tax base and the governmental activity. We have already referred to the most obvious real-world example: the financing of roads from gasoline and/or automobile taxes. Government broadcasting financed by taxes on receivers offers another. When possible, the argument suggests that fees and tolls should be used in the governmental sale of partitionable services, perhaps even at the cost of some underutilization of facilities; it is unlikely that there could be tax bases for a good more complementary than the good itself.

Less conspicuous examples are worth mentioning. Earl Thompson has argued for taxes on capital to finance defense on the grounds that capital accumulation leads to the threat of external aggression.[7] A similar argument might be made as concerns internal law and order. Thompson's argument is that there will be excessive accumulation of coveted capital in the absence of capital taxation. One implication is that capital and defense outlay are complementary. Leaving aside the major objections to capital taxes discussed in Chapter 5, our analysis could point toward a similar conclusion to Thompson's, but for somewhat different reasons. A tax on new capital formation might be justified on the grounds that it would encourage outlay on defense against external aggressors and on internal provision of law and order.[8]

The analysis can also be employed normatively to identify perverse elements in observed fiscal arrangements, elements that tend to create incentive structures that oppose those which efficiency in revenue disposition would require. Once again, we can find a good example in transportation. Since 1974, a portion of the U.S. federal tax on gasoline (and indirectly on highway usage) has been allocated to the financing of urban mass transit systems (bus, rail, subway lines). In this case, the base of tax (highway usage) is a *substitute* rather than a complement for the public good (transit facility) that the government is supposed to provide. It is clearly in the direct interest of the urban-transit bureaucrats to reduce rather than to increase the supply of public good (to reduce the value of α) because in so doing they will be able to increase the amount of revenue available for disposition.

Our purpose in the discussion above was to suggest examples for possible application of our analysis. We have made no attempt to determine whether or not the norms suggested for tax policy can be extended to cover all components in the budgets of modern governments. And we have not examined the severe informational requirements necessary for rational choice in a gen-

7. Earl Thompson, "Taxation and National Defense," *Journal of Political Economy,* 82 (July–August 1974), 755–82.

8. In this general sense, it is clear that the analysis is related to the discussion and analysis of the capitalization of public-goods benefits and taxes into land values, especially in the context of a set of local governments among which persons may move.

uine constitutional setting. However, the general institution of earmarked taxes is familiar. The conventional wisdom in normative public-finance theory has condemned earmarking essentially on the grounds that any restriction on revenue usage tends to reduce the flexibility of the budgetary decision maker who is charged with the responsibility of allocating total governmental outlay among activities. This normative argument against earmarked bases is conceived in a benevolent despot image of governmental process, one that envisages a centralized decision maker divorced from the citizenry but always motivated to act strictly in the interests of the latter, in the "public interest." Such an image is not consistent either with models of democratic decision making or with models that allow some role for the self-interest of politicians and bureaucrats. Once the government is perceived in an institutional setting that bears any remote resemblance to reality, the role of earmarking as one means of securing more efficient fiscal outcomes must be reexamined.

An argument in support of earmarked taxes has been advanced in post-Wicksellian, public-choice theory,[9] and it will be useful to compare this with that argument which emerges here. If decisions on public spending are assumed to be made democratically even at the postconstitutional level, there is a self-evident argument for requiring that benefits be tied directly to costs. Voters, or their representatives, are likely to choose outcomes more rationally, more efficiently, if they can compare costs and benefits for each separate activity rather than for a multicomponent budget. General-fund financing ensures that fiscal choices are made under almost maximal uncertainty.

Our analysis differs from the standard public-choice model in its basic assumption about postconstitutional political process. We explicitly drop the central assumption that budgetary spending and taxes are determined through an effectively democratic voting process in postconstitutional periods. The argument for the behaviorally induced earmarking that emerges is derived directly from the political model in which in-period fiscal decisions are made by revenue-maximizing politicians-bureaucrats who may have at least some power to secure a share of tax revenues as surplus for themselves. A consti-

---

9. See James M. Buchanan, "The Economics of Earmarked Taxes," *Journal of Political Economy,* 71 (October 1963), 457–69. Also see James M. Buchanan, *Public Finance in Democratic Process* (Chapel Hill: University of North Carolina Press, 1967), especially chap. 6.

tutional utilization of the relations between tax bases and the provision of desired public goods becomes a means of exerting discipline on those who do make fiscal decisions. As such, it is not at all out of place in a democratic decision model, and it may be interpreted as reinforcing other arguments noted above. One plausible model of democracy involves attempts by rotating majority coalitions to maximize net fiscal transfers to their members at the expense of members of minorities. The disciplinary argument for earmarking applies equally well to this model as to the more cynical model of bureaucratic domination. All that is required is that the words "majority coalition" be substituted for the word "king" in the earlier parts of the chapter.

Our basic argument is indeed simple. Effectively designed earmarking may limit the extent to which government, any government, can exploit the taxpaying public; government may be given a positive incentive to provide the goods and services that taxpayers want. The decision makers, whoever these may be, can be kept "honest."

8. The Domain of Politics

What a *government* ought to do, is a mysterious and searching
question, which those may answer who know what it means; but
what other men ought to do, is a question of no mystery at all. . . .
The question is not why governments are bound not to do this or
that, but why other men should let them if they can help it. The
point is not to determine why the lion should not eat sheep, but
why men should eat their own mutton if they can.

—Perronet Thompson, "Greatest Happiness Principle,"
Westminster Review, 21 (July 1829); reprinted in *Utilitarian Logic
and Politics,* p. 141

Our concern in this book is with the fiscal constitution, with alternative means
of constraining government's power to tax and to spend. We are not directly
concerned with *nonfiscal* constraints on governmental powers, whether these
be constitutionally or otherwise imposed. Our analysis would, however, be seriously incomplete if we did not recognize the relationship between fiscal
and nonfiscal constraints. The potential substitutability between fiscal and
nonfiscal constraints keeps us from claiming that the former are in all circumstances absolutely essential for keeping governments within appropriate
limits. Conversely, the complementarity between fiscal and nonfiscal constraints keeps us from extending to wild extremes the argument that fiscal
limits alone will accomplish the purpose of constraining Leviathan.

The construction of this book can perhaps best be interpreted as being
predicated on the assumption that an appropriate set of nonfiscal rules is operative, setting the context within which alternative *fiscal* constraints can be
analyzed and evaluated. Broadly speaking, the nonfiscal constraints in existence are simply assumed to be those that we generally observe in modern

Western democracies. Beyond this, however, our analysis requires the assumption that the imposition of specifically fiscal constraints will not itself generate successful "escape" from fiscal limits through nonfiscal channels. Although we shall make no attempt at exhaustive analysis here, this chapter is devoted to an examination of the interdependencies between those means of limiting Leviathan which involve restrictions on the taxing power and those which do not. In particular, we include in the latter category restrictions on the domain of government spending, as well as specific types of procedural restrictions on the nature of political process.

8.1. Procedural Constraints on Political Decision Making

As we have noted earlier, our analysis departs from the conventional public-choice framework in which the government is modeled as a relatively passive responder to the demands placed upon it by voters-taxpayers-beneficiaries. We have argued in Chapter 2 that constitutional guarantees of electoral competition among politicians and parties are not sufficient to ensure that the Leviathan-like proclivities of governments are always kept in bounds. In that earlier discussion, we assumed a setting for electoral competition characterized by majority-voting rules both in elections among candidates for office and in choices among policy actions within legislative assemblies.

Once the inadequacies of electoral competition are acknowledged, there are two directions for reform. We might think of imposing constitutional constraints directly on the taxing-spending power, which is our basic subject matter in this book, or we might think of imposing constitutional changes in the *procedures* or *rules* through which political decisions are made. With some reforms of this latter type, resort to direct fiscal constraints may be neither necessary nor desirable.

By way of illustration, we can do no better than look to the seminal work of Knut Wicksell—work that has already been referred to several times in this book. Wicksell did not seek reform in the fiscal constitution, as such, but he did seek to achieve more responsive government through changes in the procedures through which taxing-spending decisions were made. In his idealized model, he proposed a rule of unanimity in legislatures. But he acknowledged the difficulties of such a rule in practice, and he seemed willing to settle for a qualified majority approval for all public outlay projects amounting to perhaps five-sixths of the total voting membership. Further, and at a more attainable level, Wicksell proposed that taxing and spending legislation be simultaneously considered. To Wicksell, legislatures should operate under an obligation to provide explicitly for the financing of each and every spending program authorized. In so doing, he recommended a form of earmarking somewhat similar to that indicated by the discussion in Chapter 7, but for rather different reasons. In the context of the modern discussion of constitutional policy, the proposal that government be required to balance its budget is perhaps a reasonably close analogue to the sort of procedural requirement that Wicksell suggested. We shall have more to say about "balanced-budget limitation" in Chapter 10; here, we simply note its status as a variety of "procedural constraint."

The characteristic feature of procedural reform lies in its explicit avoidance of imposing constraints or limits on the results or outcomes of collective decision making. The proposals listed above, and others that might be discussed, operate directly on the *process* of reaching or making collective decisions; they do not restrict directly the particular range of outcomes that might be attained. This is not, of course, to deny that there must exist some feedback relationship between the predicted effects of procedural changes and the direction of predicted results. Indeed, some such predictions must be used to inform any choice among alternative procedures. But an advantage of purely procedural reform lies in the outcome flexibility that is retained.

In earlier chapters, we have found it to be convenient to model government as a monolithic entity that seeks to maximize net revenue or surplus. This model is useful in allowing us to discuss alternative tax constraints; the single maximand offers a device that allows predictions to be made about the behavior of an unconstrained Leviathan. It is clear that any discussion of procedural reform, as a possible substitute for fiscal constraints, must depart somewhat from such simplistic Leviathan construction. In the earlier analysis, the objective for constitutional change was one of limiting governmental behavior, of fencing government in, so to speak, without at the same time changing its "character." The procedural changes suggested by Wicksell, however, are directed at modifying the structure of governing itself and, hence, changing the behavioral model appropriate to describe governmental actions.

The surplus-maximizing objective would not be appropriately assigned to a government that operated within the Wicksellian procedural constraints. Such a government would not evoke the Leviathan metaphor, and the whole analysis and discussion of possible constitutional reform would be quite different from that presented in this book.

We have written this book about potential change in the fiscal constitution on the presumption that major changes in governmental procedures for reaching decisions do not occur, and that government, as we observe it to operate, will continue essentially as it is now institutionally characterized. As our other works should have indicated, the stance taken here does not suggest that we personally prefer the strictly fiscal constraints over the procedural ones. Both means of controlling governments must be analyzed and examined. Our efforts here reflect nothing more than a division of labor.

8.2. The Rule of Law: General Rules

A different, if somewhat related, approach to that previously discussed as procedural may be examined under the rubric of the "rule of law." This approach, perhaps best identified by the arguments of F. A. Hayek in his *The Constitution of Liberty* (1960) and subsequent writings, aims to restrict the structure or pattern of allowable outcomes rather than either the procedures for reaching outcomes or the specific outcomes themselves. This objective is to be accomplished by requiring that outcomes of the fiscal process conform to the familiar and time-honored "rule of law." By this Hayek means that all rules involving taxes must be *general*. They must be universally applicable to *all* members of the political community, whether or not these persons are inside or outside the subset of persons that make the governmental decisions. This approach essentially reflects the specific application of the traditional legal norm of "equality before the law" to the taxing activities of government.

Historically, the constitutional requirement that taxes be uniform seems to stem directly from this legal norm. As our earlier analysis has indicated, tax uniformity may be generated as one means of restricting the revenue-gathering potential of government. In our analytic setting, such uniformity was taken to require nondifferentiation in tax rates among persons or among groups or among different tax bases. However, insofar as this sort of uniformity is to be found in modern fiscal systems, it probably reflects residues of the legal equality norm rather than any overt consciousness of the need to restrict Leviathan's fiscal appetite. The tenuousness of existing uniformity precepts is evident; taxes do and may vary among persons and among groups; different tax bases are subjected to differing levies. At best, existing legal norms, as currently interpreted, serve only to rule out totally arbitrary discrimination in taxation. For example, the United States government could not (or at least has not, to date, been able to) impose one rate of income tax on Catholics and another rate on Protestants, one rate on blacks and another rate on whites, one rate on women and another rate on men. If the government tried any such tax discrimination, it seems likely that it would be ruled out of court on constitutional grounds. Of course, were government able to discriminate beyond currently allowable limits, it could generate more revenues from its current sources, as our analysis in Chapter 4 indicated. The accepted legal norms do, therefore, limit Leviathan. The taxing power is not unrestricted.[1]

This Hayekian interpretation of the rule of law as requiring generalized uniformity suggests two questions. How effective are existing legal limits? And how could a generalized extension of the legal norm of uniformity be used so as to constrain Leviathan beyond those limits already discussed?

These questions immediately raise issues of definition. How is uniformity or equality to be defined for tax purposes? Should "equality before the law" in taxation require equal payments by all persons in the polity? Or should such equality be interpreted to require that all persons in the jurisdiction confront equal *rates* of tax, hence allowing for proportional but not regressive or progressive tax structures? Hayek's argument to the effect that a proportional tax structure would meet the requirement for generality whereas a progressive rate structure would not do so seems to be dangerously arbitrary. To defend such a position requires considerably more analysis than Hayek has provided.

If we leave the questions of definition aside, however, does the generality requirement impose checks on the taxing proclivity of Leviathan? Would the stipulation that persons who are inside the ruling coalition face the same tax

---

1. For a general discussion of the fiscal constitution, see Kenneth W. Dam, "The American Fiscal Constitution," *University of Chicago Law Review,* 44 (Winter 1977), 271–320.

structure as those who remain outside the ruling coalition restrict the taxing power as such? With no accompanying constraints, would the mere fact that members of the ruling group themselves pay taxes like everyone else effectively result in less total tax gathering?

It seems clear that it would, at least in some plausible settings. Consider a simple example in which Leviathan takes the form of an exploitative majority coalition. Suppose further that the uniformity requirement on the tax side involves the requirement that revenues be raised by a completely general income tax. To avoid definitional questions of the type indicated above, suppose that all citizens-taxpayers have identical tastes and pretax incomes, so that the choice between progression and proportionality involves no question of discrimination between individuals. Given here that the majority and minority are of virtually identical size, the contribution that members of the majority make to each dollar of revenue collected is virtually 50 cents. It may therefore seem as if the majority would rationally vote for maximum revenue: it makes a net gain of almost 50 cents for every dollar of revenue collected. This conclusion would be valid if taxes were lump-sum. Uniformity in and of itself—specifically in the absence of any restrictions on the power to tax—would not limit Leviathan at all: the exploitative majority would end up with *all* the income. In the presence of base limits of the sort we have analyzed earlier, however, the uniformity requirement does serve as an additional means of constraint. For where the tax to be levied involves limited revenue, it also involves an excess burden for all taxpayers. This excess burden is present because each of the taxpayers, including those in the majority coalition, will rationally attempt to minimize his own tax payment by substituting away from the taxed good. At some level, the marginal excess burden sustained by members of the majority coalition will be equal to the marginal transfer received from members of the minority. The majority coalition will not seek to push the extent of redistribution beyond this point, because they lose more in additional excess burden from the tax system per dollar of additional transfer received than they gain in transfers.

Consider a simple example. The tax base is taken to be money income, X, leaving leisure exempt. The "demand" curve for X for the economy as a whole is depicted as the D curve in Figure 8.1. Given the assumption of identical tastes, this "demand" for X can be divided into two (virtually) identical parts, with D_m being the aggregate demand for X over all members of the

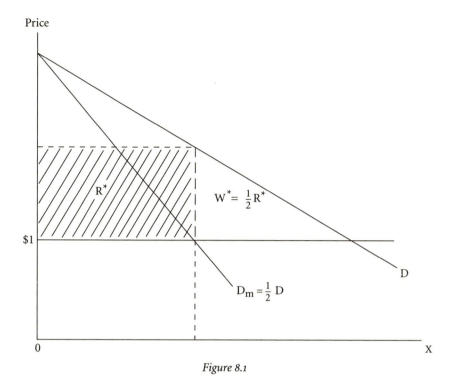

Figure 8.1

majority coalition. With uniform taxes, the most revenue that can be obtained from the taxation of *X* is shown by the shaded areas, R^*, in Figure 8.1: one-half of this revenue (or one-half of any other quantity of revenue, for that matter) will be paid by members of the majority coalition. The welfare loss sustained by taxpayers at this maximal level of revenue will, in the linear case, be precisely one-half the maximum revenue yield (as demonstrated in Chapters 3 and 4).

We can transfer the information in Figure 8.1 into a more usable form by depicting in Figure 8.2 the costs to majority members of any transfers they receive. Such costs are of two parts: first, since taxes are uniform and the majority is a bare 50 percent of the population, majority members pay in taxes 50 cents out of every dollar of transfer revenue. This is shown as the horizontal line at 50 cents in Figure 8.2. Beyond this, however, there is the excess burden of the tax system. One-half of this excess burden, also, will be borne by the decisive majority. To determine total marginal costs to the majority, including excess burden, of higher transfer levels, we need to add to the 50-cent line in Figure 8.2 the marginal excess burden per dollar of revenue raised. Clearly, the addition to welfare cost or excess burden associated with an extra dollar of revenue approaches infinity as revenue approaches its maximum. For as the tax rate approaches the revenue-maximizing rate t^*, the excess burden is increasing at an increasing rate while the revenue level is increasing at a decreasing rate. For tax-rate increases in the neighborhood of t^*, excess burden rises while the revenue increase is zero: the *extra* welfare loss associated with an additional dollar of transfers (or an additional dollar of revenue) is quite literally infinite.

On this basis, we can draw from the 50-cent line upward a curve labeled *TMC* in Figure 8.2 that depicts the *total* marginal cost to majority members of various levels of transfer, including that part of the excess burden of the tax system that majority members bear. At R^*, the *TMC* curve will approach

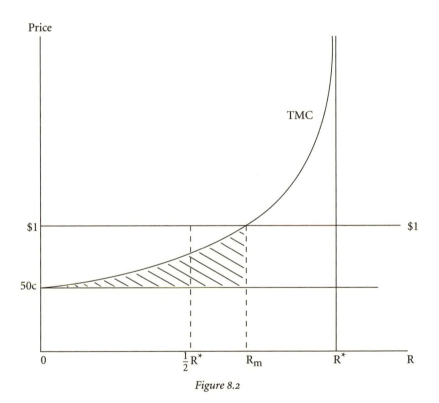

Figure 8.2

infinity, indicating that the excess burden per dollar of extra revenue is approaching infinity. The area between *TMC* and the 50-cent line up to R^* measures the total excess burden of R^* borne by majority members: since the majority is one-half of the electorate, this will be one-half of aggregate excess burden, or $\frac{1}{2} W^*$ in Figure 8.1.

Given *TMC*, we are in a position to predict the level of transfers that the decisive majority will rationally vote for. Since the value of a dollar transfer to the majority is always $1, the level of transfers emergent under majority rule will occur where the *TMC* curve intersects the $1 line. At this point, the cost of an extra dollar's transfer, including the excess burden of taxes that the majority pays, is exactly $1. We depict this point by R_m in Figure 8.2. Clearly, R_m will be to the left of R^*: the majority will not push taxes to the revenue-maximizing limit. The revenue level R_m depicts the total revenue raised for transfers in the presence of a generality requirement on the tax side.

Let us now suppose that the generality requirement does not apply. The majority will now apply taxes to the minority alone, and will do so up to the revenue-maximizing limit. Since the minority is one-half the population, revenue will be $\frac{1}{2} R^*$; and the majority will receive all that revenue in transfers. The excess burden sustained by minority members will be one-half of this maximum revenue, or $\frac{1}{4} R^*$, given linearity assumptions.

The implications of the generality requirement for a given tax base can now be gauged by appeal to a direct comparison of the two equilibria. In the absence of generality: aggregate tax revenue is $\frac{1}{2} R^*$ dollars; the net benefit of transfers to the majority coalition is $\frac{1}{2} R^*$ dollars; and total excess burden is $\frac{1}{4} R^*$. In the presence of the tax generality requirement: aggregate tax revenue is R_m; the net benefit of transfers to the majority coalition is the area between *TMC* and the $1 line up to R_m in Figure 8.2; and total excess burden is twice the area between *TMC* and the 50-cent line up to R_m in Figure 8.2. Since R_m is less than R^*, and the benefits to majority members in the generality case are less than $\frac{1}{2} R_m$, those benefits are also less than $\frac{1}{2} R^*$. Majority members lose by the generality constraint. In the case of general taxation, however, both majority and minority members sustain excess burdens due to taxation, and the total excess burden in this case *may* exceed that in which only minority members pay taxes. In sum, the generality requirement clearly reduces the fiscal exploitation of the minority, but it will increase total tax revenue and it may increase the aggregate excess burden attributable to taxation. The net effects of the generality rule on the tax side are therefore not entirely un-ambiguous.

The model outlined here in some sense makes the case for the effectiveness of uniformity constraints in its most generous form. As the size of the decisive coalition falls from one-half of the electorate to an even smaller proportion of the citizenry—to a ruling class, a bureaucratic elite, a president-premier-king—the bite of any uniformity constraint falls: the contribution of the decision makers to the cost of transfers to themselves becomes smaller and smaller. In terms of Figure 8.2, a reduction in the size of the dominant or ruling coalition would have the effect of displacing the TMC curve downward throughout its range, and hence shifting the solution toward R^*.

In the discussion of this section, we have set aside the possibility that the Leviathan surplus should itself be subject to tax. Although this is not inconceivable in the case of the exploitative majority, it becomes rather strained where the transfers take the form of public expenditures of particular benefit to the ruling class or the bureaucratic elite.

8.3. The Domain of Public Expenditures

The ambiguity of the uniformity norm when applied only to the tax side of fiscal operations should not be taken to prejudice the question of its extension to the expenditure side. As it happens, requirements for Hayekian equality of treatment or generality have historically never been applied to the spending side: on the contrary, quite arbitrary discrimination in the distribution of the benefits of public spending among persons and groups seems to be characteristic of modern fiscal systems.[2] But this fact of fiscal experience, in itself, offers no logical basis for rejecting legal requirements for uniformity on the spending side of the fiscal account as a possibility to be considered. But other types of constraint on the spending side deserve some attention here, and are historically more common. In this section, we seek to explore briefly some of these restrictions on expenditures, along with the implications of generality requirements.

2. For a discussion of the legal-constitutional asymmetry in the treatment of taxes and benefits, see David A. Tuerck, "Constitutional Asymmetry," *Papers on Non-market Decision Making*, 2 (1967), 27–44.

If we imagine, in the foregoing example, that restrictions on generality were extended to the spending side of the account, it is clear that the potential for redistribution in the majority's favor would be entirely removed: the requirement of an identical share in revenue for all would obliterate the possibility of *any* individual obtaining more than he paid in taxes. This would not, to be sure, hold in a slightly more general setting in which pretax incomes differ, provided that uniformity on the tax and expenditure sides is defined asymmetrically. For example, if proportional taxation is taken to satisfy the uniformity rubric on the tax side, but equal per capita shares are required on the expenditure side (a structure the so-called "linear negative income tax" simulates), some redistribution would still occur. There would clearly be *less* redistribution than where no uniformity restrictions were imposed on the transfer pattern, since richer majorities could never transfer income in their own direction; but where uniformity is defined symmetrically on both sides of the fiscal account, exploitation of a minority by a decisive majority is removed.

Somewhat similar restrictions on the power of an exploitative majority are achieved by the requirement that the spending activities of government be restricted to the provision of genuinely "public goods" of the pure Samuelsonian type. Such goods are by definition *equally* (and totally) consumed by all citizens; consequently, if there is uniformity on the tax side, the possibility of a majority redistributing resources in its own favor is substantially removed. It could indeed be argued that the restrictions on the domain of government activity which are extant in most written constitutions were drafted with such considerations in mind—they can certainly be *rationalized* along such lines.

In fact, the requirement that government spending be restricted to pure public goods is unnecessarily strict. The domain of government activity could be extended to those goods which are nonexcludable, even if jointness is incomplete: the crucial characteristic for these purposes is that each individual's consumption—or access to consumption—be identical. Indeed, government could be allowed to finance and provide fully partitionable "private" goods and services embodying no jointness efficiencies at all provided that equal quantities be made available to all. In all such cases, the distributional consequences are essentially the same as when transfers are made to all on an equal-share basis. To the extent that uniformity on the tax side is interpreted to require anything other than equal absolute amounts of tax per taxpayer, possibilities of redistribution remain but are substantially restricted by the equal-share requirement on the expenditure side.

Two somewhat different and more general points should be made in relation to this discussion. First, we have interpreted the power to redistribute negatively, in the sense that such power offers Leviathan the opportunity to redistribute in its own direction. This interpretation is consistent with the basic thrust of our model of constitutional choice: in this model, there are no preferences for redistribution as such at the constitutional level, although of course some redistribution might emerge to the extent that taxpayers-donors *wish* to make transfers to recipients in-period.[3] It is, however, clear that if the individual exhibits preferences over distributional matters at the constitutional level—whether they be Rawlsian, or otherwise—there is no guarantee that assigning the power to redistribute to government will be desirable: the transfer patterns that emerge from the assignment of such power may not at all satisfy any set of moral norms.

Second, restrictions on the domain of public spending of the sort we have been discussing may be implemented under an umbrella of rules against bureaucratic and political "corruption." That such rules exist and that institutions for their enforcement exist under most constitutions can hardly be questioned. These rules clearly restrict the domain of public activity in one sense. Their significance lies in the inhibitions they place on the ability of those exercising discretionary power to appropriate resources *directly*. Neither such rules nor the restrictions on spending discussed earlier serve to prevent Leviathan's appropriation of revenue surplus by *indirect* means— perquisites of office, overexpanded bureaucracies, and so on. For this reason, even if such restrictions could be expected to be totally effective—which seems unlikely—there would remain a role for tax limits of the type we have explored in preceding chapters.

8.4. Government by Coercion

To this point, we have examined nonfiscal constraints that might serve as possible substitutes for fiscal constraints on the activities of government. We

---

3. See Harold Hochman and James Rodgers, "Pareto Optimal Redistribution," *American Economic Review,* 59 (September 1969), 542–57, for a discussion of this possibility.

have been interested in determining the extent to which the presence or potential introduction of such nonfiscal limits might reduce the need for any imposition of constitutional controls over the power to tax. A wholly different set of interdependencies emerges when we look at nonfiscal constraints as necessary complements to the fiscal controls. Here the issues to be analyzed concern the potential effectiveness of overtly fiscal constraints in view of their critical dependence on the maintenance and enforceability of nonfiscal instruments that will serve to prevent the former from being successfully avoided by government with Leviathan proclivities.

If we remain strictly within the revenue-seeking model of government, the problems to be discussed here do not formally arise since, by our somewhat artificial assumption, the single maximand is *tax* revenues. Hence, any constraint on the power or authority to tax must be effective by definition. Once we depart from this artificial construction, however, to grant that Leviathan's instrumental desire for tax revenues is for the purpose of ultimately acquiring command over real goods and services, the possible avoidance of any explicit tax limit or constraint must be reckoned with. If, when confronted with a legal limit on its taxing power, government should find it relatively easy to secure real goods and services by nontax means, there would be little purpose in the whole tax-limit exercise.

As we have noted, there exist legal-constitutional restrictions on the government's power to *take,* and, indeed, without some such restrictions there would presumably be no *raison d'être* for the institution of taxation itself. The government could, in the absence of legal constraints on the taking of power, simply coerce persons into relinquishing possession of the goods and services it wants. In the established legal traditions of Western nations, governmental coercion of this variety has been and continues to be considered beyond the legitimate exercise of state authority. Certain exceptions prove the rule—conscription for military services and eminent domain are two. In the latter case in particular, governmental taking is accompanied by the legal requirement for "just compensation," which becomes a part of the more general legal requirement for "due process."

The existence of legal limits to the taking power does not, of course, guarantee against an extension of such power. And it must be acknowledged that any imposition of constraining tax limits on government will create additional incentives for the direct "taking" of goods and services from persons, independently of the fiscal channel that involves first, taxation, and subsequently, governmental purchase of such goods and services in the market-place. If tax limits are expected to be effective at all, legal restrictions on governmental taking power must be maintained in the face of increased incentives.

If the agents of Leviathan, the rulers, seek to use the fiscal system or the taking power for the purpose of acquiring command over goods and services for their own direct consumption or use (over and above that share which they might legally be required to return to members of the community as public-goods benefits), the potential dangers embodied in dramatic extensions of the taking power may not loom as significant. Established legal traditions are important, and overt coercion on the part of governmental agents could presumably be held within reasonably narrow limits, despite enhanced incentives offered to such agents. But a much more severe, and possibly intractable, problem arises when we allow the agents of Leviathan to incorporate what we may call "nonpersonal" arguments in their utility functions, when we allow these agents to promote or to seek to further a set of "objectives" that can be plausibly "legitimized" on what may be called "public interest" or "general welfare" grounds. In such a setting, tax limits per se may be ineffective in containing government. This seems to be a fact that must be squarely faced.

Consider a familiar example. Prior to the mid-1960s, individual citizens in the United States were, for the most part, unconstrained in their access to and their usage of the air- and waterways except to the extent that limits were inherent in the laws of nuisance as carried down from the English Common Law. In a reconstructed scenario different from the one actually followed, the government could have, in recognition of the pollution-environmental problems, declared "clean air" and "clean water" to be "public goods." It could have then levied taxes for the financing of such "goods," which in this case would have involved the purchase of individuals' agreements to reduce polluting activities. As we know, such a scenario was not followed; government did not utilize the fiscal route to the accomplishment of its avowed and newly found environmental objective. Instead, the government simply enacted laws that embodied direct prohibitions on specific types of activity, or in lieu of this, enacted laws that authorized administration agents (bureaucrats) to define the scope of prohibited activities. Individuals were simply prevented from being allowed to do things that had previously been available to them.

In a real sense, government used the taking power; it took valued rights from persons, and without questions of due process being raised, and without compensation. The alleged "public good" was secured without resort to taxing and spending.

It seems evident that the presence or the absence of tax limits would have had, and could have, relatively little effect on extensions of governmental activity of the sort exemplified in the wave of environmental regulation of the late 1960s and the 1970s in the United States—air and water pollution, automotive and occupational safety, and consumer protection. Indeed, it may be persuasively argued that the interferences with personal freedoms reflected in regulatory laws of this nature present more serious issues than the more indirect extensions of governmental power by means of the fiscal process and reflected in explicit taxation.[4]

There are, of course, relationships between the extension of direct governmental regulation and the size of the budget. Regulatory action implies regulatory agency, and agency in turn implies a regulatory bureaucracy, which, in its own turn, implies bureaucrats who work for money rather than peanuts. And as they impinge on agency budgets, tax limits can have a constraining influence. As the pollution control examples reveal, however, differing means of accomplishing differing governmental objectives have widely differing budgetary implications. The environmental regulatory bureaucracy requires financing, and from tax revenues, but the fact that it is empowered to regulate directly rather than through the fiscal process of spending on compliance very substantially reduces the bureaucracy's demands on the government treasury. It is relatively easy to envisage a federal budget making up no more than 20 percent of GNP that would reflect more interference with personal liberties than an alternative budget of 40 percent of GNP, but with substantially less direct regulation.

As economists here, we might call upon *ceteris paribus* and suggest that,

---

4. The phenomena discussed here need not be restricted to "environmental regulation," even if this rubric is broadly and inclusively defined. All that is required is that, at some stage of the legitimization argument, appropriate reference is made to "public interest" sufficient to surmount minimal legal standards of acceptance. In his important paper "Taxation by Regulation," *Bell Journal of Economics and Management Science*, 2 (Spring 1971), 22–50, Richard A. Posner stressed the internal subsidization aspects of such things as the regulation of rail passenger service, local airline service, and natural gas pricing.

under a given legal environment concerning direct regulatory action by government, the imposition of fiscal constraints must remain potentially effective. The government that commands 20 percent of GNP is less intrusive in the economy than the government that commands 50 percent, provided that the legal setting for direct regulation in the two cases is at all comparable. But this sort of argument would ignore the very real feedback that exists between the government's proclivity to regulate directly and to tax. A government subjected to tax-limit pressures will surely be predicted to exert more efforts through the legal process toward opening up direct regulatory channels.

There is little that we can do here other than to acknowledge the "limits of tax limits" in this respect. Tax limits, or fiscal constraints generally, can be expected to curb government's appetites to the extent that the utility function of governmental decision makers contains arguments for privately enjoyable "creature comforts," for final end items of consumption. Such constraints become much less effective, and may well be evaded, if the motive force behind governmental action is "do-goodism." The licentious sinners we can control; the saintly ascetics may destroy us.

Acknowledging the limits of tax limits amounts to saying that there are other elements of the political-legal constitution that warrant attention, over and beyond those that we analyze in this book. In particular, we should note that some of the procedural constraints discussed earlier in this chapter can serve to constrain direct regulatory behavior as well as the taxing power. As such, these procedural constraints are more general in their impact since they modify the decision-making structure itself. If such more general procedural changes are not within the realm of the possible, fiscal constraints will require the accompaniment of legal limits on the exercise of direct regulation. The argument for the imposition of fiscal limits, derived from the choice calculus of the individual who places himself behind the veil of ignorance at some constitutional stage of decision, takes on meaning only to the extent that it lends support, at the same time, to the companion imposition, or enforcement, of severe restrictions on the range of direct regulation.

9. Open Economy, Federalism, and Taxing Authority

It is better to keep the wolf out of the fold, than to trust to drawing his teeth and claws after he shall have entered.

Thomas Jefferson, *Notes on Virginia: The Writings of Thomas Jefferson*, p. 165

Implicit in all of the analyses of earlier chapters has been the assumption that the polity and the economy are perfect mappings of each other with respect to geography, membership, and the extent of trade and resource allocation. That is, we have assumed the economy to be closed: neither trade nor migration extends the economy beyond the boundaries of the political unit. Consequently, all fiscal activities are carried out exclusively within the polity.

In this chapter we propose to relax the closed-economy–closed-polity assumption. We shall do so in two stages, the first of which contains two parts. In Section 9.1, we allow the economy to be open to trade; hence, citizens may buy and sell goods from citizens of other polities-economies. In that section, however, we continue to assume that migration across governmental boundaries does not occur. The model is the relatively familiar one of a small, independent, national state whose citizens trade in an international market but who remain resident within the small state. In Section 9.2, this model is modified to allow for interunit migration. The analysis of this section provides a bridge between the first and second stages of the analysis of this chapter. In the remaining sections, we examine the prospect of deliberate constitutional partitioning of the political power (and hence of the taxing power) within the confines of a larger and more inclusive political jurisdiction, within which internal trade and migration are unrestricted. Federalism is a means of constraining Leviathan constitutionally; hence, it becomes a topic of some importance in the framework of our analysis.

9.1. Toward a Tax Constitution for Leviathan in an Open Economy with Trade but without Migration

The analysis of this section is obviously related to that which has been developed by international and public-finance economists under the rubrics of "optimal tariffs" and "tax exportation." As before, however, the difference between our discussion and that of the orthodox literature lies in our concentration on the constitutional calculus of the potential taxpayer under Leviathan-like assumptions about the workings of the political process. A Leviathan government, interested solely in maximizing net revenue surplus for its own purposes, need not make any significant distinction between citizens and foreigners. This distinction is, however, quite crucial to the potential taxpayer, in his determination of the range and extent of taxing powers granted to government. The reason is straightforward: to the extent that government can be assigned taxing powers that impose costs on foreigners rather than on citizens, resources both for the provision of public goods and for the generation of Leviathan's net surplus are not drawn directly from the private incomes of citizens.

Recall our simple algebraic formulation, in which Leviathan's maximand, S, is determined by the difference between revenues, R, and G, the amount that it must spend on providing public goods:

$$S = R - G. \tag{1}$$

If, as we previously postulated, government must spend a fixed share, α, on G, we get

$$S = (1 - \alpha)R. \tag{2}$$

If R can be increased without any increase in domestic taxation, it follows that G can be increased without cost, no matter how small the value of α may be. Of course, it remains true that the citizen-taxpayer would prefer α to be as large as possible and will take appropriate constitutional steps to increase its value whenever possible. But for a given α, the citizen-taxpayer will rationally attempt to raise maximal taxes from foreigners.

The potentiality for shifting the burden of taxes from citizens to foreigners depends on the degree to which domestic demand and supply may be separated from foreign demand and supply and upon the relative elasticities of the relevant demand and supply functions. In considering possible tax bases that might be assigned to government, the individual would favor those for which foreign demand looms large relative to domestic demand, and for which domestic supply is relatively elastic. Hotel rooms in Bermuda offer an example. At a constitutional level, the Bermuda government might be assigned the authority to levy taxes on hotel rooms with the assurance that only a relatively small part of the cost will fall on Bermuda citizens. In such a case, there need be little or no concern about the size of the aggregate revenue potential in relation to some globally efficient level of public goods and services. At essentially zero cost, the ideally desired level of public goods provision for local citizens may be very high indeed.

The domestic supply elasticity of the possible tax bases is, however, of critical importance. If domestic supply is available at sharply increasing costs, or if supply is such as to ensure that prices embody large elements of economic rents, any attempt to export tax burdens to foreigners may fail. Regardless of demand elasticities, the potential taxpayer (who will also be potential supplier of the taxed good and, hence, a potential rent recipient) may not want to allow government to have access to a tax base characterized by low supply elasticity.

The conclusions above relate to taxes on domestically produced goods and services, on exports, broadly considered. The same sort of analysis may, of course, be applied to imports, with the obverse relationships being relevant. If foreign supply to the domestic market is relatively inelastic whereas domestic demand is relatively elastic, the levy of a tax on such a good would be borne largely if not exclusively by foreign citizens rather than those who are resident of the tax-levying jurisdiction. Burden shifting by means of taxes on imports may not be an important instrument for exploitation by a small country, however, since foreign supplies of most goods, to that country, may be highly elastic. On the other hand, when large countries are considered, the whole problem of possible retaliation among a small number of trading countries must be incorporated into the analysis.

Detailed consideration of various possible cases need not be worked out here. It should be clear that the constitutional assignment problem in an open economy involves a set of different prospects from those that are relevant to the closed economy setting. With precisely the same model of political process, and with the same preferences for publicly provided goods and services, an individual in an open economy will select a differing range and mix of taxing powers to be allowed to government. He will allow Leviathan access to tax bases that promise a higher potential revenue yield than would be true in a closed economy, and he will tend to choose different bases in accordance with the export-potential criteria sketched out above.

The "prisoners' dilemma" aspects of tax competition among separate states cannot substantially modify these general results. The individual, at the constitutional choice stage when initial taxing authority is assignable to government, may recognize that if different governments try to export tax burdens to citizens beyond their jurisdictions, the net result, for citizens of all jurisdictions, may be harmful. It would be better, for everyone, if each government should be constrained so that no tax burden exportation could exist. But the individual is not placed in a position, even conceptually, to choose "the tax constitution for the world." At best, he can partially constrain the taxing powers of his own national state by constitutional means. In such a choice setting, the individual must consider tax exportation prospects, regardless of the dilemma created by a world regime of mutual retaliation. If he fails to do so, if he selects domestic tax rules on some Kantian-like principle of generalization, he must reckon on being exploited fiscally by the taxing powers assigned to governments other than his own and over which he has no control. The individual will find himself, and his fellow nationals, paying the ultimate costs of public goods and services enjoyed by citizens of other states and also financing the surpluses of the Leviathan rulers of those governments. At the same time, citizens of other countries will be escaping possible payments for at least some share of domestically supplied public goods and some share in the financing of the home-grown Leviathan's surplus. In a world of dog eat dog, the dog that does not eat gets eaten.

9.2. Tax Rules in an Open Economy with Trade and Migration

The economic interdependence among persons in different political jurisdictions changes dramatically when trade in final goods is supplemented by the prospects of resource mobility across governmental boundaries. If persons are free not only to engage in trade but also to shift capital and labor resources in response to differential economic signals, the economy becomes genuinely international, even if political units remain separate. It should be evident that the constitutional choice problem concerning the initial grant of taxing authority becomes different in this setting from that faced in either the closed-economy–closed-polity model of earlier chapters or the open economy-with-trade model examined above.

Freedom of trade and migration among separate governmental units acts as a substitute for overt fiscal constraints. In this sense, free trade and migration parallel in effect some of the Wicksell-like procedural rules examined in Chapter 8. By contrast with the latter, however, the indirect controls over Leviathan exercised by free international economic exchange seem closer to the realm of the institutionally politically feasible, at least in Western nations, than do the required procedural departures from majoritarian electoral processes.

The limiting case of free trade and migration is the idealized Tiebout world.[1] Assume a world of competing governments, each one of which supplies some public goods to its citizens, public goods whose benefits do not spill over beyond the boundaries of the individual polity. Each "national" government is, we assume, modeled as a revenue-seeking, surplus-maximizing Leviathan. Migration across governmental boundaries is, however, also assumed to be costless. Further, let us assume that persons are motivated exclusively by the economic returns available to them. No persons exhibit personal preferences as to jurisdiction of residence, and no persons earn locational rents. In this extreme case, there is no surplus available for potential exploitation by any potential Leviathan in the resource equilibrium generated by the voluntary decisions of persons in the whole international economy. Each governmental unit, regardless of its motivations to maximize net revenue surplus, will find it necessary to offer public goods in the efficient quantities desired and to finance these goods efficiently. In this limiting case, freedom of trade and migration will render any overt fiscal constraints unnecessary.

Once we depart ever so slightly from this extremely restrictive model,

---

1. Charles M. Tiebout, "A Pure Theory of Local Government Expenditures," *Journal of Political Economy*, 60 (October 1956), 415–24.

however, the idealized Tiebout process will not fully substitute for constitutional tax rules or limits, even if we continue to allow for costless migration.[2] If locational rents accrue to persons in particular places of residence or occupation and/or if personal preferences as among the separate locations are known to exist, a potential surplus for governmental exploitation becomes available. Interestingly, the governmental jurisdiction that is most "favorably situated" in terms of the generation of locational rents, on the production or the utility side of the individual's choice calculus, opens up the prospect for the relatively greater degree of fiscal exploitation. Those governmental jurisdictions that are "pedestrian" in the sense that they offer no locational rents at all, in utility or in production (they have neither sunny beaches nor oil beneath the rocks), may remain immune from the fiscal inroads of Leviathan.[3]

At the constitutional stage of consideration, the individual who looks upon his jurisdiction as possessing, actually or potentially, the capacity to generate locational rents, may seek to impose overt constraints on the taxing power. But even in such cases, the effectiveness of freedom of trade and migration in serving as a substitute for such direct constraints should not be overlooked. On the other hand, unless free trade and free migration are themselves constitutionally guaranteed, the indirect limits that these controls might impose on the fiscal proclivities of Leviathan cannot be predicted to operate. Nor is an individual, at some initial constitutional stage, likely to prefer open migration on a one-way basis. That is, the individual may not want to ensure that migrants from other jurisdictions can freely enter into his own unless reciprocal guarantees of free outmigration and immigration into other jurisdictions are also offered. These latter guarantees cannot, of course, emerge in the constitution making for a single jurisdiction. Further, even in a world where such guarantees might emerge from some multinational convention, predicted disparities in income and wealth levels among persons of separate

---

2. David Friedman has analyzed a regime of competitive revenue-maximizing nations, with costless migration, but with attractiveness related to population density. See his "A Competitive Model of Exploitative Taxation," mimeographed, Virginia Polytechnic Institute and State University, August 1979. See also Dennis Epple and Allan Zelenitz, "Competition among Jurisdictions and the Monopoly Power of Governments," Working Paper, Graduate School of Industrial Administration, Carnegie-Mellon University, March 1979.

3. Does Hong Kong offer a real-world example? Interestingly, we observe little or no fiscal exploitation of Hong Kong citizens by the Hong Kong government.

jurisdictions may make free migration undesirable for members of particular jurisdictions. The protection against the fiscal exploitation of Leviathan that the opening up of governmental boundaries offers may not outweigh the predicted costs in locational rents destroyed by such action.

For the foregoing and other considerations, the full substitutability of trade and migration for explicit constraints on governmental fiscal authority does not seem likely to characterize the constitutional calculus. Although he might well recognize the relationships here, the person who has an option at the constitutional stage would presumably select some constraint on governmental taxing power even in a world that is predicted to be characterized as truly international or interjurisdictional.

9.3. Federalism as a Component of a Fiscal Constitution

The analysis of Section 9.2 provides a useful introduction to that of federalism. In the earlier analysis, we adopted a model that contained a large number of political jurisdictions, each one of which defined the "range of publicness" for the goods and services to be supplied governmentally, but all of which were contained within a suprajurisdictional economy, characterized by open migration and free trade among persons in all the governmental units. Here we introduce a different model. We define the inclusive jurisdictional-political boundary to be coincident in both membership and territory with that of the economy. In this respect, we are back to the implicit closed-economy–closed-polity models of earlier chapters. There are no "independent nations" to be considered; there is only one political community. We want, however, to examine the prospect of using *federalization* of the political structure as an indirect means of imposing constraints on the potential fiscal exploitation of Leviathan. It may be possible that an explicit constitutional decision to decentralize and hence to disperse political authority may effectively substitute for overt fiscal limits. In conducting this discussion, we wish to contrast both the approach and the results with the reigning orthodoxy in the economic theory of fiscal federalism. We begin, therefore, with a brief descriptive statement of the main elements of that theory.

The conventional theory of fiscal federalism. In what might be called the conventional or orthodox "economic theory" of federalism, the various functions of government are assigned to different levels (central, state or provincial, local) in accordance with the spatial properties of the public-goods externalities embodied in the carrying out of these functions.[4] In terms of the efficiency norm of the economist, this theory places or specifies for any particular public good or service a *lower bound* on the size of the political (or administrative) jurisdiction that should be assigned powers to finance and supply that good or service. In this framework, assignments to jurisdictions of smaller size (below such a boundary limit) would generate interunit spillovers. Efficiency in the overall organization of public-goods financing and supply, therefore, seems to dictate "merger" into "optimal-sized" units.

Note, however, that this argument does not establish any case for federalism, per se, because there are no logical grounds against assigning functions to jurisdictions larger or more extensive than the lower bound determined by the appropriate ranges of publicness. There would seem to be no reason why strictly localized public goods should not be provided by supralocal governmental units, which might, of course, decentralize administratively as the relevant externality limits dictate. In other words, the conventional theory offers no basis for deriving an *upper bound* on the size of political jurisdictions. There is no analysis that demonstrates the superiority of a genuinely federal political structure over a unitary structure, with the latter administratively decentralized.

This result is not, in itself, surprising when we recognize that the "economic theory" of federalism is no different from standard normative economics in its implicit assumptions about politics. The normative advice proffered by the theory is presumably directed toward the benevolent despotism that will implement the efficiency criteria. No support can be generated for a politically divided governmental structure until the prospects for non-

4. For a clear example, see Albert Breton, "A Theory of Government Grants," *Canadian Journal of Economics and Political Science*, 31 (May 1965), 175–87. But also see Gordon Tullock, "Federalism: Problems of Scale," *Public Choice*, 6 (Spring 1969), 19–29; Mancur Olson, "The Principle of 'Fiscal Equivalence,'" *American Economic Review*, 59 (May 1969), 479–87; Albert Breton and Anthony Scott, *The Economic Constitution of Federal States* (Toronto: University of Toronto Press, 1978); Richard A. Musgrave, "Approaches to a Fiscal Theory of Political Federalism," in National Bureau of Economic Research, *Public Finances: Needs, Sources, and Utilization* (Princeton: Princeton University Press, 1961), pp. 97–122; and Charles M. Tiebout, "An Economic Theory of Fiscal Decentralization," in *Public Finances: Needs, Sources, and Utilization*, pp. 79–96.

idealized despotism are acknowledged. Once government comes to be modeled either as a complex interaction process akin to that analyzed in standard public choice or, as in this book, in terms of Leviathan-like behavior, an argument for a genuinely federal structure can be developed. Further, the normative theory that emerges can be as "economic" as the conventional one. The individual, at the initial stage of constitutional deliberation, may find it "efficient" to decentralize and to disperse the effective taxing power as between the central and the subordinate units of government.

The central government and protective-state functions. Let us continue to model government in Leviathan terms. Whether central, provincial, or local, we assume that government will try to maximize net surplus within the set of internal and external constraints that it confronts. The question to be examined is whether or not explicit constitutional decentralization and dispersal of fiscal authority can provide effective substitutes, in whole or in part, for direct controls over the taxing power.

We must first take account of the initial leap out of Hobbesian anarchy, the primal establishment of government as the enforcer of individual rights and contracts, sometimes called the minimal or the protective state.[5] The protective functions will almost necessarily be assigned to the governmental unit that is coincident in area and membership with the area of the potential economic interdependence. Political subdivision into fully sovereign national units will create prospects for internal conflict, quite apart from internal barriers to trade and migration.[6] If protective-state functions are assigned to the central government, with no constraints on the taxing power, the individual will predict Leviathan provision of protective-state services (internal security, enforcement of rights and contracts, and external defense) but that taxes will be imposed so as to maximize the net surplus over and above the costs of supplying such services. Since the size of the potential tax base (income and

5. For further discussion, see James M. Buchanan, *The Limits of Liberty* (Chicago: University of Chicago Press, 1975). Also, see Robert Nozick, *Anarchy, State, and Utopia* (New York: Basic Books, 1974).

6. Historically, of course, federalized political structures have emerged from some coordination between previously independent units rather than from the deliberative dispersal of political power at a constitutional stage of decision. For our purposes, however, the conceptualization of the latter model of origination of federalisms is more helpful analytically.

wealth in the economy) is clearly dependent on the size and quality of the protective-state services offered, government may well be in the position discussed in Chapter 7. (See, particularly, Figure 7.2 and related discussion.) At the constitutional stage, the individual will clearly seek to restrict the central government's power to tax while leaving it with sufficient authority to finance the desired level of protective-state services. This objective may be accomplished by assigning to the central government a relatively narrow revenue potential through an appropriate base-rate restriction, one that directly relates revenue potential to the services provided.[7]

Productive-state functions: "national" public goods, costless migration, no locational rents. Our concern is not primarily with the financing of protective-state functions assignable to the central government. It is, instead, centered on the possible extension of central government competence beyond such limits with the corresponding extension of taxing power. For purposes of analysis in this and succeeding subsections, we assume that the central government carries out its protective-state functions satisfactorily. It guarantees rights of property and contract, protects against external threats, and ensures free internal trade and migration within its boundaries. It finances these activities by some appropriately limited taxing power, one that restricts the central government's possible exploitation of taxpayers within relatively narrow bounds.

We shall develop our argument in a series of models, arrayed in some rough order of increasing complexity (and realism). In the first three models discussed below, we shall make the extreme assumption that migration is costless. There are no moving costs, and no one has personal preferences as to location within the inclusive territory. Further, there are no locational rents to be earned anywhere in the economy.

In the first case, let us assume now that there is a single public good poten-

---

7. Earl Thompson has implied that protective-state services are directly related to "coveted wealth." From his argument a case can be made for allowing a central government to tax nonhuman wealth, presumably with designated rate limits. See Earl Thompson, "Taxation and National Defense," *Journal of Political Economy*, 82 (July–August 1974), 755–82. Thompson derives his theory from the predicate that governments are totally efficient and entirely constrained to produce results desired by the electorate. Our alternative model of public choice generates a quite different normative evaluation of the wealth tax. (See Chapter 5.)

tially desired by citizens, a good that is technologically nonexcludable throughout the whole "national" territory. Further, we assume complete nonrivalry in consumption. The good is ideally Samuelsonian. (No such good may exist, but the polar case is useful for expository purposes.)

From the precepts of the orthodox theory of fiscal federalism, the financing and provision of such a "national" public good under these conditions should be assigned to the central government rather than to subordinate units of less-than-optimal size for the function. In the latter assignment, interunit spillovers emerge to generate inefficiency, and total supply of the good will tend to be suboptimal. What emerges from the Leviathan perspective?

Assignment of the "national" public good to central government fiscal authority will require constitutional constraints to ensure both that revenues will be expended on provision of the good and that there will be limits on total revenue collections. Some such constraints could surely be constructed, in accordance with the norms emergent from the analyses of earlier chapters, and as we have already assumed to be present with respect to protective-state services. Nonetheless, as the analyses have also suggested, the constraints that might be imposed will accomplish these purposes only within certain tolerance limits and cannot be expected to ensure "efficiency" in any narrowly defined sense. Government could, in other words, be expected to secure some net surplus, a surplus that represents net efficiency loss to taxpayers.

The problem to be posed is one in comparative institutional analysis. It would be possible, at the constitutional stage, to assign the financing and provision of the "national" public good to subordinate units rather than to the central government, despite the "national" range of both nonexcludability and nonrivalry. The predicted results of such a *federal* assignment may then be compared with centralized assignment.

Under the extreme conditions postulated, the equilibrium solution under the federal assignment will be zero taxation along with zero provision of the public good. Any attempt on the part of any single subordinate unit of government, under Leviathan motivation, to levy taxes, even for the provision of the good, will result in total and immediate outmigration to the remaining jurisdictions in the economy. There will be no tax or fiscal exploitation in this solution. But the net efficiency loss will be measured by the potential difference between the benefits of the public good and its costs. There is no way of determining a priori whether these efficiency losses will be greater than, equal to, or less than those that are to be expected under centralized assignment. For our purposes, it suffices to demonstrate that the federal assignment *may* involve lower efficiency loss than the equivalent assignment of the function to the central government authority. The mobility constraint that prohibits local governments from exploiting citizens is tantamount to a constitutional rule that restricts the domain of public spending in such a way as to prohibit provision of the public good.

Productive-state functions: costless migration, no locational rents, complete "national" jointness efficiency but with provincial excludability. The efficiency argument for federal assignment increases dramatically if we drop the nonexcludability assumption from the model considered above while leaving all other assumptions of the model invariant. Let us continue to assume that the "range of publicness" defined in terms of costs of provision over numbers is genuinely "national." We assume now, however, that subordinate units of government may, without undue cost, effectively exclude noncitizens from enjoying the public-goods benefits from localized provision.

In this model, by contrast with that examined above, any single unit of government can tax-finance and supply the public good without motivating mass outmigration from its boundaries to other units within the inclusive territory. To the extent that taxes are imposed so as to leave citizens with more surplus than they could obtain in competing jurisdictions, individuals will be motivated to remain in the fiscally responsive jurisdiction.

The equilibrium solution in this model will involve the concentration of all members of the inclusive jurisdiction into only *one* of the subordinate governmental units. This concentration will be necessary to exploit fully the jointness efficiency aspects of the public good. The single government that remains fiscally viable, however, will, in the extreme conditions postulated, be unable to secure any net fiscal surplus. Taxes will be levied on citizens strictly in terms of their relative public-goods evaluations; all taxes will tend to approximate Lindahl prices. Any attempted departure from this pattern of taxation will immediately set up the potentiality for a competing government to offer better terms to everyone; immediate mass outmigration from the unit that tries to undertake any fiscal exploitation will result.

In this model, therefore, there is a clear efficiency gain in adopting the *fed-*

eral rather than the centralized assignment for the public good, even though the range of publicness defined in the jointness sense remains "national." There are no efficiency losses in the federal solution, whereas, as earlier indicated, there may be efficiency losses in the centralized solution stemming from the failure of taxing constraints to eliminate all Leviathan surplus prospects. Note that the federal assignment secures the reduction of predicted efficiency loss to zero without the introduction of any overt fiscal constraints on the authority of the local governmental units. The fiscal discipline that is forced upon these units in the solution emerges from the mobility of resources across subordinate governmental boundaries within the inclusive territorial jurisdiction. These units of government cannot spend revenues for other purposes than public-goods provision, and they cannot tax in any arbitrary way so that net surplus may be generated.

Production-state functions: costless migration, no locational rents, localized public goods. If we now modify the model by relaxing the assumption concerning the range of publicness, and allow for local-governmental limits on the jointness efficiency in public-goods provision, we are back in the idealized Tiebout world discussed earlier in this chapter. Elaboration at this point is unnecessary. The equilibrium solution differs from that immediately above in that, with localized public goods, population will not be concentrated in single units but will instead be dispersed among separate units, with each unit producing an efficient level of public goods, and with each unit imposing essentially Lindahl tax prices. As in the earlier case, the solution will be fully efficient. A federal assignment is dictated, both from our Leviathan set of assumptions about government and from the set of assumptions that characterize the orthodox theory of fiscal federalism.

Locational value, costs of mobility, and localized Leviathans. The models introduced to this point in our discussion of federalism are grossly unrealistic in their assumptions about locational value and costs of mobility. They should be considered to be preliminary to more realistic models that incorporate locational preferences of taxpayers, locational rents earned by economic resources, and positive costs of moving as between locations. Once any or all of these elements are allowed for in the distribution of people and resources throughout the territory of an economy, the efficacy of the indirect constraint in reducing or eliminating fiscal exploitation by subnational units of government is decreased. If a person, for any reason, simply prefers to live in *X* rather than in *Y*, within an inclusive jurisdiction containing both *X* and *Y*, he becomes vulnerable to some fiscal exploitation by the government of *X*, even if it remains in "competition" for people and resources with the government of *Y*.

The existence of locational value implies that local governments should not be allowed unconstrained taxing power, as might have been implied by some of the extreme models when this value was assumed away. Acknowledgment of the existence of positive locational value does not, however, directionally modify the argument for federal assignment of functions sketched out in the simpler models given above. To the extent that the indirect mobility constraint is operative at all, subordinate governments will be limited in their fiscal powers in comparison with centralized government powers.

Toward an "optimal" federal structure. The argument for a constitutional-stage federal assignment of functions, with accompanying taxing powers, under certain conditions may be accepted, and the suggested modification of the "range of publicness" mappings implicit in orthodox analysis may be rejected. But we have not, to this point, offered a definitive set of suggestions concerning "optimality" in the design of a federalized structure itself, given our Leviathan assumptions about political process. How small or how large should competing subordinate units of government be? How many subordinate units should be contained within the inclusive protective-state jurisdiction?

There are at least four elements that need to be considered as relevant to any answer to this question: costs of mobility, potentiality for collusion, ranges of publicness, and economies of scale in administrative organization.

The costs of moving presumably increase with geographical distance. "Costs of moving" include here not only actual costs of shifting among locations, but, also, subjective or psychological costs involved in shifts among locations along scales of preference. (A person may be relatively indifferent as between Broward and Dade County in Florida. She may place a high value on Florida over any other state.) Empirical evidence confirms the simple analytical results here; persons tend to shift among jurisdictions more readily if these jurisdictions are geographically close one to another. From this fact it follows that the potential for fiscal exploitation varies inversely with the number of competing governmental units in the inclusive territory. This element, taken alone, implies the efficacy of a large number of subordinate governmental units.

A second element also points toward the desirability of a multiplicity of jurisdictions. For reasons equivalent to those familiar in oligopoly theory, the potentiality for collusion among separate units varies inversely with the number of units. If there are only a small number of nominally competitive governments, collusion among them with respect to their mutual exercise of their assigned taxing powers may be easy to organize and to enforce. On the other hand, the costs of organizing and enforcing collusive agreements increase disproportionately as the number of competitors increases.

The "range of publicness" or "economies of scale in consumption" element offsets the first two elements, at least to some degree and for some functions. As the orthodox analysis suggests, the equivalence mappings between the size of political jurisdictions and the range of publicness is of relevance, if not necessarily of dominating importance. It is worth noting as an analytic footnote in this connection that it is the nonexcludability characteristic of public goods rather than the economies of scale in consumption as such that is the more crucial limit on the capacities of decentralization.

A final element involves the costs of administration and organization, which tend to point in the direction of a smaller number of units and toward a combination of functional authorities within single units. There is economic content in the familiar argument for fiscal consolidation among localized jurisdictions. What is often neglected in discussions of consolidation, however, is the offsetting potential for fiscal exploitation, a potential that only emerges when something other than the benevolent despotism model of government informs the analysis.

A normative theory of the "optimal" federal structure would have to incorporate each of the elements noted, along with other relevant considerations, among which would be the locational fixity of productive resources, the homogeneity of the population, and the predicted efficacy of explicit constitutional constraints on central-government and local-government taxing powers. Our purpose here is not to offer such a "theory," even in the form of a few highly abstracted models. Our purpose is the much more limited one of suggesting a rationale for introducing a dispersal of fiscal authority among differing levels of government as a means of controlling Leviathan's overall fiscal appetites.

9.4. An Alternative Theory of Government Grants

The orthodox theory of fiscal federalism includes as one of its parts a theory of intergovernmental grants. The traditional justification for such grants can take three forms: first, certain functions of government allocated to lower levels may generate interjurisdictional spillovers, which can be internalized only by payments between jurisdictions, or appropriate transfers from higher levels of government; second, economies of scale in the administration of taxation may be obtained if central (or higher-level) governments are responsible both for revenue raising and for disbursing funds to lower-level jurisdictions for expenditure; or third, interregional disparities in income (or possibly population) may be seen to require interregional redistribution on more-or-less standard "equity" grounds, by higher-level governments.

As elsewhere in this book, we set aside this third possible justification as lying outside the domain of the current discussion. The other two arguments are, however, of a type that would make them relevant to the constitutional calculus of the typical voter-taxpayer as we have posited it. In principle, they are arguments that ought to bear weight, but like other aspects of the economic theory of federalism, they presume a model of government as the benevolent despot—far removed from our own.

The Leviathan model does, however, readily enough generate a theory of "government grants," with both positive and normative aspects. Within a constitutionally designed federal structure, we would predict that there would be constant pressures by competitive lower-level governments to secure institutional rearrangements that would moderate competitive pressures. One obvious such arrangement would be one that established a uniform tax system across all jurisdictions: this would remove one major element of the competitive government process. And the logical body to administer any such agreement is the higher level of government. In return for an appropriate share of the additional revenue, the central government would act as an enforcer of the agreement between lower-level governments, doling out financial penalties to those jurisdictions which attempted to breach the agreement. Appropriate "fiscal effort" would become an important criterion for determining the share of total revenue that went to each lower-level government: if some state-province levied a low rate of tax in relation to some revenue instrument over which it retained jurisdiction, other states would need to be able to penalize it by means of its grant appropriation by the central government.

With revenue-raising powers thus reassigned to the central government, we would expect both some pro rata return of revenues to state governments and some remaining "special" grants to particular states. The reason for these latter "redistributions" in this model lies in the presence of differential locational rents among states. Those states where locational rents are high, and which could therefore charge higher taxes in the genuinely competitive setting, would no doubt expect a larger share of total revenues per capita in the cartelized case where the central government organizes revenue collection. Correspondingly, in those states where locational rents are lowest, we would expect states to obtain a lower per capita share of total revenue. Additionally, since any lower-level government unit can effectively break the cartel by remitting taxes and attempting to attract extra residents-taxpayers thereby, one might expect that some proportion of the additional tax proceeds from cartelization would be shared on a more-or-less equal-share basis. In this sense, we ought to expect small states to obtain a larger per capita share than large states. There are, then, clear empirical implications here that could be tested to determine the extent to which this explanation of revenue sharing and the structure of grants is an acceptable one. In this connection, there is one observation that deserves mention. With conventional explanations-justifications of intergovernmental grants, one would expect that a considerable amount of intergovernmental transfer could and would occur bilaterally between governments at the same level: interjurisdictional spillovers, for example, would seem to be most appropriately handled in this way. With our alternative theory of the central government as monitor of a cartel among lower levels of government, simple bilateral negotiation between particular jurisdictions would be almost useless since it increases monopoly power only modestly, and we would expect it to be a rare phenomenon. In practice, of course, it is: in very few federations do we observe any significant transfer of funds between jurisdictions at the same level—virtually everything is channeled through the higher level of government.

The normative implications of our alternative theory are clear. Revenue sharing is undesirable, because it subverts the primary purpose of federalism, which is to create competition between jurisdictions. Each jurisdiction must have responsibility for raising its own revenue and should be precluded from entering into explicit agreements with other jurisdictions on the determination of uniform rates. This conclusion is, of course, congruent with the one that emerges from more familiar models of public choice; in a setting where electoral choices are constraining, it is desirable to have expenditure and revenue decisions determined at the same jurisdictional level. The Leviathan construction, however, arrives at similar conclusions from a quite different route.

9.5. A Tax Constitution for a Federal State

It is interesting to consider here the nexus between the structural constraints imposed by an internally competitive federal polity discussed in this chapter and the explicit revenue limits that have been our concern in earlier chapters. To do so, we pose the question: How will (or how should) the power to tax be allocated among jurisdictions? The answer to this question seems clear. Recognizing that mobility will constrain governments at lower levels more severely than governments at higher levels, the citizen will, in making his constitutional determinations, be forced to rely more heavily on fiscal constraints at those higher levels. Assignment of taxing powers to jurisdictions should reflect this. At the lowest level of government, access to even minimally distorting taxes (such as head taxes, or possibly property taxes) may be appropriate, because the discipline of mobility restricts the capacity of government to exploit those tax instruments to the fullest. Equally, at the central level, since there will be little discipline exerted by the possibility of mobility, tax limitations of the sort discussed in earlier chapters remain crucial. Therefore, we would expect that, at this level, the taxpayer-citizen would select tax instruments with limited revenue potential (excises on specific items, perhaps), and otherwise choose fiscal rules designed to limit central government spending.

The tax recommendations that are derived here are, of course, somewhat at variance with practice: central governments have access to broad-based in-

struments with enormous revenue potential, whereas in many cases more localized governments have much more modest revenue instruments, though
the property tax—widely a local government revenue instrument—does have
substantial revenue potential. The fact that the property tax is not in practice
levied at revenue-maximizing levels is perhaps a casual test of the severity of
the mobility constraint.

9.6. Conclusions

The predicted intergovernmental competition for fiscal resources and the
predicted mobility response of persons and resources to the exercise of governmental fiscal authority provide the relationship between the open economy
and the federal political structure and, hence, the basis for this chapter's organization. The constitutional-level choice facing the individual in a potentially open economy–open polity is significantly different from that faced in a
closed system. Intergovernmental competition for fiscal resources and interjurisdictional mobility of persons in pursuit of "fiscal gains" can offer partial
or possibly complete substitutes for explicit fiscal constraints on the taxing
power. In prospect rather than retrospect, however, the individual cannot
constitutionally ensure that his economy-polity will remain open to trade and/
or migration with differing national entities. Critical dependence on "open-
ness" of the economy seems, therefore, unlikely to characterize the rational
constitutional choice of an individual.

The substitutability between intergovernmental competition for fiscal resources and explicit constitutional constraints on governmental taxing power
becomes important, however, even in a closed-economy–closed-polity setting,
once the possibility of federalization is introduced. Since the constitutional
rules are, in this setting, presumed to remain binding, the individual may
choose to rely on the indirect mobility constraints guaranteed by dispersed
political-fiscal power in partial substitution for the more direct constraints
that would otherwise have to be imposed. Protective-state functions would,
presumably, be assigned to the central government, along with some appropriately restricted powers to tax sufficient to finance these functions. Beyond
this minimal limit, however, the intergovernmental competition that a genuinely federal structure offers may be constitutionally "efficient," regardless

of the more familiar considerations of interunit spillovers examined in the orthodox theory of fiscal federalism.

The normative "theory of federalism" that emerges from our analysis differs sharply from the orthodoxy which places primary emphasis on the spatial properties of public goods. These properties become only one of several elements worthy of consideration in a constitutional choice among alternative functional assignments. And as our analysis has indicated, federalization may be efficient even when the desired public goods are estimated to be "national" in the polar Samuelsonian sense. Our emphasis is on federal assignment as a means of ensuring that individuals have available options as among the separate taxing-spending jurisdictions, and on the effect that the potential exercise of these options has on the total fiscal exploitation in the system.

In much modern policy discussion, local governments are allegedly "starved" for funds. Our analysis suggests that this situation is perhaps dictated by the competitive setting within which such governments find themselves, and, indeed, the analysis implies that this situation may well be efficient in the constitutional sense. Total government intrusion into the economy should be smaller, *ceteris paribus,* the greater the extent to which taxes and expenditures are decentralized, the more homogeneous are the separate units, the smaller the jurisdictions, and the lower the net locational rents.

Possibilities for collusion among separate governmental units, either explicitly organized and enforced by the units themselves or mandated by the central government, must be included in the "other things equal." When the central government collects and administers taxes on behalf of the subordinate units, the effect is identical to explicit collusion on the part of these units. Local units should tax and spend independently. But the point here is not the traditional one to the effect that jurisdictions should be responsible for both the tax and expenditure decisions in order to ensure some proper balancing of the two sides of the account, as driven by some cost-benefit–public-choice model of electoral choice. Our point is the quite different one to the effect that tax *competition* among separate units rather than tax collusion is an objective to be sought in its own right. The argument is, of course, obvious when the parallel is drawn with the monopoly-competition relationship in economic theory. But notions that are obvious in one area are often neglected elsewhere, and restatement of the familiar from one setting becomes a challenge to orthodoxy in another. The modified vision of federalism that emerges here suggests, once again, the critical relationship between the normative evaluation of institutions and the political model that is employed in positive analysis.

10. Toward Authentic Tax Reform
Prospects and Prescriptions

No doubt the raising of a very exorbitant tax, as the raising as
much in peace as in war, or the half or even the fifth of the wealth
of the nation, would, as well as any gross abuse of power, justify
resistance in the people.

—Adam Smith, *Lectures on Jurisprudence,* p. 324

The analytical setting in this book is dramatically different from that which
informs most of the literature of tax policy. One of our central purposes is
simply to shift the grounds for discussion and debate, quite apart from any
specific policy prescriptions that might subsequently emerge. Tax reform deserves to be examined in a constitutional perspective and not as some prize
to be captured in a partisan political struggle over relative shares nor as some
abstracted exercise within the political naiveté of the economist's study.

In order to discuss tax reform constitutionally, however, an analytical dimension must be introduced over and beyond that within which orthodox
analysis has been conducted. Comparatively speaking, it is relatively easy to
discuss alternative tax instruments in a normative manner when the operation of the political-governmental process can be assumed away or put to
one side, either by the partisan advocate who seeks to capture political power
for his own ends or by the economist who blindly assumes government to be
benevolent as well as despotic.

The constitutionalist, quite independently of his own ideological or normative predispositions, cannot even begin argument until and unless he first
models the operation of government in the postconstitutional sequence. A
"theory of politics," defined as the theory of the working properties of the

political process under alternative sets of rules, is logically and necessarily prior to any responsible discussion of constitutional alternatives themselves. An acknowledgment of this methodological principle confronts us with difficulties. In a very real sense, all of the public-choice theory and analysis that has been painstakingly developed over the course of three decades becomes prolegomena to analysis of constitutional design, including design for tax reform. But public-choice theory itself remains a long way from its own long-term equilibrium, potentially described by established and widely accepted paradigms.

By necessity we are required to restrict our scope and range. To do so, we have modeled politics in an admittedly extreme, and indeed simplistic, framework, one that we have called "Leviathan." The analysis of preceding chapters has demonstrated that, given this model of government, many of the standard norms for tax reform, for idealized tax arrangements, are totally unacceptable. And by "unacceptable" we mean that the arrangements would never be selected by the rational person in a genuine constitutional choice setting where he is assumed to be empowered to choose as among alternatives for constitutional policy. It is perhaps worth noting that this conclusion of our analysis emerges directly from our positive examination of the individual's constitutional calculus, given the model of politics that is plugged in. The conclusion does not stem from any ideological mind-set that we presume the individual to possess and certainly not from any presuppositions of our own.

Objections to the normative implications, assuming that the technical analysis holds up against possible criticisms, may properly be directed at the Leviathan model of politics. In such a sense, these objections may be at least similar in kind to those that we have ourselves advanced, in this book and elsewhere, against the benevolent despotism model that has for too long informed the orthodox analysis of tax reform. We have argued in Chapter 2 that "natural government" embodies Leviathan-like properties. There is, however, an important difference between the application and use of our model and the application and use of that model implicit in the orthodox policy discussion. In the latter, government is modeled as a benevolent despot, as an imaginary entity that can listen to, accept, and act upon the policy advice proffered by the economist. By contrast, our use of the Leviathan model of politics does not involve any offer of advice or counsel to governments. We use this model to generate predictions of a "worst-possible" sequence of outcomes, predictions that facilitate our analysis of ways and means of ensuring that such "worst-possible" results will not, in fact, be realized. In a very real sense, our whole effort is in close affinity with a Rawls-like minimax strategy.[1] We should also note, at least in passing, that our whole exercise is within the spirit of the classical political economists and the American Founding Fathers, some of whom are cited at the beginning of our chapters.

Even if, operationally, our Leviathan model of politics should be wholly rejected, however, there seems to be no reasonably legitimate basis for jumping to another extreme and acquiescing in the benevolent despotism presumption. Once the latter is called into question, a constitutional approach is almost necessarily required. For example, a model of politics described by the domination of the median voter under majoritarian rules might be introduced as a substitute for our Leviathan. In this case, some of the implications for tax reform would, of course, be different from those that emerge from our analysis. But they would also, and perhaps more sharply, diverge from those that are implied from the standard treatment.

Tax reform must be analyzed constitutionally. But we need to go beyond suggestions for an approach; we need to look somewhat more directly at tax-policy alternatives as these have entered into the political discussions of the later 1970s and 1980s. Our critique, whether direct or implied, of the proposals for tax "reform" that have emerged from orthodox tax-policy discussion is sufficiently contained in earlier chapters. What these chapters have not contained is any treatment of the various proposals for constitutional change that have now surfaced to command positions of reckoned importance in current public-policy debates. Constitutional changes have been made, and many more changes are being quite actively discussed, within a realm of popular-public-political discourse that has remained isolated from the "in-house" talk of tax economists and tax lawyers. Professionals in these groups find themselves unable to articulate their own positions largely because constitutionalism is alien to their thought patterns. The so-called "taxpayers' re-

---

1. Our use of minimax, however, seems more justifiable than that of Rawls because we are explicitly modeling the behavior of the "adversary player," the Leviathan government, rather than "nature," which presumably distributes talents and capacities with no malign intent.

volt" of the late 1970s, brought into focus by California's Proposition 13 in June 1978, has been populist and constitutional rather than elitist and legislative in its origins. And it has taken substantial form in actual or proposed changes in constitutional rules that impose constraints on the taxing powers rather than changes in legislated tax-rate levels and tax-structure arrangements.

It should be evident that our whole analysis is directly relevant to the policy options that have been discussed in the context of the taxpayer revolution, whether real or presumed. It is, however, also important to recognize that the proposals for explicit constitutional changes in tax rules that have emerged in the course of the shift in attitudes characteristic of the late 1970s have not represented the outcome of analysis like that we have attempted in this book. As noted in the Preface, our book is two or three years late in serving this function. The taxpayer revolution has indeed been born without an analytical blueprint or even an analytical map. Nonetheless, the potential usefulness of our effort seems evident. We try to assess critically some of the proposals under popular discussion from a more sophisticated, but still constitutional, perspective than that offered by more orthodox public-finance specialists. From this assessment, our own prescriptions for authentic tax reform follow straightforwardly.

10.1. Taxation in Constitutional Perspective

We stated above that tax reform deserves to be discussed constitutionally. To justify our argument, the differences between the nonconstitutional and the constitutional setting must be emphasized. What does it mean to say that taxes and tax reform are sometimes treated nonconstitutionally? In such a context, tax rules and institutions are considered to be subject to period-by-period changes; they are not treated as permanent or quasi-permanent features of the political structure. In the limiting case, the allocation of tax shares among individuals and groups in the economy and the choice of tax instruments that generate the imputations of such shares are considered "up for grabs" during each and every new budgetary period. In such a nonconstitutional setting, the prospective taxpayer is, of course, vulnerable to exploitation by government to the maximum limits of his taxpaying capacity. Under anything resembling our Leviathan assumptions about governmental processes, the prospective or potential taxpayer will clearly have some interest in imposing constitutional constraints on the taxing power in advance of the budgetary period, constraints that will act to bind the exercise of fiscal authority over the whole postconstitutional sequence.

Even if we relax the Leviathan assumptions, however, and allow for some genuine electoral in-period controls to be exercised by a majority coalition of taxpayers, the single individual must face the prospect that, within any given budgetary-fiscal period, he may find his tax obligations arbitrarily settled by the dominant political coalition which may act contrary to his own interests. Under almost any set of projections or predictions about governmental processes, even those that model politics as ideally benevolent in some respects, the individual would prefer that basic tax rules be considered to be constitutional. There is positive value in predictability. And, indeed, a constitutional interpretation of tax rules implicitly informs much of the tax practice in Western countries. Tax arrangements, once in being, tend to be relatively long-lived, and the adage that "an old tax is a good tax" is a part of a more general attitude toward tax practice even if it does not seem to have been recognized widely in the economic analysis.[2]

In a sense, our argument becomes a plea for a more explicit constitutional attitude toward tax reform. Tax rules should be considered, analyzed, and discussed as a set of quasi-permanent arrangements within which persons can anticipate making appropriate behavioral adjustments, including those that require a long planning horizon. As earlier analysis has indicated, one means of constraining Leviathan lies in the restriction of its ability to modify tax rules with such frequency that taxpayers must face continued uncertainty as to just what the rules will be period by period. If government can succeed in keeping taxpayers off balance in their planning, additional revenue potential may be available for exploitation, provided, of course, that the fiscal uncertainty itself is not pushed beyond revenue-maximizing limits.

The categorical distinction between tax rules as elements in the basic constitutional contract and tax rules as pawns in in-period conflicts over tax shares emerges only in a non-Leviathan context. If electoral politics is assigned the task of imputing or reimputing relative shares in total tax liability

---

2. For a specific discussion of this adage, see James M. Buchanan, *Public Finance in Democratic Process* (Chapel Hill: University of North Carolina Press, 1967), chap. 5.

as among differing groups of taxpayers in each budgetary period, or even if such reimputation is treated as being available for consideration, the analytical model becomes that of a never-ending, negative-sum, n-person game. Continual manipulation of the basic tax-share distribution can be judged to be an undesired attribute of "tax reform," even in the most "democratic" electoral-political process, even when political outcomes sensitively mirror the true demands of members of effective majority coalitions among voters and, hence, among taxpayers. In such a setting, "tax-reform" advocacy largely takes on the pattern of mutually offsetting attempts to shift tax shares among groups. Little or nothing is gained by any group in the process and, over a sequence of periods, all groups would reasonably expect to lose. In playing off groups against each other, the opportunities available to any revenue-seeking authority can be effectively exploited.

It is essentially in the context of a presumed "democratic" model of politics that F. A. Hayek has advanced two distinct proposals for fiscal reform worthy of brief discussion here. In his treatise, *The Constitution of Liberty*,[3] Hayek strongly argued against progressivity in rate structures of income taxation. His argument for proportionality in rates was related directly to his more general argument for the "rule of law." Proportional taxation was classified as falling within his normative requirement that all rules or laws be general in the sense that all persons in the community be equally subjected to their impact and effect. By contrast, progression in tax rates was held to violate this basic precept of generality.

As our earlier analysis in this book has indicated, a requirement for tax-rate proportionality may not seriously constrain a governmental Leviathan bent on maximizing surplus, either because the decision makers are effectively isolated from the taxpaying citizenry or because the public-spending structure can be manipulated to achieve any result desired. If, however, we shift out of the extreme Leviathan model, as we move toward more "realism" with models that contain Leviathan-like elements but which also require that decision makers (politicians and bureaucrats) remain as members of the taxpaying citizenry and which, further, restrict the range for overt transfers, the proportionality restriction might well serve to constrain discrimination among different groups of taxpayers. One effect would surely be to reduce,

---

3. F. A. Hayek, *The Constitution of Liberty* (Chicago: University of Chicago Press, 1960).

or even substantially to eliminate, the debate-conflict over relative tax shares (over the "degree of progressivity") that characterizes much modern discussion of alleged "tax reform."

In his more recent work, *Law, Legislation and Liberty,* vol. 3,[4] Hayek proposes a different, and more structural, reform of political process that relates directly to the taxing power. He proposes that the structure of taxation, the distribution of relative tax shares among persons and groups, be chosen in the deliberations of a new and differently elected and differently organized assembly, an upper house, whose sole function is limited to the enactment of general laws or rules, which would presumably, once enacted, remain in force over long periods of time. Hayek's "general laws" seem equivalent to what we should here call "constitutional rules." He would then allow the other assembly, the ordinary legislature or parliament, to choose levels of taxation and, of course, levels of outlay along with the allocation among uses.[5] As with his earlier proposal for tax proportionality, the structural reform suggested by Hayek is designed primarily to reduce or to eliminate the in-period political squabbles over the distribution of relative tax shares. In a sense, both of Hayek's proposals have as their objective some insurance that tax rules be treated constitutionally rather than nonconstitutionally.

10.2. Tax Reform as Tax Limits

> I would add, however, that there are certain tax "reforms" under discussion that threaten *to contract rather than to augment* net tax revenues and therefore *tend in the wrong direction.* [Italics added.]
>
> —E. S. Phelps, "Rational Taxation," *Social Research,* p. 666

The intellectual integrity of E. S. Phelps, as indicated in the citation above, is to be applauded. But in his candor, he has really let the cat out of the bag of orthodox tax-reform advocacy. As our earlier analysis has revealed in more

---

4. F. A. Hayek, *Law, Legislation and Liberty,* vol. 3, *The Political Order of a Free People* (Chicago: University of Chicago Press).

5. We should note that the political structure that Hayek is implicitly suggesting be modified is one of parliamentary government, akin to the British structure. His suggestions for change fit less readily into the U.S. context.

technical detail, many of the orthodox proposals for "tax reform," especially those that are alleged to be directed toward the achievement of enhanced economic efficiency, may be reinterpreted as directives that suggest how Leviathan may secure additional revenues. "Minimization of excess burden" and "maximization of net tax revenues" become, in many instances, the two sides of the same coin. Income-tax-reform advocacy provides the simplest, and most important, illustration. The dominant emphasis is on making the tax base more comprehensive rather than less, a suggested "reform" that would, if enacted, tend to ensure a larger total tax take under political assumptions that allow any scope at all for Leviathan proclivities. Similarly, proposals for commodity taxation involve the introduction of differential rates that are related to the different degrees of substitutability between taxed and nontaxed outlays.

These, and other, suggestions for "tax reform" are justified within the strict confines of the economists' ivory tower by the equi-revenue framework imposed on analysis. The suggested changes are made to appear almost *wertfrei*, and they seem to allow the "oughts" of tax reform to be derived from the minimal ethical postulate required for the acceptance of the Pareto criterion. However, the very usage of the equi-revenue constraint depends upon the acceptance of the benevolent despotism model of politics, a proviso that is rarely made explicit and may not even be realized by many of those who participate in the discussion. Such an acceptance is not merely something that is convenient for analysis and without substantive importance. It has implications for the real fiscal world of taxing and spending.

We may illustrate by analogy. "It is costly to build a fence or to purchase a chain. It is possible to prove that the no-fence, no-chain solution is more efficient than either, *provided* that we model the behavior of our dog in such a way that he respects the boundaries of our property." As we have put this example from personal experience, the exercise seems, and is, absurd. But is it really very different from that procedure which argues that tax structure X is more "efficient" than tax structure Y provided that we model the behavior of government in such a way that it seeks only to further efficiency in revenue collection?

Once the benevolent despotism model of governmental behavior is abandoned, the orthodox suggestions for tax reform that tend to emerge from the equi-revenue analytical framework cannot stand alone. Alternative tax institutions and rules must be evaluated on criteria other than efficiency and equity, although, of course, these standard objectives remain relevant. If, for example, the comprehensiveness in income-tax base suggested by the efficiency criterion is predicted to offer Leviathan the opportunity to extract more revenues from taxpayers, this instrumental target for reform may well be discarded in favor of some alternative that produces more effective predicted results consistent with the political model adopted. As the analysis of earlier chapters has indicated, a change in the political model may turn many of the orthodox precepts for tax change on their heads.

In almost any nonbenevolent model of political process, which need not, of course, be so severe as the specific Leviathan constructions we have introduced, the choice of the desired "tax constitution" arises, and this constitution is defined by the constraints or limits that it places on government's power to tax. The tax-reform exercise becomes categorically different from that which posits the giving of normative advice to the benevolent and all-wise government. In the latter, and standard, version, any constitutional-legal constraint on the ability of the fiscal authority to respond directly to the advice so proffered can only be negatively valued. "Good" government can only be limited from doing "good." The desire to limit government constitutionally, to define in advance the range and scope for the subsequent implementation of the taxing authority, arises only from a presumption-prediction that government may, at least on some occasions, act in ways that are not within the interests of taxpayers. In this setting, the tax-reform exercise becomes that of choosing among alternative sets of limits.

We shall, in subsequent sections of this chapter, examine some of the fiscal limits that have been discussed in the "tax revolt" of the late 1970s. Before launching into such an institutional array, however, it is useful to look briefly at the possible objectives for "constitutional tax policy," considered in their more general sense. On the assumption that the potential taxpayer, at the stage of constitutional choice, does not model government in idealized terms, what protections will he try to secure through constitutional limits on the power to tax? We may distinguish between *relative* and *absolute* guarantees. The individual may be interested in his own position in the postconstitutional budgetary sequence relative to other persons in the political community. He also may be interested in his position vis-à-vis the fiscal authority defined or described in absolute terms.

Some insurance that the fisc will not arbitrarily discriminate against the individual, any individual, may be a desired feature of almost any acceptable constitutional-policy set. This objective is, of course, the same as that which appears in different guise under the horizontal equity norm of the traditional tax literature and also under the more inclusive "legal equality" norm familiar in the discourse of jurisprudence. The methodological advantage of the veil-of-ignorance–constitutional analysis is that it allows us to derive the logical basis for such a norm from the choices of the individual rather than from some presumed external ethical standard. As we have noted in earlier chapters, existing fiscal or tax constitutions in Western nations incorporate some of the limits against arbitrary discrimination in the distribution of tax shares that almost any person's "efficient" constitution would embody.

Existing constitutions do not, however, embody protections to the potential taxpayer in the absolute dimension. In the United States, existing constitutional law would presumably prevent the levy of a confiscatory tax on Mr. *A* while allowing Mr. *B* to remain free of tax, assuming that both persons are, somehow, "equally situated" as deemed relevant for tax purposes. By contrast, there is nothing in existing constitutional law or its interpretation that would deter government from levying a confiscatory tax on *both* Mr. *A and* Mr. *B*. Much of the support for new and additional constitutional constraints on government's fiscal powers stems from a general, if vague, sense of the existence of this anomaly in the fiscal constitution.

Our Leviathan construction is helpful in isolating and identifying the potential value of constitutional protection against absolute exploitation of the individual by the state. The requirement for uniformity in treatment, or insurance against relative tax deprivation, has been shown to complement constraints aimed at limiting absolute revenue potential in many cases. The significant exception here lies in the possible revenue productivity of progressive and proportional taxation. If the uniformity or legal equality precept is interpreted to require rate proportionality, as it is by Hayek and as it was by the U.S. judiciary prior to the passage of the Sixteenth Amendment in 1913, the shift to nonuniformity in the direction of rate progression may well tend to reduce rather than to enhance the *maximum* revenue potential available to the fiscal authority. This possible relationship tends to be obscured by the American historical experience in which the twentieth-century federal government revenue explosion was facilitated by the introduction of progressivity in rate structures. Rate progression serves to ensure that revenues increase disproportionately with real economic growth and with inflation, but this relationship would also operate under proportionality if rates should be set and adjusted continuously to revenue-maximizing levels.

It is inappropriate in this summary chapter to expand and elaborate analysis that has been developed earlier. But it is useful to remind those who seek to move toward tax-rate uniformity as a means of constraining overall revenue growth that the relationship may sometimes be reversed. The aggregate revenue potential of a broad-based proportional tax (e.g., a value-added tax) tends always to be greater than the aggregate revenue potential of a highly progressive tax on a roughly comparable base. The argument here is not to suggest that movement toward more restrictive constitutional guarantees of tax-rate uniformity may be undesirable. Our point is only that, in some cases, the guarantee of equality of tax treatment may be secured at the partial expense of tighter guarantees against absolute revenue limits.

One further qualification should be made before we discuss specific proposals for constitutional constraints on the taxing power, as these have variously emerged in the 1970s. For the most part, and almost necessarily, the debates over constitutional tax policy have proceeded in a setting where the economic positions of individuals and taxpaying groups are well identified, at least over short-term planning horizons. In such a setting, self-interest dictates, of course, that individuals and groups favor policy actions that promise to yield the most advantageous results. That is, the conflict over the assignment of tax shares implicit in all the orthodox tax-reform advocacy is not absent from the conflict over constitutional tax policy.

Nonetheless, this conflict is necessarily reduced in the constitutional choice setting. When tax rules are treated as quasi-permanent features of the legal structure, individuals are naturally more uncertain about the effects of differing rules on their own positions.[6] Further, the conflict need not emerge at all, whereas it must emerge in the alternative tax-share allocation context.

6. For a comprehensive analysis of the effects of extensions in the time sequence of tax rules on the prospects for securing agreement among persons, see Antonio Pinto Barbosa, "The Constitutional Approach to the Fiscal Process: An Inquiry into Some Logical Foundations," Ph.D. Dissertation, Virginia Polytechnic Institute and State University, 1978.

10.3. Tax-Rate Limits: The Logic of Proposition 13

The most significant fiscal event of the late 1970s was the approval of Proposition 13 in California in June 1978. In a state-wide referendum, voters by a two-to-one margin approved a constitutional limit to restrict the tax on real property to 1 percent of market value. There were many features of Proposition 13 peculiar to the California fiscal-political environment in 1978 that need not be examined here. It is instructive, however, to try to look at this event within the analytical framework of this book. From a truly constitutional perspective, is there any logical basis for imposing maximum limits on rates for specific taxes? Are there plausible reasons for predicting that maximum rate limits will be imposed on real property taxes but not on other taxes? What are the predicted consequences of constitutional rate constraints on some but not all of the tax instruments within a government's fiscal bag? Can rate limits alone restrict total spending? Can rate limits offer any guarantee of equal relative treatment?

It is first of all necessary to distinguish clearly between constitutionally imposed limits on rates for specific taxes and constitutionally imposed limits on overall revenue collections, defined as some share of product or income and, hence, as some inclusive "rate" of tax. We shall postpone discussion of the latter type of limits until Section 10.5. In this section, we shall discuss rate limits for specific taxes.

If the potential taxpayer in some constitutional choice setting conceives of government in Leviathan terms, he will recognize that the imposition of maximum rates for any particular tax will result in a diversion of fiscal pressures toward those taxes that may not fall under the rate-limit constraint. However, any rate limit on one tax from among the allowable set available to government must reduce the total revenue potential collectible by government from the whole set. Whether or not the introduction of specific rate limits offers a desirable or efficient means of achieving the overall absolute constraint on revenues that may be desired is another issue.

There may be desired objectives of constitutional tax policy that are at least partially independent of the aggregate results defined in terms of total revenue potential. Rate or base limits may be aimed at some of these peripheral objectives, even if the taxpayer is not primarily concerned with the absolute levels of revenue potentially extractable from the citizenry. In the analysis of Chapter 5, the announcement effects of taxes were discussed with special reference to taxes on wealth. Emphasis was placed on the temporal dimension, which separates the taxpayer's decisions on saving and capital accumulation from the potential tax levy by government. The extreme vulnerability of the individual to fiscal exploitation in this setting relative to that in which he can make behavioral adjustments after taxes are announced will be recognized by the individual at the constitutional state of deliberation. The analysis of Chapter 5 suggested that the individual would be reluctant to grant government the constitutional authority to levy taxes on wealth and capital.

The most important tax on wealth in most fiscal systems is the tax on real property. We observe that this tax is largely concentrated within the fiscal authority of localized units of government. And there is a sound, logical reason for such a constitutional assignment of tax base, as our analysis makes clear. The prospect for interunit resource mobility, human and nonhuman, tends to restrict the potential exploitation of the real property tax. If, however, local units are not sufficiently competitive, one with another, and if strictly locational rents are significant, localized assignment alone may not provide effective guarantees. In this case, individuals may reasonably demand some imposition of maximum rate limits in order to allow the making of long-term decisions concerning investments in real assets.

Individuals save in order to accumulate wealth, but the rate of saving in any one period is small relative to the total value of wealth potentially accumulated. A rational saving plan, projected forward through many periods, requires that the individual possess some reasonably accurate expectations concerning the tax liabilities that asset ownership will involve. He cannot readily adjust his desired portfolio to changing tax burdens. And for most taxpayers, the purchase of real property represents a commitment to a long-term saving-investment profile, and one that is not readily adjustable at the margins of value. Some constitutional guarantee that the tax claims against such assets will not exceed a specific share of market value may be desired by substantially all potential taxpayers, quite independently of personal persuasion concerning the proper size of government or the proper place of a property tax within the overall tax mix.

It should not, therefore, be surprising that Proposition 13 embodied rate limits on the tax on property values and that other tax-protest emphases have been somewhat differently orchestrated. The assessment here does not, of course, enable us to say anything at all about the appropriateness of the particular rate limit adopted. The argument suggests only that there may be a logical basis for imposing maximum rate limits on taxes on wealth. We should predict, therefore, that this approach toward fiscal constraints, generally, will be more likely to surface with respect to wealth and capital taxes, along with specific limits on public-debt issue, which involves somewhat comparable logical support.

10.4. Tax-Base Constraints

Proposals to introduce new constitutional restrictions on the bases for taxation made available to government were not within the set of suggestions for practical constitutional reform in the late 1970s. However, as our analysis, particularly that developed in Chapters 3 and 4, suggests, base constraints warrant more serious consideration. Moreover, one important reason for directing attention to tax-base questions is that orthodox tax advocacy is preoccupied with this aspect of tax reform. The policy stance that emerges from the conventional treatment, and that is now taken for granted in virtually all professional discussion of tax policy, leads inexorably to broader tax bases and correspondingly larger potential tax revenues. Much of our discussion is designed to indicate the extent to which such policies depend on heroic political assumptions. Apart from our intellectual and academic purposes, however, we believe that tax-base limitations may have a practical role to play in "tax-limit" policy.

One way of looking at tax-base assignment is in terms of "governmental property rights." As we noted, the constitutional delegation of that base amounts to the assignment of a monopoly franchise in the exploitation of that base. The behavior of government, in possession of such a franchise, becomes predictable in a manner analogous to that of the profit-seeking monopoly firm. And with an ability to make such predictions, individuals can anticipate and plan for their own adjustment responses. If the tax-base assignment is made with care, individuals will be protected against undue fiscal exploitation without more complex constraints on the fiscal authority.

The individual will not, of course, want to allow government access to taxable bases that are sufficiently general (inclusive, comprehensive) to allow the generation of revenues far in excess of estimated public-goods financing requirements, given some complementary estimates for the share of collected revenues likely to be expended on goods provision. To ensure that base restrictions will indeed be constraining on governmental action, the individual must try to ensure that government will limit its tax-rate imposition because of the predicted behavioral responses of taxpayers, responses that will, beyond certain rate limits, reduce rather than increase total revenues.

If we translate this relationship into the tax-reform jargon, we can say that the individual at the constitutional stage will seek deliberately to build certain "loopholes" or "escape routes" into the tax structure. These provide the protection or guarantee against undue fiscal exploitation that the individual wants the constitution to embody. This argument in favor of loopholes and against comprehensiveness in tax base runs directly counter to the norm or principle that is central to much of the orthodox tax-reform advocacy.

In this summary section, it may be useful to specify precisely what sort of "defense of loopholes" our analysis implies, and to discuss this defense in the context of existing tax systems. The argument for leaving open avenues for flexibility in behavioral response to tax rates suggests the rationality of *constitutional* loopholes. But what about a possible postconstitutional opening up of loopholes or maneuvering of an agreed-on tax base? Is this action a desirable or undesirable characteristic of in-period political "reform"? The answer to this question must be ambiguous. On the one hand, unless the rate structure is effectively constrained, a Leviathan government could, through a combination of high nominal tax rates and a set of tax preferences, move toward the discriminating monopoly level of revenue analyzed in Chapter 4. On the other hand, governments may seek to further particular objectives other than straightforward revenue maximization by manipulation of tax rules. "Tax preferences" may be granted to citizens in "exchange" for certain modifications in their behavior. To the extent that affected taxpayers respond, they are clearly better off than they would be without the tax preference. Other taxpayers need be no worse off; their tax treatment by a Leviathan government would be unaffected; and the activities of others encouraged by the tax preference will, presumably, exert favorable spillover effects at least equal to any reduction in public-goods financing necessitated by the reduction in tax revenues. Our analysis suggests, therefore, that there may be an important normative distinction between constitutionally and postconstitutionally imposed tax loopholes.

10.5. Aggregate Revenue and Outlay Limits: Ratio-Type Proposals for Constitutional Constraint

Most economists who support some constitutional constraints on governmental fiscal powers beyond those in being tend to favor that set of proposals that attempts somehow to relate aggregate revenues or outlays to some aggregate economic base, such as total income or product. In 1973, one of the first of this type of proposals, Proposition 1 in California, was soundly defeated in a referendum. In 1978, proposals of this nature were made parts of the state constitutions in Tennessee, by convention, and in Michigan, by a referendum vote. In early 1979, the National Tax Limitation Committee sponsored a proposed amendment of this type to the U.S. Constitution. As drafted, and as introduced for consideration in the U.S. Senate, this amendment would restrict percentage increases in rates of federal government outlays to percentage increases in gross national product over preceding years, with a tempering adjustment designed to penalize government for generating inflation. The state proposals, somewhat more simply, tie state tax revenues or state outlays directly to state income, in proportionate terms, more or less at the status quo of the date of enactment.

Aggregate revenue and outlay constraints, defined in relative terms, appeal to economists because they seem to be directed at the central objective, which is one of limiting the overall size of government, of keeping the Leviathan-like proclivities that seem to have surfaced only in recent years from further encroachment on the private sector of the economy. By contrast with these apparently direct approaches, rate and base limits necessarily seem to leave more scope for governmental manipulation and evasion, still within the allowable fiscal powers of the constitution. With some effective aggregate revenue or outlay limits, governments would be forced to nonfiscal alternatives in order to evade the constitutional requirements.

On the other hand, ratio-type proposals have major disadvantages which may well prevent their effective implementation. The proposals seek to establish some constitutionally enforceable relationship between revenue or outlay totals (R and/or G) and the total income or product in the economy (NI or GNP). Both elements in this sort of relationship are aggregates that require, first, abstract definitions, and, second, expert measurement by specific criteria. Neither element in the relationship carries direct meaning for the taxpayer other than as an abstract idea. Neither element means much in personally measurable value. By sharp contrast, a rate or base limit is readily translatable into personal terms. The taxpayer knows roughly what the Jarvis-Gann ceiling of 1 percent of market value implies for her tax bill next year. And a taxpayer also would know what it means when the government is not allowed to tax interest on municipal bonds or on the rental value of owned homes. Generalized taxpayer support for base and rate constraints falls within the realm of the possible in the constitutional tax-policy debates. Comparable support for ratio-type proposals to limit government's fiscal powers may be exceedingly difficult to organize.

Another difficulty with ratio-type proposals lies in the relationship between the specific ratios or shares that are normally suggested and the currently existing status quo. There is little other than historical accident that determines the government's current share in aggregate product. Why should this share necessarily be frozen at its 1980 limits? Arguments may be advanced concerning the appropriate share, quite independently of the present limits, but the constitutional-policy discussion has not, to this point, taken this form. It becomes difficult, therefore, to assess the whole ratio-type approach to fiscal constraint on analytical grounds that are comparable to our earlier discussion of rate and base limits.[7]

10.6. Procedural Limits: Qualified Majorities and Budget Balance

All of the proposals for constraining the fiscal powers of government that have been examined in Sections 10.3 through 10.5 can be classified as result- or end-state-directed, in one sense or another. They are designed to set specific limits on what government can and cannot do. They involve the setting

---

7. For a general discussion of tax limits in the context of the 1978 issues, see Geoffrey Brennan and James M. Buchanan, "The Logic of Tax Limits," *National Tax Journal,* 32 (June 1979), 11–22.

of maximum rates on specific tax rates, the defining of the bases upon which government is to be allowed to levy taxes, and the maximum shares in total economic income or product that government is to be allowed to take and to spend. None of these proposals is directed at the governmental decision structure as such. None of the proposals is aimed at processes or procedures through which end-state results are produced. An alternative, and conceptually quite distinct, approach to constraining government's overall fiscal powers is to modify and to limit the structure within which governmental outcomes emerge.

Mention was made earlier in this chapter of Hayek's proposal to separate the power for setting the tax-share distribution among individuals and groups and the power of setting the level of tax rates, given the tax-share distribution. This proposal falls within what we shall call here the set of *procedural* constraints on fiscal powers. Earlier in the book we have, on several occasions, made reference to Knut Wicksell's proposals for constitutional change which took the form of requiring qualified majority approval of spending legislation by members of legislative assemblies. Wicksell moved from his idealized process requiring unanimous approval to the qualified majority process which involves the approval of as much as five-sixths of the members. Some participants in the discussion of the 1970s have called for constitutional requirements that dictate three-fifths, or two-thirds, approval of spending legislation in legislatures. Proposition 13 in California, in one of its less familiar clauses, requires a two-thirds majority in the state legislature for the enactment of new taxes. Further, almost all of the specific proposals previously discussed are framed in such a way as to include escape clauses, for overriding restrictive limits in times of war or national emergency. These escape clauses are almost all stated in terms of qualified majority approval in state or national legislative bodies.

These procedural reform proposals seek to constrain fiscal outcomes indirectly by modifying the process through which governments are allowed to reach fiscal decisions. One particular proposal that falls within this set has received widespread support and warrants brief discussion here. In early 1979, thirty state legislatures had approved resolutions calling for a constitutional convention for the purpose of adding a budget-balance amendment to the U.S. Constitution. Some thirty members of the U.S. Senate had sponsored resolutions that would have proposed such an amendment to the con-

stitution but without the convention route. In effect, the proposal for requiring the federal government to balance its budget is designed only to ensure
that government cover its outlays with tax revenues rather than with public-
debt issue or with new money creation. It does not aim directly at the level
of revenues or outlays. In a sense, this proposal may also be interpreted as
falling within the base-limit set; this would be the case if we should treat
public-debt issue and money creation as forms of taxes. The amendment
would effectively deny these "tax bases" to government. In a more fundamental sense, however, the amendment for budget balance may be interpreted in procedural terms. It seeks to modify the governmental decision
process by requiring that decision makers, whoever these may be, balance off
costs against benefits.

It may be argued that budget balance was a part of the existing fiscal constitution of the United States prior to the Keynesian revolution in the theory
of economic policy. Even if the constitution did not contain a formal, written
requirement for budget balance, governmental decision makers acted as if
such a constraint did limit their fiscal behavior. The effect of the Keynesian
revolution was to repeal this part of the fiscal constitution.[8] Much of the support for the introduction of an explicit constitutional provision for budget
balance in the 1970s stems from a widening recognition that, in the absence
of such a constraint, governments will revert to their quite natural tendency
to generate budget deficits almost continually.

In comparison with the more restrictive proposals for constitutional
change, the budget-balance amendment, if approved, would not seriously
constrain Leviathan's fiscal appetites. On the other hand, proponents of the
amendment predict that the electoral checks on governmental process will
work much more effectively if governments are prevented from concealing
the genuine costs of governmental outlays through deficit creation. In one
sense, budget balance might be considered as a first step toward more comprehensive constitutional constraints on the fiscal powers of modern governments.

8. This theme is developed at length in James M. Buchanan and Richard E. Wagner,
Democracy in Deficit (New York: Academic Press, 1977).

10.7. Toward Authentic Tax Reform

Our basic purpose in this summary chapter is not to support or to reject any one or any set of the various proposals for constitutional reform that have been advanced to impose constraints on government's fiscal power. Our whole analysis, however, may properly be interpreted as offering analytical argument in support of *some* appropriately designed set of limits. Our extreme Leviathan model of politics is not critical for this conclusion. This model, which we introduced to allow us to develop our analysis with some logical rigor, may be substantially modified in the direction of more "realistic" political assumptions without undermining the general conclusion in support of constitutional constraints.

To the extent that our analysis bears on "tax reform" at all, it does so with reference to "constitutional tax reform," and, as noted, with particular reference to "tax limits." We have little or no interest, here or elsewhere, in proffering our own private and personal advice to existing governments about taxes or indeed about anything else.

If we can succeed in shifting the grounds for debate in tax reform, we shall have opened the way toward the only authentic tax reform worthy of serious consideration.

Given this somewhat restrictive methodological stance, it would be inconsistent for us, at this stage, to lay down our own pet prejudices as to "ideal tax arrangements," whether these be supported on efficiency, equity, or some other grounds. We hope to have been able to demonstrate that the individual, as potential taxpayer, placed in a hypothetical position where he is allowed to select among alternative sets of constraints on the taxing power of government, will rationally choose to exercise his option and impose some such constraints. In a broadly defined perspective, therefore, our whole analysis may be interpreted as providing positive argument in support of almost any one of the currently discussed proposals for constitutional fiscal limits. To go further than this, and to try to isolate supporting arguments for any one of the proposed set of prospects that have been suggested, would require more analysis than we have been able to muster. We do not want to make the mistake of suggesting that a unique constitutional solution will necessarily emerge even from the most idealized modeling of constitutional choice.

As we noted in the Preface as well as earlier in this chapter, this book is both badly and excellently timed. Perhaps a two- or three-year advance date in writing and in publication might have allowed some of our analysis to inform more fully some of the current discussions of constitutional change. But a ten-year advance would have surely meant a neglect of our whole argument. The "taxpayer revolution" of the 1970s has been politically exciting regardless of the final tally in terms of ultimate change in the political framework of society. And this political event has offered intellectual challenges that too few of our fellow economists and other scholars have chosen to accept. To the extent that our analysis in this book prompts others, regardless of ideological persuasion, to take up the gauntlet, tax-reform discussion will have moved beyond the realm of partisan advocacy toward authenticity in the desired debate over constitutional alternatives within which we should allow government's fiscal powers to be exercised.

Epilogue

There is a science of economics that embodies conceptually refutable hypotheses to the effect that persons act so as to maximize objectively measurable value (net wealth) subject to the constraints that they confront. The constraints are presumed to be exogenous to the persons whose behavior is to be predicted. Empirical tests of these hypotheses are necessarily limited to behavior under constraints that have been historically experienced. The boundaries of predictive science are logically set by those of reality, quite apart from any considerations of practical issues concerning data meaning, collection, and usage.

It is perhaps not surprising that modern economists do not feel at home outside these boundaries. They become uneasy when issues about choices among constraints are raised. How can individual choice behavior outside the standard paradigm be modeled? How can a positive science of rules be derived?

The first step lies in the elementary recognition that the constraints that bound behavior within a social order are not exclusively exogenous. At least some proportion of the constraints are of man's own making, the results of deliberative choice behavior. Some of the rules we live by are grounded neither in physical reality nor in the social evolutionary process but are, instead, the product of design and intent. From this recognition it follows that some rules of social order must be subject to modification and change, to "reform."

But what criteria may be adduced to guide judgment? Clearly, empirical science is exhausted once behavior within existing and past rules is fully described. A change in rules necessarily requires that we "fly to others that we know not of." Choice among rules is inherently speculative.

Speculation may, however, be reasoned. Analysis that models individual choice behavior under alternative sets of potential constraints becomes an essential part of a positive science of rules, where the hypotheses are only conceptually refutable rather than empirically testable. Choice among constraints embodies greater uncertainty about the properties of the alternatives than does choice within constraints. But the suggested transference of the modern economists' analysis of "choice under uncertainty" to the choice among rules cannot be made without a full appreciation of the leap from one choice setting to the other. The criterion of expected utility maximization, widely held to be applicable to choice under uncertainty within constraints, may not be relevant or appropriate to choice among constraints themselves. The distinction here was sensed by John Rawls but was overlooked by most of his economist critics.

Rules may be chosen that place limits on extremes, even at some accurately reckoned cost in value. We need not predict that each child will fall off the cliff to justify the installation of railings. Minimax is descriptive of deeply felt human precepts of rationality. We seek to ensure that the best remains a potentiality by guarding against the worst. We seek "freedom within constraints."

At a fundamental methodological level, our plea is not for a particular set of changes in existing rules. It is, instead, a plea that the choice of rules receives the attention it deserves in modern discussions of policy reform. Neglect of rules ensures drift into constitutional anarchy, a state of affairs that many modern diagnoses suggest has already been attained. In such a setting, confusion abounds, and the tentacles natural to a Hobbesian jungle take root, grab, and hold.

Modern man did change his sociopolitical rules; he did once emerge from the Dark Ages. In doing so, he was guided, not solely by science and not primarily by blind evolutionary change, but by the reasoned speculation of persons who dared to think in terms of rules other than those under which they lived. They dreamed of possible futures, and some of their dreams were realized. It is not without significance that the chapter-beginning citations included in this book are predominantly drawn from eighteenth- and early-nineteenth-century writers.

Selected Bibliography

Andrews, W. D. "A Consumption Type or Cash Flow Personal Income Tax," *Harvard Law Review*, 87 (April 1974), 1113–88.

Arrow, Kenneth. *Social Choice and Individual Values.* New York: John Wiley & Sons, 1951.

Atkinson, A. B., and Stern, N. H. "Pigou, Taxation and Public Goods," *Review of Economic Studies*, 41 (April 1974), 119–28.

Auster, Richard D., and Silver, Morris. "The State as a Firm: An Economic Approach to Political History." Mimeographed, University of Arizona, Tucson, 1978.

Bailey, Martin. "The Welfare Cost of Inflationary Finance," *Journal of Political Economy*, 64 (April 1956), 93–110.

Barbosa, Antonio Pinto. "The Constitutional Approach to the Fiscal Process: An Inquiry into Some Logical Foundations." Ph.D. Dissertation, Virginia Polytechnic Institute and State University, 1978.

Barlow, Robin, and Sparks, Gordon R. "A Note on Progression and Leisure," *American Economic Review*, 54 (June 1964), 372–77.

Baumol, W. J., and Bradford, D. F. "Optimal Departures from Marginal Cost Pricing," *American Economic Review*, 60 (June 1970), 265–83.

Bergson, A. "A Reformulation of Certain Aspects of Welfare Economics," *Quarterly Journal of Economics*, 52 (February 1938), 314–44.

Brennan, Geoffrey. "Second Best Aspects of Horizontal Equity Questions," *Public Finance/Finances Publiques*, 27, no. 3 (1972), 282–91.

Brennan, Geoffrey, and Buchanan, James M. "Towards a Tax Constitution for Leviathan," *Journal of Public Economics*, 8 (December 1977), 255–74.

———. "Tax Instruments as Constraints on the Disposition of Public Revenues," *Journal of Public Economics*, 9 (June 1978), 301–18.

———. "The Logic of Tax Limits," *National Tax Journal*, 32, no. 2 (June 1979), 11–22.

———. "The Logic of the Ricardian Equivalence Theorem," *Finanzarchiv*, Heft 38/1 (1980), 4–16.

Brennan, Geoffrey, and McGuire, T. G. "Optimal Tax Policy under Uncertainty," *Journal of Public Economics*, 4 (February 1975), 205–9.

Breton, Albert. "A Theory of Government Grants," *Canadian Journal of Economics and Political Science*, 31 (May 1965), 175–87.

———. *The Economic Theory of Representative Government*. Chicago: Aldine-Atherton, 1974.

Breton Albert, and Scott, Anthony. *The Economic Constitution of Federal States*. Toronto: University of Toronto Press, 1978.

Buchanan, James M. "The Theory of Monopolistic Quantity Discounts," *Review of Economic Studies*, 20 (1952), 199–208.

———. "La scienza delle finanze: The Italian Tradition in Fiscal Theory," in *Fiscal Theory and Political Economy*, pp. 24–74. Chapel Hill: University of North Carolina Press, 1960.

———. "The Economics of Earmarked Taxes," *Journal of Political Economy*, 71 (October 1963), 457–69.

———. "Externality in Tax Response," *Southern Economic Journal*, 33 (July 1966), 35–42.

———. *Public Finance in Democratic Process*. Chapel Hill: University of North Carolina Press, 1967.

———. "The Samaritan's Dilemma," in *Altruism, Morality and Economic Theory*, edited by E. S. Phelps, pp. 71–85. New York: Russell Sage Foundation, 1975.

———. *The Limits of Liberty*. Chicago: University of Chicago Press, 1975.

———. "Barro on the Ricardian Equivalence Theorem," *Journal of Political Economy*, 83 (April 1976), 337–42.

———. "Taxation in Fiscal Exchange," *Journal of Public Economics*, 6 (July 1976), 17–29.

Buchanan, James M., Tollison, Robert D., and Tullock, Gordon, eds. *Toward a Theory of the Rent-Seeking Society*. College Station: Texas A & M University Press, 1980.

Buchanan, James M. and Tullock, Gordon. *The Calculus of Consent*. Ann Arbor: University of Michigan Press, 1962.

Buchanan, James M. and Wagner, Richard. *Democracy in Deficit*. New York: Academic Press, 1977.

Cagan, P. "The Monetary Dynamics of Hyperinflation," in *Studies in the Quantity Theory of Money*, edited by Milton Friedman, pp. 25–117. Chicago: University of Chicago Press, 1956.

Corlett, W., and Hague, D. "Complementarity and the Excess Burden of Taxation," *Review of Economic Studies*, 21 (1953–54), 21–30.

Cowling, Keith, and Mueller, Dennis C. "The Social Cost of Monopoly Power," *Economic Journal*, 88 (December 1978), 727–48.

Dam, Kenneth W. "The American Fiscal Constitution," *University of Chicago Law Review,* 44 (Winter 1977), 271–320.

Davis, O., Hinich, M. J., and Ordeshook, P. C. "An Expository Development of a Mathematical Model of the Electoral Process," *American Political Science Review,* 64 (June 1970), 426–48.

Denzau, A., and Mackay, Robert. "Benefit and Tax Discrimination by Monopoly Bureaus," *Journal of Public Economics,* 1980.

Denzau, A., Mackay, Robert, and Weaver, Carolyn. "Spending Limitations, Agenda Control and Voter Expectations," *National Tax Journal,* 32 (June 1979), 189–200.

de Viti de Marco, Antonio. *First Principles of Public Finance,* trans. by E. P. Marget. London: Jonathan Cape, 1936.

Downs, Anthony. *An Economic Theory of Democracy.* New York: Harper & Brothers, 1957.

Epple, Dennis, and Zelenitz, Allan. "Competition among Jurisdictions and the Monopoly Power of Governments." Working Paper, Graduate School of Industrial Administration, Carnegie-Mellon University, March 1979.

Fasiani, Mauro. *Principii di scienza delle finanze,* 2nd ed. Turin, 1951.

Fisher, Irving, and Fisher, Herbert W. *Constructive Income Taxation.* New York: Harper & Brothers, 1942.

Friedman, David. "A Competitive Model of Exploitative Taxation." Mimeographed, Virginia Polytechnic Institute and State University, August 1979.

Friedman, Milton. "The Optimum Quantity of Money," in *The Optimum Quantity of Money and Other Essays.* Chicago: Aldine-Atherton, 1969.

Hailsham, Lord. *The Dilemma of Democracy.* London: William Collins Sons & Company, 1978.

Hansen, Bent. *The Economic Theory of Fiscal Policy.* London: George Allen & Unwin, 1958.

Harberger, Arnold. "Taxation, Resource Allocation and Welfare," in *The Role of Direct and Indirect Taxes in the Federal Revenue System,* pp. 25–70. National Bureau of Economic Research/Brookings Institution. Princeton: Princeton University Press, 1963.

Hayek, F. A. *The Constitution of Liberty.* Chicago: University of Chicago Press, 1960. *Denationalization of Money: An Analysis of the Theory and Practice of Concurrent Currencies.* London: Institute of Economic Affairs, 1976.

————. *Law, Legislation and Liberty,* vol. 3, *The Political Order of a Free People.* Chicago: University of Chicago Press, 1979.

Head, John G. "A Note on Progression and Leisure: Comment," *American Economic Review,* 66 (March 1966), 172–79.

Hobbes, Thomas. *Leviathan.* London: J. M. Dent & Sons, Everyman's Library, 1943.

Hochman, Harold, and Rodgers, James. "Pareto-Optimal Redistribution," *American Economic Review,* 59 (September 1969), 542–57.

Hotelling, Harold. "The General Welfare in Relation to Problems of Taxation and of Railway and Utility Rates," *Econometrica,* 6 (July 1938), 242–69.

Hume, David. "Of the Independency of Parliament," in *Essays, Moral, Political and Literary,* edited by T. H. Green and T. H. Grose, vol. 1. London: Oxford University Press, 1963.

Jefferson, Thomas. *Notes on Virginia: The Writings of Thomas Jefferson,* Memorial Edition. Washington, D.C.: Thomas Jefferson Memorial Association, 1905.

Johnson, David B., and Pauly, Mark V. "Excess Burden and the Voluntary Theory of Public Finance," *Economica,* 36 (August 1969), 269–76.

Johnson, Harry G. "A Note on the Dishonest Government and the Inflation Tax," *Journal of Monetary Economics,* 3 (July 1977), 375–77.

Keynes, John Maynard. *The Economic Consequences of the Peace.* New York: Harcourt Brace, 1920.

Krueger, Anne O. "The Political Economy of the Rent-seeking Society," *American Economic Review,* 64 (June 1974), 291–303.

Lerner, Abba. "On Optimal Taxes with an Untaxable Sector," *American Economic Review,* 60 (June 1970), 284–96.

Lively, Jack, and Rees, John, eds. *Utilitarian Logic and Politics.* Oxford: Clarendon Press, 1978.

Lucas, Robert E. "Econometric Testing of the Natural Rate Hypothesis," in *The Econometrics of Price Determination Conference,* edited by O. Eckstein. Washington, D.C.: Board of Governors of the Federal Reserve System, 1972.

Mackay, Robert. "Agenda Control by Budget Maximizers in a Multi-bureau Setting." *Public Choice* (Summer 1981).

Mackay, Robert, and Weaver, Carolyn. "Monopoly Bureaus and Fiscal Outcomes: Deductive Models and Implications for Reform," in *Deductive Reasoning in the Analysis of Public Policy,* edited by Gordon Tullock and Richard E. Wagner. Lexington, Mass.: Lexington Books, 1978.

Madison, James. *The Federalist No. 51, The Federalist Papers,* edited by Roy P. Fairfield. New York: Doubleday & Company, 1966.

Meade, James E. *The Structure and Reform of Direct Taxation.* Report of a committee chaired by J. E. Meade. London: George Allen & Unwin, 1978.

Migué, Jean-Luc, and Bélanger, Gérard. "Toward a General Theory of Managerial Discretion," *Public Choice,* 17 (Spring 1974), 27–42.

Mill, John S. *Principles of Political Economy.* London: Longmans, Green, 1926.

———. *Considerations on Representative Government,* in *Essays on Politics and Society,* vol. 19, *Collected Works.* Toronto: University of Toronto Press, 1977.

Miller, James C. "A Program for Direct and Proxy Voting in the Legislative Process," *Public Choice,* 7 (Fall 1969), 107–13.

Montesquieu, C. *De l'esprit des lois,* Book XI, Chap. 4. Paris: Garnier Frères, 1961.

Musgrave, Richard A. *The Theory of Public Finance.* New York: McGraw-Hill Book Company, 1959.

———. "Approaches to a Fiscal Theory of Political Federalism," in *Public Finances: Needs, Sources and Utilization,* pp. 97–122. National Bureau of Economic Research. Princeton: Princeton University Press, 1961.

Ng, Yew-Kwang. "Towards a Theory of Third Best," *Public Finance/Finances Publiques,* 32, no. 1 (1977), 1–15.

Niskanen, William A. *Bureaucracy and Representative Government.* Chicago: Aldine-Atherton, 1971.

Nozick, Robert. *Anarchy, State, and Utopia.* New York: Basic Books, 1974.

Olson, Mancur. *The Logic of Collective Action.* Cambridge: Harvard University Press, 1965.

———. "The Principle of Fiscal Equivalence," *American Economic Review,* 59 (May 1969), 479–87.

Orton, W. A. *The Economic Role of the State.* Chicago: University of Chicago Press, 1950.

Pesek, Boris P., and Saving, Thomas R. *Money, Wealth, and Economic Theory.* London: Macmillan, 1967.

Phelps, E. S. "Inflation in the Theory of Public Finance," *Swedish Journal of Economics,* 75 (March 1973), 67–82.

———. "Rational Taxation," *Social Research,* 44 (Winter 1977), 657–67.

Pigou, A. C. *A Study in Public Finance.* London: Macmillan, 1928.

———. *The Economics of Welfare.* London: Macmillan, 1932.

Posner, Richard A. "Taxation by Regulation," *Bell Journal of Economics and Management Science,* 2 (Spring 1971), 22–50.

———. "The Social Cost of Monopoly and Regulation," *Journal of Political Economy,* 83 (August 1975), 807–27.

Rawls, John. *A Theory of Justice.* Cambridge: Harvard University Press, 1971.

Riker, W. H., and Ordeshook, P. C. *Introduction to Positive Political Theory.* Englewood Cliffs, N.J.: Prentice-Hall, 1973.

Robertson, Dennis H. *Economic Commentaries.* London: Staples Press, 1956.

Robinson, Joan. *The Economics of Imperfect Competition.* London: Macmillan, 1933.

Rowley, Charles K., and Peacock, Alan T. *Welfare Economics: A Liberal Restatement.* London: Martin Robertson, 1975.

Samuelson, Paul A. *Foundations of Economic Analysis.* Cambridge: Harvard University Press, 1947.

————. "The Pure Theory of Public Expenditure," *Review of Economics and Statistics,* 36 (November 1954), 387–89.

————. "Diagrammatic Exposition of a Theory of Public Expenditure," *Review of Economics and Statistics,* 37 (November 1955), 350–56.

————. "Aspects of Public Expenditure Theories," *Review of Economics and Statistics,* 40 (November 1958), 332–37.

Sargent, Thomas, and Wallace, Neil. "Rational Expectations and the Theory of Economic Policy," *Journal of Monetary Economics,* 2 (April 1976), 169–83.

Schotter, Andrew, and O'Driscoll, Gerald P. "Why Rational Expectations May Be Impossible: An Application of Newcomb's Paradox." Discussion Paper, Center for Applied Economics, New York University, November 1978.

Shefrin, A. M., and Thaler, Richard. "An Economic Theory of Self-control." Working Paper No. 208, Center for Economic Analysis of Human Behavior and Social Institutions. Stanford, Calif.: National Bureau of Economic Research, October 1977.

Shoup, Carl S. "Collective Consumption and Relative Size of the Government Sector," in *Public and Urban Economics,* edited by Ronald E. Grieson, pp. 191–212. Lexington, Mass.: Lexington Books, 1976.

Siegel, Jeremy J. "A Note on Optimal Taxation and the Optimal Rate of Inflation," *Journal of Monetary Economics,* 4 (April 1978), 297–305.

Simons, Henry. *Personal Income Taxation.* Chicago: University of Chicago Press, 1938.

Sjaastad, Larry A. "Why Stable Inflations Fail: An Essay in Political Economy," in *Inflation in the World Economy,* edited by Michael Parkin and George Zis, pp. 73–86. Manchester, England: Manchester University Press, 1976.

Smith, Adam. *The Wealth of Nations.* New York: Modern Library, 1937.

————. *Theory of Moral Sentiments.* Oxford: Clarendon Press, 1976.

————. *Lectures on Jurisprudence,* edited by R. L. Meek, D. D. Raphael, and P. G. Stein. Oxford: Clarendon Press, 1978.

Thompson, Earl. "Taxation and National Defense," *Journal of Political Economy,* 82 (July–August 1974), 755–82.

Thompson, Perronet. "Greatest Happiness Principle," *Westminster Review,* 21 (July 1829). Reprinted in *Utilitarian Logic and Politics,* edited by Jack Lively and John Rees. Oxford: Clarendon Press, 1978.

Tiebout, Charles M. "A Pure Theory of Local Government Expenditures," *Journal of Political Economy,* 60 (October 1956), 415–24.

————. "An Economic Theory of Fiscal Decentralization," in *Public Finances: Needs, Sources and Utilization,* pp. 79–96. National Bureau of Economic Research. Princeton: Princeton University Press, 1961.

Tinbergen, J. *On the Theory of Economic Policy.* Amsterdam: North-Holland Publishing Company, 1952.

Tuerck, David A. "Constitutional Asymmetry," *Papers on Non-market Decision Making*, 2 (1967), 27–44.

Tullock, Gordon. *The Politics of Bureaucracy.* Washington, D.C.: Public Affairs Press, 1965.

————. *Toward a Mathematics of Politics.* Ann Arbor: University of Michigan Press, 1967.

————. "The Welfare Costs of Tariffs, Monopolies and Theft," *Western Economic Journal*, 5 (June 1967), 224–32.

————. "Federalism: Problems of Scale," *Public Choice*, 6 (Spring 1969), 19–29.

————. "Can You Fool All of the People All of the Time?" *Journal of Money, Credit and Banking*, 4 (November 1972), 424–30.

Wicksell, Knut. *Finanztheoretische Untersuchungen.* Jena: Gustav Fischer Verlag, 1896.

Index